Lonely planet

DREAM TRIPS

of the

WORLD

100 Destinations and Itineraries

TO MAKE YOUR

Bucket List a Reality

Contents

Introduction

WE ALL HAVE A WISH LIST at the back of our minds (or stuck to the refrigerator). Will this be the year to see gray whales in the wild or the Northern Lights swirl above the Arctic? Or tour the temples of Kyoto or perhaps the ruins of Angkor? This book brings together 100 trips, curated by Lonely Planet's expert editors and writers, to fulfil every travel dream and features destinations that define the extraordinary variety of our world. Not all are famous but every single one, from the Galápagos islands to South Africa's Garden Route, is unforgettable.

Dream Trips of the World is organised by region, usually by continent. Within each chapter, our pick of the destinations are covered in differing degrees of detail. The regular At a Glance section suggests where to stay and shop, the dishes and drinks to try, and what to do. The Practicalities panel provides details of how to get there and get around; the best time of year to visit; and what else to note about the destination. A planned itinerary maps out an ideal route through the region, stopping at the undisputed highlights.

Travel allows us to engage with the world and experience the wonder of a place for the first time. That, of course, is a rare

Opposite: the temple of Saturn in the Forum, Rome; *This page top:* Yellowstone National Park's Grand Prismatic; *Bottom:* springtime in Kyoto's Higashiyama district

privilege that brings with it responsibility: to stay longer; use sustainable transport where that option is possible; to spend money in a way that benefits local communities. In short, to travel more slowly and deeply. Many of the destinations profiled in this book are immensely popular, to a problematic degree in some instances. We would always encourage travel to them outside of their peak periods: Rome in winter is as beguiling as it is in the pell-mell summer holiday season.

Having travel goals helps us plan to achieve them but first you have to know what it is that would mean the most to you. In *Dream Trips of the World*, you'll find many of the world's great natural wonders: Yellowstone's geysers, the Northern Lights dancing above Svalbard in Norway, Oman's Empty Quarter, the Great Migration, cherry blossom sweeping across Japan, Australia's Great Barrier Reef. Five of what are among the best national parks in the world are in Utah's Red Rock Country. Or you could test yourself further in the alien landscape of Chile's high-altitude Atacama desert.

Wildlife is often the big appeal of some destinations, whether you've always wanted to meet mountain gorillas in Rwanda, gray whales off Mexico's Baja California peninsula or spirit bears in the Canadian rainforest.

There are the trips that are just downright deliciously indulgent: hopping between Greece's Ionian Islands or touring around Australia's wine regions.

Or it might be journeys into our human history and culture that are most illuminating. This book dives into New Zealand's Māori culture, walks in the footsteps of Lutruwita's (Tasmania's) traditional custodians, reveals the influence of the Renaissance in Italy, the melding of cultures in Moorish Andalucía, and explores the Mayan civilisation of Mexico.

But wherever you wish to start your own list, each trip is a reminder that we live on a uniquely beautiful and precious living planet.

Americas

CHILE AND ARGENTINA

Trek Into *the* Wilds *of* Patagonia

WHEN YOU'RE ON THE ROAD to nowhere at South America's southern tip, keep going. There's no reaching Patagonia in a hurry, whether you arrive bleary eyed by plane, on a rumbling overnight bus or by choppy ferry. But it's instantly worth it when you first see its toothy granite peaks, piercing-blue lakes, booming glaciers and buff-coloured steppe veined with silver rivers. This hefty chunk of Chile and Argentina is where South America's wilderness raises the bar.

Sparsely populated and out on its lonesome, Patagonia is truly deserving of its 'epic' label. A region whittled out of rock, ice and desert-like steppe, with brutal gale-force winds to knock you off your feet, thundering rivers to traverse and *lenga* (southern beech forests) where you can walk in solitude for days, peering up at cloudless skies where condors wheel. It's beautiful, but the terrain is harsh and the weather ridiculously fickle, so you'll have to earn that beauty by pitting yourself against the elements. Rock up in anything but thermals, waterproofs and trekking gear and you'll attract a few strange looks.

Topping every Patagonia must-trek list is Torres del Paine and its much-raved-about, four-day, 50-mile (80km) 'W' hike.

Opposite: a Patagonian gaucho rounds up his sheep; *This page top:* a waterfall plunges into Torres del Paine national park, Chile; *Bottom:* hiking in El Chaltén, Argentina; *Previous page:* Arenal volcano in Costa Rica

AT A GLANCE

EAT

Try *cordero al palo*, whole lamb spit-roasted over an open fire with chimichurri salsa, or *empanadas de cordero*, flaky pastry pockets filled with lamb, onions and garlic.

DRINK

Calafate sour is a twist on the pisco sour, laced with calafate berry syrup. Legend has it that if you try the calafate berry you're guaranteed to return to Patagonia.

STAY

Pack an extreme-weather tent or book your dorm in a *refugio* or ecolodge well in advance. *Estancias* offer traditional ranch life. Gateway towns like Puerto Natales (in Chile) and El Chaltén (in Argentina) have tons of choice.

EXPERIENCE

Hit the road and get off the beaten track on Argentina's legendary Ruta 40, which unravels through Patagonia's vast, beautiful pampas with the snowcapped Andes hovering on the horizon.

SHOP

Buy a pair of super-soft Patagonian merino wool socks and hand-knitted jumper, or a bottle of purple-hued, herby, berry-forward Last Hope Calafate Gin.

A Traveller's Tale

Day breaks on the Huemul Circuit and the sky looms grey and menacing as I crawl out of my tent to face the day's first challenge: the Río Túnel. The river is fast-flowing, the water icy and waist-deep. The wind bends me double as I grapple for a foothold on slippery rocks, heart hammering, poles digging into pebbles. One wrong step and I'm a goner. As I reach the other side, a rainbow appears and relief floods my body. But the battle has just begun, with nature unleashing its full force as I traverse the crevasse-riddled Lower Túnel Glacier, gusts catching me unawares as we approach the Mordor-like peaks of the Cerro Grande. The wind howls and rain pounds on a relentless climb to Paso del Viento (Windy Pass). My reward at the top is a break in the weather and an astonishing view of the Southern Patagonian Ice Field that quite literally blows me away.

KERRY WALKER

"Patagonia is truly deserving of its 'epic' label. A region whittled out of rock, ice, desert-like steppe and thundering rivers"

Left: the sun rises over a lake in Patagonia's Torres del Paine

And rightfully so. While this national park in southern Chile is no secret, it is unmissable – a ravishing spread of granite towers, raging rivers, azure lakes and golden pampas where guanacos graze. The masterstroke is the vast, iceberg-calving, crushed-meringue-like expanse of the Grey Glacier. These days, you can choose your level of comfort, from wind-pounded tent to *refugio* dorm bed to luxe lodge where you can round out a day's hike over steaks and pisco sours. For fewer crowds, sidestep peak season (November to February) or tackle the tougher, remoter, less-hyped eight- to 10-day 'O' circuit.

Torres del Paine gets all the love but it's tip-of-the-iceberg stuff – Patagonia is more than a one-hike wonder. Argentina lures intrepid folk to Parque Nacional Los Glaciares for challenging treks like the four-day, 40-mile (65km) Huemul Circuit, heading deep into the wilderness nudging the Southern Patagonian Ice Field. With more time, you can embark on the long-distance Huella Andina, a 372-mile (600km) stomp across Northern Patagonia from Neuquén to Chubut, rounding up five national parks. Chile knits together 17 national parks on its 1740-mile (2800km) Ruta de los Parques between Puerto Montt and Cape Horn, allowing walkers to easily dip into the country's most extraordinary landscapes.

Trek in Patagonia and you'll curse the wicked winds and cruel climbs. But you'll be back, bearing muddy boots, as there's no place on Earth quite like it.

This page top: guanacos in Torres del Paine, Chile; visitors at a lookout point over Perito Moreno glacier in Argentina

PRACTICALITIES

GETTING THERE AND AROUND

Patagonia is well known for its rough *ripio* (gravel) roads and seemingly never-ending bus rides. In Chile, there are daily direct flights between Santiago and Punta Arenas, the closest airport (about a five-hour drive) to Torres del Paine. In Argentina, you can reach El Chaltén by flying to El Calafate, with daily flights from hubs including Buenos Aires and Ushuaia.

WHEN TO GO

November to April (late spring to autumn) is best for hiking in Patagonia, with lots of colour in wildflowers and foliage respectively, though be prepared for wild weather and wind year-round. Crowds peak from December to February. Snow and flooding render many trails inaccessible in winter when *refugios* close.

THINGS TO NOTE

This is tough terrain so some experience is necessary and, depending on the trek, possibly a guide, such as Swoop (swoop-patagonia.com). In summer, reserve accommodation well in advance. Pack wind and waterproof gear for the unpredictable weather, a pair of sturdy boots, hiking poles, good topographic maps – not all trails are perfectly waymarked – and a compass.

Two Week Itinerary

>

Touch down in El Calafate, then take a 3½-hour bus ride to El Chaltén. If you're driving, it's a dramatic road trip on Ruta 40, which blazes through rust-tinged pampas towards the gnarly, snow-frosted peaks of Cerro Fitz Roy.

>>

Spend a couple of days in El Chaltén, Argentina's chilled-out hiking capital. Enlist a good local guide to strike out into the savagely beautiful Parque Nacional Los Glaciares on the Huemul Circuit. Battling fierce winds, raging rivers, glacier traverses and thigh-burning mountain passes, the four-day, wild-camp hike is often billed as Patagonia's toughest trek.

>>>

Bus it or drive back to El Calafate. From here, you're a short hop from the national park's showstopping centrepiece: the 19-mile-long (30km), 197ft-high (60m) Perito Moreno Glacier, where giant icebergs (some as big as houses) fall in thunderous booms. Join a guided tour to slip on crampons for a glacier hike. El Calafate is a five-hour bus ride from Puerto Natales, gateway to Parque Nacional Torres del Paine, south of Los Glaciares.

MORE TIME? Get a solid night's sleep in an *estancia* or *refugio* before embarking on the 'W' trek to be wowed by its guanaco-grazed steppe, granite pillars, jewel-coloured lakes and one vast, radiant blue glacier.

BRAZIL

Journey Down *the* Amazon

IN THE ROADLESS TRACTS of the Amazon, highways are made of water and oversized ferries are floating buses carrying people and produce from place to place. Huge transit hubs such as Manaus see passenger boats arriving from far-flung corners of northern Brazil, while oceangoing vessels travel up and down the famed river to the Atlantic, some 930 miles (1500km) to the east. Near the bustling waterfront, Manaus' historic core is sprinkled with grand buildings from its past, including the Teatro Amazonas, a Renaissance Revival opera house with an elaborately tiled dome painted in the colours of the Brazilian flag.

Manaus is also the epicentre for adventures into the jungle. Dozens of lodges lie within a half-day boat journey from the city, including riverside spots where the days are spent tracking monkeys, macaws and pink river dolphins, and the nights offer immersion in the wondrous cacophony of the rainforest's nocturnal wildlife.

It's a slow, four-day journey to Belém aboard a triple-decked wooden vessel strung with hammocks. Impromptu communities form as everyone chats with their neighbour, swaying

Opposite: the Uakari Lodge in Brazil's Mamirauá Reserve promotes ecotourism;
This page: kayaking in the Amazon rainforest

just a few inches on either side of them. Delicious breezes give respite from the tropical heat as thick jungle rolls past, and the meditative quiet is pierced by the occasional roar of a howler monkey. Along the way, there are several worthwhile places to break up the trip, including Santarém, which has a pleasant riverside promenade, leafy parks and open-sided restaurants serving up fresh fish from the Amazon. Just west of Santarém is Alter do Chão, a village fronting an astonishing lagoon complete with white-sand beaches and limpid waters ideal for snorkelling.

A Traveller's Tale

As I stepped onto the rickety boat, I felt both excitement and dread. The voyage from Santarém to Belém seemed like a rite of passage, but I wasn't sure how I'd deal with two days sitting idly as we chugged along. I needn't have worried. I quickly made friends with chatty families and other solo travellers bunking in hammocks around me. And the evenings, drinking cold beers while watching the stars, were unforgettable.

REGIS ST LOUIS

AT A GLANCE

EAT
Try *tacacá*, a soup of shrimp, *tucupí* (made from cassava) and lip-tingling *jambú* leaves.

DRINK
Enjoy smoothies made with açaí and other Amazonian fruits.

SLEEP
Set in Mamirauá Reserve, sustainable, community-run Uakari Lodge is one of Brazil's ecotourism pioneers.

EXPERIENCE
Near Manaus, take a boat to see the Meeting of the Waters, where the dark Rio Negro and milky-coffee-coloured Rio Solimões flow side-by-side without mixing.

This page: the attractive city of Belém, capital of the Brazilian state of Pará

The boat journey ends at Belém, a captivating city near the mouth of the river. Much like Manaus, Belém has a vibrant waterfront. By day, shoppers crowd into the vast belle époque Ver-o-Peso Market, the stalls heaving with exotic Amazonian fruits, medicinal plants and the fresh catch of the day. In the evening, friends and couples gather at the open-air bars and eateries of shore-hugging Estação das Docas, the perfect spot to watch the sunset over Guajará Bay.

PRACTICALITIES

GETTING THERE
AND AROUND
Manaus has a few direct flights to the US, while Belém has flights to Lisbon. Both are also well-connected to other cities in Brazil. Once there, riverboats motor between towns, although if time is limited you can fly.

WHEN TO GO
During the dry season (June to November), water levels fall and it's a prime time for wildlife viewing. The wet season (December to May) brings torrential downpours, though there's plenty of sunshine in between showers.

THINGS TO NOTE
If you're travelling by riverboat, bring drinking water and a hammock (you can purchase quality hammocks in Brazil). There are also cabins, but these are often hotter and more confining than the breezy decks. Food is available, though it's good to bring snacks.

11 Day Itinerary

> In Manaus, spend a day exploring the historic sights, including a tour of the Teatro Amazonas, before heading to the Museu da Amazônia to get close-up looks at the rainforest's flora and fauna.

>> From Manaus, spend three full days (or more if you can) at a jungle lodge, enjoying kayaking, guided hikes and wildlife watching, followed by memorable sunsets and evening excursions to see (and hear) nocturnal wildlife.

>>> Spend days five and six aboard a public boat trundling its way to Santarém. Once there, take the one-hour bus trip to Alter do Chão where you'll spend a delightful seventh day paddling, snorkelling and relaxing on the white-sand beach fronting Lago Verde.

>>>> Back in Santarém, it's another two days to Belém by boat. Once you arrive, wander the old city, visiting museums and old sights, before rounding off your river odyssey at restaurant- and bar-lined Estação das Docas on the waterfront.

MORE TIME? From Belém, take a three-hour ferry to Ilha do Marajó, a massive river island sprinkled with sleepy villages, deserted beaches and abandoned Portuguese-era estates.

BRAZIL

Live It Up *in* Rio de Janeiro

RIO DE JANEIRO HAS an idyllic setting for a metropolis. Wedged between forest-covered mountains and golden beaches, human life mixes with marmosets skittering through leafy parks and capybara grazing along the shores of Lagoa, while street markets heave with exotic fruits. The wonders of the tropics seem deeply woven into the urban fabric here. When the sun is high overhead, there's no better place to be than Ipanema Beach. Surfers jockey for space off rocky Arpoador as vendors wind through the bikini- and *sunga* (Speedo)-clad crowds proffering *agua de coco* (coconut water), *cerveja* (beer) and other cold drinks. Bronzed bodies are everywhere – kicking footballs, jogging along the water's edge and cycling the promenade. In the evening, life takes a different form. Samba's rapid rhythms draw revellers to Lapa's dancehalls, and a bohemian crowd heads for Santa Teresa's hilltop cocktail lounges. With so much on offer, it's no wonder Cariocas (locals) joke that 'Deus é Brasileiro' (God is Brazilian) and couldn't imagine living anywhere else.

AT A GLANCE

EAT
Weekends mean *feijoada*, a traditional pork and black-bean stew.

DRINK
The much-loved caipirinha cocktail serves as potent refreshment on the beach.

PRACTICALITIES

Rio has an excellent metro system, but you can also get around with Bike Itaú, an easy-to-use bicycle-sharing network.

CHILE

Visit Other Worlds
in the Atacama Desert

AT A GLANCE

EAT

Unique to the Atacama, *patasca* is a meat, potatoes, onions and corn stew.

DRINK

Sip a pisco sour, the national drink, under a starry sky.

PRACTICALITIES

Tour operators in the town of San Pedro de Atacama offer a range of excursions, including sandboarding, geyser walks and mountain biking.

STEAM SPILLS FROM GURGLING mud pools as a geyser blasts superheated water into the frosty air. The sun peaks over the mountains bathing the geothermal field of El Tatio in golden light. Walking amid these sputtering features high in the Andes, it's easy to feel like you've left Earth behind and landed on another planet. To the west, the wind creates artful, undulating patterns in the red-gold sand dunes of the aptly named Valle de Marte (Mars Valley). Nearby lie the dramatic multihued rock formations of the Valle de la Luna (Moon Valley), and shimmering salt lakes that seem as lifeless as the surrounding desert – until a flock of brilliant pink flamingos arrives to feed on brine shrimp and other microorganisms. These are just a few of the many astonishing landscapes of the Atacama, one of the oldest and driest deserts in the world – and the otherworldly wonders don't end at sundown. With clear skies and little light pollution, the region is also renowned for stargazing.

COLOMBIA

Venture from *the* Desert *to the* Jungle

COLOMBIA'S 1000-MILE (1600KM) Caribbean coastline is way more than just a string of palm-fringed beaches. Behind the strips of sand lies a mix of strident cultures, diverse ecosystems and moulded-in-stone history.

As you stand amid the stark coastal desert of La Guajira Peninsula, it's hard to imagine how quickly and dramatically the scenery will change as you head west. Flush up against the border with Venezuela, La Guajira stands at the northern tip of the South American continent. The scrubby landscapes, best navigated in an off-road vehicle, are inhabited by the Indigenous Wayuu people, famed for their intricate weaving and forthright resistance to colonisation.

The coast's biggest lure for first-time visitors is the well-preserved walled city of Cartagena, 249 miles (400km) to the west, its basic structure unaltered for centuries, and its charm and mystique unrivalled anywhere in the country. With intimate plazas and sturdy fortifications, the former trade port is an evocative place for lovers of history, romance and good food. You'll find grittier and less crowded urban action in Santa Marta, to the east, a slightly older city with strong connections

A Traveller's Tale

It's hard to emulate the historic charm of Cartagena, where horses' hooves echo down cobbled streets and bougainvillea spills over wrought-iron balconies, but I've always found myself experiencing equally blissful sensations in Capurganá in the Darien Gap. Hemmed in by jungle, and bereft of motor traffic, this small, insular settlement is the perfect place to while away indolent hours strolling along steamy jungle paths looking out for toucans and howler monkeys.

BRENDAN SAINSBURY

AT A GLANCE

EAT
Savour warm *arepas* stuffed with melted cheese, the ultimate Colombian street food.

DRINK
Head up to Minca, near Santa Marta, for some of the best coffee in Colombia.

STAY
Gravitate to a small historic hotel in the Centro or San Diego neighbourhoods of Cartagena.

EXPERIENCE
Go river-tubing in Palomino, a rustic beach haven with cheap accommodation between Riohacha and Santa Marta.

Opposite: blooms on the beach near Riohacha on Colombia's Caribbean coast;
This page: the spire of the 17th-century cathedral in Cartagena's old town

to celebrated South American liberator Simón Bolívar, who died here in 1830. The coast around Santa Marta, at the foot of the coffee-growing Sierra Nevada, is lush and humid, culminating in the small, forested swathe of Parque Nacional Natural Tayrona, a paradise of meandering coastal trails leading to idyllic swimming spots. The city is used as a base for excursions into the misty mountains of Minca and the isolated trek-in ruins of Ciudad Perdida, a one-time citadel of the pre-Columbian Tayrona civilisation.

West again, past Cartagena, the coast is less touristy until you reach the Gulf of Urabá, beyond which lies the thin jungle-covered Darien Gap isthmus, where North and South America meet. Tricky to reach by land, this mostly roadless enclave is still little-visited by non-Colombians. Most people arrive by boat, heading for the small community of Capurganá, huddled against the border with Panama. Still imbued with an island-like, under-the-radar feel, this magical region is beloved for its exotic birdlife and hidden natural pools surrounded by unblemished rainforest.

Opposite top: somewhere to take it easy as the sun sets over Colombian sands; *Bottom:* the ancient ruins of Ciudad Perdida

Two Week Itinerary

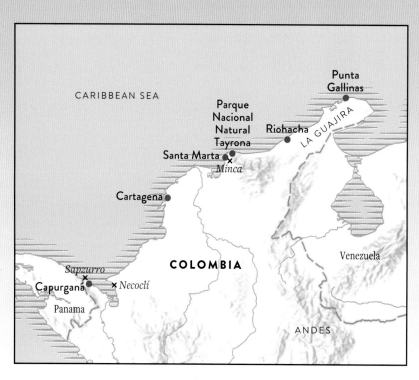

> Start in Riohacha, gateway to La Guajira, where the desert kisses the Caribbean. Stay a couple of days and get a jeep to whiz through sand dunes to Punta Gallinas, where you can sleep in a hammock and sample local seafood.

>> Bus southwest for a day in the Parque Nacional Natural Tayrona, whose panoramic coastal trails link unblemished beaches ideal for swimming. It's a short bus ride to Santa Marta, a mesh of cool cafes and Bolívar-related historical sites. Spend two days here, making time for a side-trip to the coffee-growing town of Minca.

>>> Next stop, Cartagena, merits four days. One for the beach, one for the walls and squares, one dedicated to forts and museums, and the last for seeking out the bars in the Gestemani quarter. Suitably relaxed, take a bus-boat combo southwest, with an overnight in Necoclí, for three days in Capurganá, a remote beach-shack village surrounded by jungle and with excellent diving.

MORE TIME?

Hike 2.5 miles (4km) from Capurganá to the village of Sapzurro and on into Panama.

PRACTICALITIES

GETTING THERE AND AROUND

The region's main international airport is in Cartagena. Riohacha has a small airport with regular flights to Bogotá. Most of the Caribbean coast is accessible by bus, except Capurganá which requires a boat ride.

WHEN TO GO

The beaches are at their best around Christmas and New Year when the humidity drops. The dry season peaks between February and April, when it's rare to experience a day interrupted by rain.

THINGS TO NOTE

There are no ATMs in Capurganá – bring plenty of cash. A 4WD vehicle and driver are essential for the deserts of La Guajira, where in most places there are no roads at all. Tours can easily be organised in Riohacha.

Further information is available at colombia.travel/en/where-to-go/ great-caribbean-colombian

CUBA

Experience Son, Sand *and* Revolution

INLAND FROM CUBA'S HANDSOME beaches is a world of syncopated music, rebellious history and Afro-Latino culture. Most visitors head directly for the sprawling resorts that line the north coast and rarely leave. But beaches are only a small part of what this complicated country is all about. Beyond Cayo Coco and Varadero lies a land of head-scratching anachronisms and jarring contradictions, that invariably throw up more questions than answers.

If it's your first time on the Caribbean's biggest island, you'll undoubtedly want to squeeze in as many quintessential experiences as possible – including rum-laced cocktails, traditional live music known as *son*, and a couple of bombastic revolutionary museums – which means tracing a meandering path west–east between the country's two largest cities, Havana and Santiago de Cuba. Both are impressionistic, vibrant places stuffed with Spanish-era forts, flamboyant cabaret acts and seductive streetscapes where life is still lived very much out

Opposite: eye-catching autos and architecture in the town of Camagüey;
This page: street entertainers in Old Havana

in the open. Havana is a great city for art and design aficionados, with one of the finest ensembles of historic architecture in the Americas. Santiago, its smaller, more seditious twin, is sometimes referred to as the 'city of revolutionaries' for having spawned a long line of political firebrands.

The towns and cities in between oscillate between the famous and infamous. Cienfuegos, Trinidad and Camagüey are all UNESCO World Heritage Sites courtesy of their striking architecture. Cienfuegos is a city of slender columns and graceful neoclassical facades that retains a definitive French flavour.

A Traveller's Tale

I could easily spend an entire trip in Havana and often do. With its wild salsa energy, spontaneous street theatre and ruggedly beautiful historic buildings, it's a hard city to leave. A typical night will see me at the Fábrica de Arte Cubano listening to spectacular live music before hitching a ride back along the Malecón sea wall at 1am, with the window open and the ocean spray blowing in my face.

BRENDAN SAINSBURY

AT A GLANCE

EAT
Dine on *ropa vieja*, shredded beef in a spicy sauce, accompanied by rice, beans and vegetables.

DRINK
Imbibe a glass of fiery local rum. The Santiago de Cuba blend is often touted as the country's best.

STAY
Bed down in an economical *casa particular* (private homestay).

EXPERIENCE
Enjoy a night of unplanned live music. Don't book, just follow the sounds on the street.

Trinidad, nestled in the Sierra del Escambray, is a time-warped tangle of sturdy mansions and cobbled streets that harks back to the settlement's history as a wealthy sugar town. Camagüey's maze of narrow, winding streets is guarded by baroque churches and giant clay pots known as *tinajones*. Santa Clara and Bayamo are two lower-key towns with strong revolutionary legacies: the former guards the mausoleum of Che Guevara; the latter is the birthplace of 'Father of the Motherland', Carlos Manuel de Céspedes.

If the beach is calling, Cuba has hundreds worth your time, but the stand-out in terms of all-round magnificence is Varadero, a 12.4-mile-long (20km) strip of sand on the north coast that's large enough to satisfy all moods, tastes and budgets.

Opposite top: the colonial town of Trinidad; *Bottom:* a Cuban musician blows his trumpet for passers-by

16 Day Itinerary

> Spend four days taking in Havana's art, history and music. Next, take a three-hour bus ride to Varadero for two days admiring the Caribbean's best beach and exploring the waters by catamaran. It's another three-hour bus ride to Santa Clara, where horse-carts will take you to the Che memorial and alternative music will draw you into Club Mejunje. The next day, head to Cienfuegos, an architectural homage to Neoclassicism.

>> After a night in its elegant bars, track 1½ hours along the coast to stuck-in-time Trinidad, where the *casas particulares* are palatial and the restaurants museum-like. Three days is enough to absorb the cobbled centre, visit the local beach and hike the nearby mountains.

>>> Heading east by bus, reserve a day for Camagüey, with its eye-catching ceramics, and another for laid-back Bayamo, with mementos of Cuba's first independence uprising. Finish with three days in Santiago de Cuba, the national capital of folkloric dance and traditional *son* music.

MORE TIME?

Press on to offbeat Baracoa on Cuba's eastern tip for spicy food and jungle walks.

PRACTICALITIES

GETTING THERE AND AROUND

José Martí International is Cuba's main airport. Another useful gateway is Varadero, 100 miles (160km) to the east. State-run Víazul buses serve all the main towns and cities.

WHEN TO GO

It's best to travel outside the June–November hurricane season. The five-month spell between November and April is the coolest and driest.

THINGS TO NOTE

Cuba is still primarily a cash economy, with a widespread black market offering highly volatile exchange rates. US-linked credit cards are not accepted. Economical accommodation can be found in the countrywide network of *casas particulares* (private homestays) that usually supply a hearty breakfast for a small extra cost. Book in advance through Airbnb or Expedia.

Further information is available at lonelyplanet.com/cuba

ECUADOR

See Evolution *in* Action *on the* Galápagos

THE WORLD HAS A LOT to thank the Galápagos Islands for. Famously connected to Charles Darwin and his theory of evolution, these islands were never part of the South American mainland, meaning plants and animals here followed their own extraordinary paths. Tortoises, free of predators, became huge. Finches, lacking competition, sub-specialised into tool users (woodpecker finch), seed eaters (ground finch) and blood suckers (vampire finch), among others. Flightless cormorants dive like porpoises, and iguanas feed in the sea. The landscapes are just as unusual, varying from island to island. Younger islands like Isabela burst with volcanic activity, while central Santa Cruz features endangered scalesia forests. Older islands to the east include Española, whose flat-topped cliffs are home to colonies of waved albatross – a bird so massive it needs a runway to get aloft. While it's impossible to see everything in one trip, on even a short cruise the days are packed with once-in-a-lifetime experiences, from spotting blue-footed boobies in a mating dance to snorkelling over lava formations.

AT A GLANCE

EAT
Enjoy fresh-off-the-boat seafood at Puerto Ayora's waterfront market.

DRINK
Coffee made from beans grown in the Galápagos' rich volcanic soils is served in some cafes.

PRACTICALITIES

Small (typically 16-passenger) cruise ships offer the best way to see the islands. Peruse a range of boats and itineraries at Happy Gringo.

BOLIVIA

Marvel at Surreal Salar de Uyuni

AT A GLANCE

EAT
The perfect snack is the *salteña*, pastry filled with meat and vegetables.

DRINK
Warm up with *api*, a hot drink of corn, cinnamon and citrus.

PRACTICALITIES
Numerous companies offer tours (typically three-day circuits) from Uyuni. It's worth paying extra for a reputable outfit like Quechua Connection.

DRIVING ACROSS THE BLINDING white landscape, it's easy to lose all sense of proportion. The horizon vanishes, and mirages form and then melt away on Bolivia's Salar de Uyuni – the largest salt flats on the planet. The surreal perspective only intensifies after a rainstorm, when a thin layer of water creates a mirror-like surface reflecting the sky overhead. Stepping out of the 4WD and across this otherworldly terrain is like walking on the clouds. Tours from the lofty town of Uyuni (elevation: a whopping 12,140ft/3700m) rumble out to the great sunbaked plains. Along the way you'll stop at a mountaintop emerging from a snow white sea – or at least that's what Isla Incahuasi resembles. This cactus-covered 'island' is all that remains of an ancient volcano that was once surrounded by a prehistoric lake. By late afternoon the blustery desert cold arrives along with a legendary sunset, as the sky and glass-like earth below light up in fiery colours.

ANTARCTICA

Board an Expedition *to* Antarctica

REACHING ANTARCTICA IS LIKE the moment Dorothy wakes up in Oz. After two days of treacherous storms and seasickness on the Drake Passage, everything suddenly shines in technicolour. The waves give way to mirror-calm waters, reflecting icebergs as big as castles and frost-white, fin-shaped mountains. Glaciers boom. Humpback whales breach and blow. Penguins skitter across snowy beaches, eyed up by hungry leopard seals. You can watch every David Attenborough documentary going, but nothing prepares you for the reality of the White Continent. Here nature is turned up to max, wildlife rules and human beings are just passing through. Antarctica isn't just random bucket-list stuff, though. It's an effort and an investment. A physically demanding adventure to a remote, cold, wondrous place at the edge of the planet and the final frontier of the imagination. Choose a small, sustainably minded ship to get to the parts that the bigger cruises can't reach, and prepare for a journey that is beautiful beyond belief.

AT A GLANCE

STAY

A 10-night trip costs around US$7500 (sharing a cabin is cheaper).

EXPERIENCE

Daily zodiac boat excursions get you up close with the wildlife.

PRACTICALITIES

Expeditions run during the short summer (November to March). March is good for marine mammals. Most voyages depart from Ushuaia at Argentina's southern tip.

BAHAMAS

Hop Islands *in the* Bahamas

AT A GLANCE

EAT
Conch salad is a mix of firm mollusc with vegetables and citrus juice.

DRINK
Try a Bahama Mama: rum, juice and grenadine served over crushed ice.

PRACTICALITIES
Avoid the Atlantic hurricane season, which runs June to November, when storms can impact boat charter and flight schedules.

HOW MANY SHADES OF BLUE can there be? As you start calculating from your beach towel looking out at the sea, the number soon starts to add up. And that can be just from a singular vantage point in the Bahamas, let alone across its 16 major islands. Each of those islands is unique and easy to reach – the country has around 40 airports, a number of ferry operators and private yacht and boat charters – and as you hop from one to another, you'll find this is a no-limits, build-your-own-adventure destination. You can splash with the swimming pigs off Big Major Cay, kayak through mangroves at Lucayan National Park on Grand Bahama and gaze at the pink majesty that is the Atlantis resort on Paradise Island. For happy faces and a bumping energy, time your visit for the annual Junkanoo festival, held the day after Christmas and soundtracked by cowbells and goatskin drums. And keep counting those blues.

PERU

Encounter Ancient Civilisations *and* Mythical Ruins

PERU'S INCREDIBLE RUINS showcase a rich tapestry of pre-Columbian cultures spread over five millennia. From fortified ridgelines in the Andes to mysterious geoglyphs in the Nazca Desert, the country is scattered with archaeological sites. The misty terraces that embellish the slopes of Machu Picchu are merely a gateway to less heralded but equally fascinating places. While none are quite as spectacular as the fabled 'Lost City of the Incas', many are significantly older, and most are a lot less crowded.

The south is a good place to start. With Cuzco as your base, pitch northwest to the ruins and museums of the Sacred Valley. A special ticket, the *boleto turístico*, covers a dozen sites here including magnificently terraced Pisac, megalithic Sacsayhuamán and geometrically aligned Ollantaytambo, famed for its aqueducts and fountains. The valley acts as a perfect overture for Peru's best-known attraction, Machu Picchu, where you can roam the mythical ruins with thousands of other speechless admirers. Save time for the Lost City's smaller sibling, Choquequirao. Sometimes referred to as a mini Machu Picchu, it's

Opposite: sculpted wall at the ancient Chimú city of Chan Chan; *This page top*: Quechua women in traditional dress; *Bottom*: a cable car returns from Kuelap Fortress archaeological site

AT A GLANCE

EAT
Sit down to *lomo saltado*, Peru's divine stir-fry dish, loaded with marinated steak strips, peppers and french fries, and served with a side of rice.

DRINK
Sip Peru's quintessential cocktail, a pisco sour, made by mixing the local pisco spirit with lime, syrup, egg white and Angostura bitters.

STAY
Seek out an Andean lodge. They can range from cheap to boutique, but all are carefully integrated with their rural surroundings and celebrate local culture with thick blankets, bright hues, Peruvian art and instant access to the mountains.

EXPERIENCE
Get acclimatised in Huaraz (altitude 10,101ft/3091m) by hiking 5 miles (8km) up to Monumento Nacional Wilkahuaín, a small, remarkably well-preserved Wari ruin dating from between 600 to 900 CE.

SHOP
San Blas in Cuzco is an artisan quarter with workshops and showrooms of local craftspeople. Jewellery shops and unique designer boutiques provide a welcome break from the ubiquitous ponchos and sheepskin rugs.

A Traveller's Tale

While all Peruvian ruins are imbued with a strong sense of history, some are more magical than others. For me, the apex of the country's archaeological sites is Kuélap, the erstwhile redoubt of the Chachapoya people, a civilisation that predates Machu Picchu by around 500 years and whose foggy history I find especially intriguing. Known as the 'Warriors of the Clouds', the Chachapoya are renowned for their haunting sarcophagi etched with humanoid faces, and a relentless fighting spirit that enabled them to push back against the colonising Inca until the 1470s. I first visited Kuélap in 2018, soon after it had opened its mountain-spanning cable car, a move that has increased traffic to the ruins without destroying the special ambience. I was transported up in an eight-person cabin that swung eerily above a spectacular river valley, and descended on foot on the Camino Herradura, a magnificent 5.6-mile (9km) trail that zigzags steeply down the mountainside.

BRENDAN SAINSBURY

"From fortified ridgelines in the Andes to mysterious geoglyphs in the Nazca Desert, Peru is a country scattered with archaeological sites"

Right: a dramatic train ride through Peru's Cuzco region; *Opposite:* Machu Picchu at sunset

more tranquil thanks to its relative isolation (it's a four-day round-trip hike), although a planned cable car could change all that.

Huge zoomorphic figures lie scattered across Peru's southern desert, left by the ancient Paracas and Nazca cultures 2000 years before the invention of the aeroplane. Today, they're (ironically) best seen on a flightseeing trip out of Nazca or Pisco. Further north, several sites are easily visited from Peru's big cities. Pachacamac, 20 miles (31km) southeast of capital Lima, is an ancient citadel with adobe and stone palaces and temple pyramids. Chan Chan, on the coast just outside handsome Trujillo, is the Americas' largest pre-Columbian town and the largest adobe city in the world.

Branching off into remote valleys in the snowcapped Cordillera Blanca, you'll have to endure long bus rides and thin air to feast your eyes upon Chavín de Huántar – it's worth the effort though. A large part of these over 3000-year-old ruins lies underground and can be explored. The ancient ceremonial centre is best viewed in tandem with a visit to the nearby museum where much of its booty is displayed. Another remote but imposing citadel is Kuélap, a hilltop fortress built by the Chachapoya people roughly 1000 years ago. Located in Peru's Northern Highlands, the remains are perched atop a 9843ft-high (3000m) limestone ridge and surrounded by a near-impassable wall that reaches a height of 66ft (20m) in places. Once notoriously hard to reach, Kuélap has been made more accessible thanks to the installation of a cable car in 2017.

This page: the Panamericana cuts through the landscape near Nazca

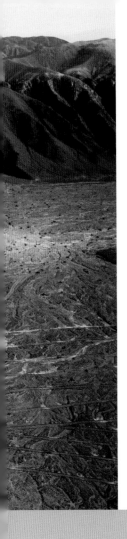

PRACTICALITIES

GETTING THERE AND AROUND

Lima International Airport is the main gateway to Peru. From here you can fly internally or catch a bus to Cuzco. Most of the country is accessible by bus, though journeys can be long. Fortunately, deluxe buses are exceptionally comfortable and run to most of the country's major towns. A train runs between Cuzco and Machu Picchu.

WHEN TO GO

June to August is the dry season in the Andean highlands and eastern rainforest, and is also the best time for festivals and activities, including treks.

THINGS TO NOTE

The Inca Trail to Machu Picchu is guided only, meaning you'll need to pre-book and acquire a permit. Entrance tickets to the site can be bought in advance in Cuzco. For the trek to Choquequirao, guides are not mandatory but recommended. For the Andes, bring shoes or boots that can tackle cobblestones and mountains, plus a rain jacket and warm layers, as it can be very chilly at altitude.

Further information is available at peru.travel

Three Week Itinerary

>

Spend two days in Cuzco, and an extra one exploring Ollantaytambo and the Sacred Valley. Next, get on a train to Aguas Calientes, the launching pad for Machu Picchu. Spend two days in the area to absorb the ruins. Then, having planned well ahead, tackle Choquequirao, which requires at least four days to hike in and out.

>>

Book a deluxe bus for the 14-hour trip to Nazca in the southern desert, where you can fly over the giant geoglyphs. Catch a bus north to Lima (eight hours) which merits three days for its cliff-lined coast, internationally lauded food and nearby Pachacamac ruins.

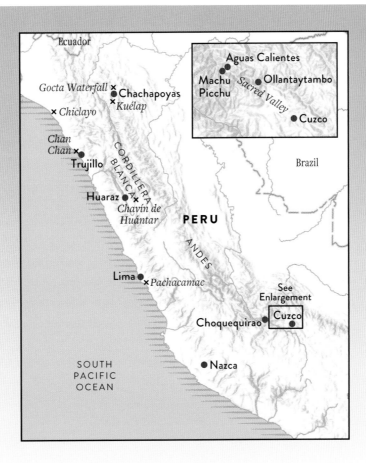

>>>

A comfortable long-distance bus will take you to the mountain nexus of Huaraz in the Cordillera Blanca, where a three-day stopover should include a day trip to the ruins of Chavín de Huántar.

>>>>

Trujillo, 5½ hours from Huaraz, deserves two days to take in its historic architecture and visit humongous Chan Chan. Head north up the coast, breaking your journey in Chicayo, where local agencies can organise trips to nearby archaeological sites. Finish your trip with three days in Chachapoyas, base camp for sorties to nearby Kuélap.

MORE TIME?

From Chachapoyas, you can arrange a trek to the 2530ft-high (771m) Gocta Waterfall.

COSTA RICA

Welcome *to the* Jungle

Opposite: Costa Rica's Playa Samara at low tide; *This page:* a three-toed sloth is one of the many animals you may spot in this wildlife-rich country

YOU'LL SEE THE EXPRESSION *pura vida* everywhere in Costa Rica. Plastered on billboards, adorning T-shirts in tourist shops and popping up regularly in conversation between friendly *Ticos* (locals) throughout the country. *Pura vida* translates as 'simple life', but its meaning extends beyond the literal to being used as a greeting and to simply say 'everything's cool'. And, indeed, everything is cool in this Central American country that's buzzing with five million residents and – fun fact, and only complementing its laid-back vibe – has no army.

Sure, people have caught on to this multifaceted, geographically blessed place over the years. The glistening white-sand beaches, the lush rainforests and the wildlife reserves where monkeys roam and toucans caw through jungles were never going to stay off the adventurous traveller's radar for long. And, more recently, museums in San José, the sprawling capital, and a host of raucous beach party towns (Jacó and Tamarindo, for example) have added to the appeal. It's a country that is visibly booming, with rising skylines in its cities, and it's all far from a secret these days.

A Traveller's Tale

I'll never forget my first trip to Costa Rica, with my Dad in 2004.
We landed at the airport in San José, rented an SUV in the middle of
the night and, for hours, drove down the curviest mountainside roads.
The route culminated along the Pacific Coast with a 28-mile (45km),
bumpy-beyond-belief, unpaved stretch from Dominical to Quepos.
The next morning, back in the car, we drove 15 minutes south to Parque
Nacional Manuel Antonio. Before arriving in the park, I remember
seeing El Avión – a Fairchild C-123 aircraft wedged into a cliff that
had morphed into a bar and restaurant, overlooking amazing blue-
green water. The wonders continued as we reached the national park's
entrance, with friendly critters popping out to say hi – tree-jumping
capuchin monkeys and nonchalant sloths among them. That's where my
Costa Rica love story began, and many chapters have been written in
the decades since.

JESSE SCOTT

AT A GLANCE

EAT
Stop at road-side *sodas* – traditional,
unpretentious Costa Rican
restaurants. Order a *casado* (typical
plate) and douse it in *salsa Lizano*,
the country's staple condiment.

DRINK
Opt for a Pilsen or Bavaria Gold
lager, full-bodied and often served
borderline frozen – you'll miss them
when you leave.

STAY
Bed down in a luxury resort on one
of Costa Rica's 58 designated wildlife
refuges. Reserva Conchal on the
Guanacaste Peninsula is in a 'blue
zone', where people statistically live
longer than average; or W Costa Rica
is an all-inclusive, modern icon with
a zip line to the beach.

EXPERIENCE
Costa Rica has eight coffee-growing
regions and tours aplenty. North
of San José, visit Doka Estate and
Hacienda Alsacia, tucked on the
slopes of Poás volcano. The latter is
Starbucks' first and only coffee farm.

SHOP
Mercado Central de San José is the
country's principal market, bustling
with *sodas*, coffee outposts and
mom-and-pop stalls selling art,
jewellery and everything in between.

"Costa Rica's glistening white-sand beaches, lush rainforests and wildlife reserves were never going to stay off the adventurous traveller's radar for long"

© KRYSSIA CAMPOS / GETTY IMAGES

Left: bathers enjoy one of Rincón de la Vieja's natural hot springs

However, more than anything, Costa Rica remains a dream destination for nature lovers who can, in one carefully planned swoop, go trekking up volcanoes, surf monster waves, float in twinkling waterfall pools and embrace underwater serenity snorkelling or diving at reefs where neon fish and blue crustaceans play in harmony. And to help things go smoothly, a sophisticated tourism infrastructure has emerged, with tour operators, transportation outfits and guides to piece together itineraries that spark your interest like never before.

To experience it all, three regions should be top of the list. The Central San José region is chock-full of mountain peaks, pine-dense forests for hiking and dormant volcanoes with turquoise lagoons to explore. The Guanacaste Peninsula features mountain-to-ocean landscapes, memorable cascades for a dip and and, at its southern tip, one of the country's vibe-iest jungle-side beach towns, Montezuma. The Pacific Coast, meanwhile, is not only home to world-class breakers but also quiet national parks brimming with biodiversity.

Costa Rica offers nature-and-wildlife sensory overload in the best way possible. The calmness of the people and serene scenery contrast with the blood-pumping exhilaration you can get from ATV-ing past sloths on remote dirt roads, zip lining through forest canopies and learning all about the gold and jade-filled history of this 300-year-old nation in museums. Begin the day with some of the country's famous coffee, grown on its many plantations, and end it, after hours of outdoor fun, with a well-earned ice-cold Imperial or Pilsen beer. *Pura vida* indeed.

This page: typically tasty Costa Rican food; chasing the surf at Playa Santa Teresa

PRACTICALITIES

GETTING THERE AND AROUND

Costa Rica is served by two international airports, central Juan Santamaría outside San José, and the less-trafficked Daniel Oduber Quirós near Liberia. For jungle-hopping, renting a 4WD vehicle is a must for coping with steep mountain landscapes and periodic gravel roads. Tour operators offer shuttles, and buses zip daily around the country, too.

WHEN TO GO

December to April is best – it's the dry season and, from jungles to beaches, there are clear skies and bright sun. This is also peak season, so count on larger crowds. Rainy season is generally May to November – note that at the end of the season debris can pile-up, drainage issues can be a problem and mudslides occur in more remote areas.

THINGS TO NOTE

Tap water is drinkable in most areas. A notable exception is most of the Osa Peninsula, so have bottled water or a purifier handy. Avoid a case of dangerous mosquito-borne illnesses like dengue fever by applying repellent and wearing long sleeves if visiting any rainforests. *Further information is available at visitcostarica.com*

Two Week Itinerary

> Land in San José and take a couple of days to acclimatise and visit the capital's museums dedicated to gold, jade and homegrown artists. Then your beachside escape begins after a five-hour drive and ferry trip to the southern tip of the Guanacaste Peninsula and bohemian Montezuma.

>> Day four involves another five-hour drive for some volcano and mountain time in Parque Nacional Volcán Arenal. Spend a couple of days in this prime spot for hot springs, rappelling and rafting, with the active peak always in the background.

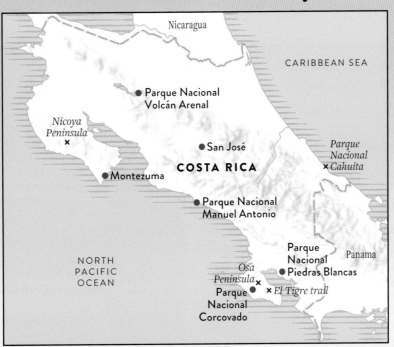

>>> On day seven, one more five-hour drive leads to Nauyaca Waterfall Nature Park, yours for three days. Sparkling waterfalls aside, book a horse ride through the rainforest, where you might hear the squawks of a great curassow (a giant, turkey-like bird). Less than three hours south, the Osa Peninsula – with Parque Nacional Corcovado and nearby Parque Nacional Piedras Blancas – equates to rainforest bliss. The El Tigre trail – an old gold-mining route – has 375 bird species to spot.

>>>> End with two days around Parque Nacional Manuel Antonio on the Pacific – look for monkeys along the beachside trail and take a surf lesson before heading back to San José.

MORE TIME? Parque Nacional Cahuita, on the Caribbean coast, is home to Costa Rica's largest coral reef.

JAMAICA

Let the Good Times Roll

JAMAICA, WITH A CULTURE steeped in rum, reggae and Rastafarian spirit, is as energising as ever it was. This is a place that doesn't give you time to slow down – here, the illusion is that life is permanently switched to holiday mode. The country's good times once began at Port Royal, formerly a stronghold of rum-swilling pirates dubbed the 'wickedest city on earth'. Magnificent ships were anchored in the harbour, but all that remains of such *Pirates of the Caribbean*-type villainy are the rusting cannons and toothy ramparts of Fort George. Kingston, meanwhile, is where Bob Marley raised the roof for reggae and fans can get nostalgic at his former home, while Appleton Estate near Black River is for rum tastings and tours at the historic distillery. Then, to the northwest is Goldeneye, once belonging to James Bond author Ian Fleming and now a swish hotel; here, naturally, cocktails are served shaken not stirred.

AT A GLANCE

DRINK
Try a Goldeneye rum cocktail, served with pineapple and hint of lime.

EXPERIENCE
Visit Tuff Gong, Bob Marley's recording studio where *Could You Be Loved* was recorded.

PRACTICALITIES
Avoid the Caribbean's hurricane season by visiting from November to March. Get around by public transport or rental car.

USA

Get Your Kicks *and* Kitsch *on* Route 66

THERE'S NO AMERICAN TRIP like a road trip. The mother of them all is Route 66 from Chicago to Santa Monica, cutting through the heart of the US on its way to the 'promised land' of California. While the original route has been mostly subsumed by modern highways, many sights remain – vintage gas stations and drive-in restaurants, blinking neon signs, kitsch roadside attractions. And then there's the landscape. Endless prairie gives way to rolling hills which lead to silvery high plains and scorched red desert. The drive can feel surreal,

miles of empty road punctuated by improbable sights. Outside Tulsa is an 80ft (24m) plaster whale beached in a pond. In Amarillo, there's a field of Cadillacs buried nose-down in the earth. The natural splendour can feel equally surreal – the rainbow-coloured fossilised trees of the Petrified Forest, the towering cacti of the Mojave Desert. By the time the Pacific appears, 2448 miles (3940km) in, a simple road trip has become an epic journey.

USA

Take a Musical Pilgrimage *in the* South

Opposite: tucking into Nashville-style hot chicken; *This page:* dancers during the Crawfish Festival in Breaux Bridge, Louisiana

COUNTRY SINGERS KNOW they've made it when they see their name in lights on venues in Nashville. 'Music City' draws both wannabe songwriters and music lovers from across the globe, eager to hear that unique Nashville sound. There are celebrated concert halls like the Ryman Auditorium and Grand Ole Opry, and famed recording studios where you can you see (and hear) what all the fuss was about. By night, visitors fill the well-worn dance floors of honky tonks as the next-big-thing takes to the stage.

A few hours west, music is the lifeblood of another venerable Tennessee town, Memphis – although here that signature sound is the blues. As the moon rises over Beale St, melancholic rhythms and the reverb of slide guitar spill out of low-slung brick buildings lit by neon signs. The atmosphere is electric as people file into lively bars and clubs. Night spots in other parts of town include Wild Bill's dive bar in historic Vollintine-Evergreen, and stylish food- and drink-loving Lafayette's, an anchor of Overton Sq. During the day, Elvis fans take the hallowed tour through the King's gaudy Graceland mansion, followed by a look at his simple but moving gravesite out back.

A Traveller's Tale

I wasn't sure quite what to expect when I made my first trip to Breaux Bridge in Cajun Country. I'd been told by a friend to get to the restaurant early, and the line was already out the door at Buck & Johnny's when I arrived at 8am. Sure you can order breakfast (the crawfish-topped grits are a perennial favourite), but most people were here to dance. Filling the warmly lit space, talented couples moved with quick-stepping footwork as they twirled on the makeshift dance floor. By the front windows, a six-piece zydeco band laid down syncopated rhythms on accordion, washboard and electric guitars as the frontman crooned his heart out in Creole French. I opted for hot coffee, rather than the bottomless mimosas and bloody Marys, to keep up my energy levels – though I still never matched that of the old timers who moved with surprising quickness.

REGIS ST LOUIS

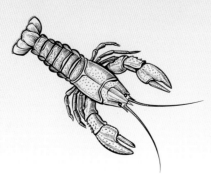

AT A GLANCE

EAT
One of New Orleans' most famous culinary offerings, jambalaya is a decadent Cajun-Creole dish of rice with spices and vegetables mixed with Andouille sausage, chicken or seafood.

DRINK
Jack Daniels, the quintessential Tennessee whiskey, is popular across the south. It's made from 51% corn mash, aged in oak barrels and charcoal filtered for a mellow flavour.

STAY
The Peabody Memphis has been a favourite hotel since 1869. Ducks swim in the indoor fountain, parading in at 11am each day.

EXPERIENCE
The National Civil Rights Museum in Memphis features powerful exhibits that chronicle the struggles and triumphs for freedom and equality by African Americans in the 1960s. It's set in the former Lorraine Motel, where Dr Martin Luther King Jr was assassinated.

SHOP
The French Market in New Orleans features crafts, artwork, clothing, jewellery and food vendors. It's been around since 1791, and is the oldest continuously operating public market in the country.

"No music-minded trip through the South is complete without a visit to New Orleans. The birthplace of jazz is home to brassy clubs and swaying crowds"

Right: a melody for New Orleans;
Opposite: architecture in the city's
French Quarter

There's more music to be heard along US Rte 61, the so-called 'Blues Highway', a 620-mile (1000km) route sprinkled with places that shaped America's musical heritage. There's Red's in Clarksdale, with a ramshackle, intimate interior that puts audiences close to the performers. In open farmland near the former Dockery Plantation, the dirt road intersection of Walker and Lusk is the alleged spot where Robert Johnson sold his soul to the devil to become a blues legend. Further south, in Indianola's reopened Club Ebony, feel the presence of the great BB King, who played here often (and later bought and donated it to the nearby BB King Museum and Delta Interpretive Center).

No music-minded trip through the South is complete without a visit to New Orleans. The birthplace of jazz is home to brassy clubs where the stages are packed with horn players weaving intoxicating tunes around the swaying crowds. Elsewhere, the streetlamps light up the night on Frenchmen St, the hub of New Orleans' ever-evolving music scene.

Bayous and wetlands flank the towns west of the Crescent City. This is the heart of Cajun Country, where accordions and washboards replace trumpets and saxophones. On weekend nights – and sometimes mornings too – floorboards rock as waltzers and two-steppers move to the lilting tunes of zydeco, another genre born in the American South, a place of unbridled creativity and heartache, where the music never stops.

Opposite: neon signs illuminate the night on Nashville's Lower Broadway

Eight Day Itinerary

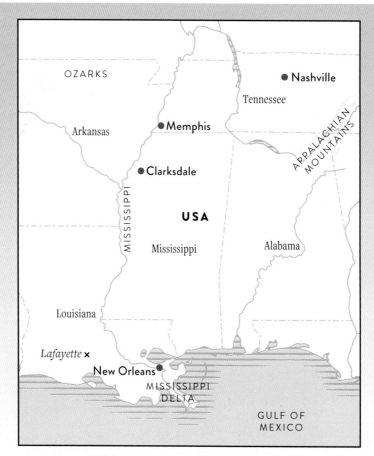

>

Start off in Nashville. Spend two days exploring the city's musical legacy, being sure to tour the fabled Grand Ole Opry. By night, hit the music-filled bars on Lower Broadway.

>>

It's a three-hour drive west to Memphis, where you can pass two enjoyable days visiting the town's music-themed museums and the buzzing blues clubs of Beale St and beyond.

>>>

On day five make the 90-minute drive south to Clarksdale. Check out the spot where Robert Johnson supposedly sold his soul to the devil, then spend the night hearing top performers sing their hearts (and souls?) out at Red's.

>>>>

Get behind the wheel again on the sixth day for the long (5½ hour) drive to New Orleans, stopping at key blues spots along the way. The Big Easy deserves at least two days of your time. By day, you can wander intriguing neighborhoods like the French Quarter, the Bywater and the Garden District. After dark, find your groove in the jazz clubs on Frenchmen St.

MORE TIME?

Continue 2½ hours west to Cajun Country. In the lively town of Lafayette, music lovers young and old hit the dance floor as zydeco bands take the stage.

PRACTICALITIES

GETTING THERE AND AROUND

Nashville and New Orleans have the busiest gateway airports, though they offer relatively few international flights. Upon arrival, you'll want to rent a car to get between places, as public transport is extremely limited. One exception is Amtrak's City of New Orleans train, which connects the namesake town with Memphis. There's also one train daily from New Orleans to Lafayette.

WHEN TO GO

The further south you go, the more intense that summer heat and humidity is (looking at you, New Orleans). Spring is ideal for visiting, featuring a packed calendar of events like Jazz Fest in New Orleans (late April and early May), Clarksdale's Juke Joint Festival (April) and Nashville's CMA (Country Music Association) Fest held in June.

THINGS TO NOTE

Guided tours add depth to the experience. The Jugg Sisters of NashTrash give a hilariously irreverent take on Nashville, while the Memphis Mojo Tour blends history with live music. Historic New Orleans Tours peel back layers of the past with insights into jazz, Black history, voodoo and more. *Further information is available at visittheusa.com/trip/blues-highway*

USA

Follow *the* Overseas Highway

MIAMI IS THE LAND of Art Deco architecture, palm-fringed beaches and Latin-infused nightlife. It's also the starting point for the fabled drive down the Florida Keys, following the Overseas Hwy past tiny islands, nature reserves and vestiges of old-school Americana. Before hitting the road, visit Miami's Wynwood Walls, where some of the world's top street artists have left their mark. From there it's 167 miles (267km) to the highway's end, bohemian Key West, a city known for its colourful Bahamian cottages and even more colourful nightlife – including the odd clothing-optional bar. While it's possible to complete the drive in under four hours, it's better spread over a few days, enjoying impromptu adventures on the way: snorkelling amid the marine life of John Pennekamp State Park, paddling the mangroves near No Name Key and strolling Bahia Honda's white sand beaches. Just be sure that when late afternoon arrives, you find a table at the nearest waterside bar – the sunsets here are legendary.

AT A GLANCE

EAT
The fish sandwich is a work of art in the Florida Keys.

DRINK
The Keys' classic cocktail is the rum runner: rum, banana liqueur and fruit juice.

PRACTICALITIES
Prices are sky-high from December to February. You'll save on accommodation (and still avoid hurricane season) by travelling March and May.

USA

Back to Nature *in the* Alexander Archipelago

AT A GLANCE

EAT

Feast on five different types of wild Alaska salmon.

DRINK

Try Spruce Tip Blonde Ale, made from handpicked, local Sitka spruce.

PRACTICALITIES

Most visitors come by cruise ship, but you can travel independently using Alaska's excellent ferries, aka the Alaska Marine Highway System.

SOUTHEASTERN ALASKA HAS changed little since the famous Scottish naturalist John Muir visited in 1879. Dense forests still cover the 1100 or so islands of the Alexander Archipelago, and dramatic fjords and glacier-carved valleys lie largely undisturbed. This is part of the world's biggest temperate rain forest, where hiking trails lead through a landscape of moss-covered boulders and gushing mountain streams, with old-growth spruce and cedar overhead. Tiny towns clinging to the water's edge are dwarfed by the wilderness beyond, and it's not uncommon to see bears or even wolves on the outskirts of state capital Juneau. Nature aside, Indigenous groups maintain deep ties to the land in places like Ketchikan, home to the largest collection of totem poles on Earth. To the north, scenic Skagway was once a bustling port during the Klondike Gold Rush, and its well-preserved downtown is lined with buildings from the early 1900s, including a restored depot from where vintage trains head up into the mountains.

USA

Ride *through* Utah's Red Rock Country

NATURE HAS LONG HAD the upper hand in southern Utah's Red Rock Country. The rippled gulches and wrinkled tablelands in this Martian wilderness are like a pop-up geological textbook. The place is a tumble – a chaos – of weird sedimentary slabs on top of way-out layers, and its seemingly eternal desertscapes appear sculpted with cinematic arches, tombstone mesas and slot canyons, as if a God had once swung a giant axe to gut the landscape. There are so many irresistible panoramas and rust-red outlooks, in fact, it's sometimes hard to believe your eyes.

On a road trip through Red Rock Country, star billing goes to the appropriately named Mighty 5 – the honeypot landmarks of Arches, Bryce Canyon, Canyonlands, Capitol Reef and Zion National Parks. Here, in a display of almost slapstick geology, hundreds of natural stone arches soar skywards, giant pinnacles teeter on canyon rims, pillars bend inwards and massive rock fins change their appearance, depending on which angle you view them from. Always, an obstacle course of rubble is strewn across the landscape.

Opposite: hiking the Narrows gorge in Zion National Park; *This page top:* on the road in Arches National Park; *Bottom:* Airstreams at Ofland Escalante

AT A GLANCE

EAT

Located beside the Anasazi State Park Museum, Magnolia's Street Food in Boulder is a taco truck (March to November only) specialising in locavore flavours, from mushroom and brisket tacos to roasted beet tostadas.

DRINK

Springdale's Zion Brewery is a stone brewpub sitting in the shadow of a gorgeous scarlet escarpment. Red Altar is its tribute to the surrounding Red Rock Country.

STAY

In a former life, Ofland Escalante was a drive-in movie theatre. Now it's anchored by Airstream trailers, cabins, pool and outdoor screen with vintage convertibles from which to watch movies under the stars.

EXPERIENCE

Come in winter and go snowshoeing among the million-year-old hoodoos in Bryce Canyon, or on a pre-dawn hike to Delicate Arch in front of the La Sal Mountains.

SHOP

Adventure capital Moab is busy with camping and desert gear retailers, and is an ideal place to stock up before heading into its rocky wonderland.

A Traveller's Tale

On a bone-gnawing pre-dawn hike to Delicate Arch in Arches National Park in late March, through a landscape that felt abandoned, fantasy rock stacks appeared out of the dark and I knew that setting the alarm for 4am had been the right decision. Soon, the sky glowed and, as the ascending sun took over from my flickering flashlight beam, the landscape filled with silhouette and spectacle. There was only a handful of other people – a world apart from the crush so commonly experienced at America's epic national parks in summer – and the impact was profound. The luxury of seeing giant rock altars and golden bridges in silence, in the company of only shadows. There were sugarloaf nuggets. Schools of knife-edge shark fins. Ghostly hoodoos. Biblical vaults. All freaks of geology. And I was left with a sense that I had one foot in the prehistoric, with time paused, and the other in the present day.

MIKE MACEACHERAN

"The place is a tumble of weird sedimentary slabs on top of way-out layers, and its seemingly eternal desertscapes appear sculpted with cinematic arches, tombstone mesas and slot canyons"

Left: Sunrise over the amphitheater at Bryce Canyon, Utah

In this homeland of the road trip, amid scenery from movie-set America, you sense that the highway is an invitation to a place of dream chasing. And from behind the steering wheel, Utah's most famous road, Scenic Byway 12, otherwise known as the Journey Through Time Scenic Byway, connects the dots through a swathe of Red Rock Country and between much of the state's most geologically immaculate terrain, including Capitol Reef and Bryce Canyon.

In the spaces between are areas where you notice the rampant dereliction more. Tropic Shale, outside the town of Tropic, has an almost incomprehensible Mesozoic geologic formation. Kodachrome Basin State Park is pockmarked with tombstone rocks and geological 'temples' of the sun. Grand Staircase-Escalante National Monument, the last area to be mapped in the contiguous US according to a presidential declaration in 1996, is an enormous chasm of seemingly limitless canyons. Off the roadside, there is nothing for it, then, but desert hiking, horse trekking, canyoneering and mountain biking. Still today, there is plenty of land here that has yet to be explored fully by hoof, boot and bike.

Understandably, summer is the season when the colours really pop: the crayon blue of the sky, the rich orange of the stone, the red oxide of the canyons. From late autumn to early spring, the parks empty, the mercury drops and the rocks change their hue, lightening in tone and covered by frost and snow. This was once the land of the Ancestral Puebloans of the American West, and you'll be blessed to step into it for a moment, leaving only footprints behind.

Opposite: the Double Arch is one of Arches National Park's many memorable sights

Eight Day Itinerary

>

Begin in Moab on your east-to-west adventure with a pre-dawn hike in Arches National Park. This slice of prehistory and nearby Canyonlands National Park deserve a couple of days for their assortment of hikes, driving loops and head-in-the-clouds photo stops. Add on a visit to Dead Horse Point State Park and you'll have the feeling that this vast desert expanse is not of this Earth.

>>

Day three brings you to Torrey and Capitol Reef National Park after around three hours driving. Factor in at least a day of exploration – hike the Chimney Rock or Hickman Bridge trails by day, later eye the dazzling gemstones of the sky on a stargazing safari.

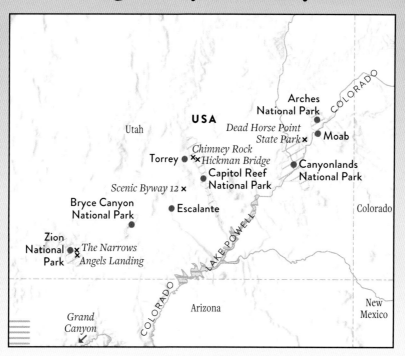

>>>

Then rise early on day four to drive Scenic Byway 12 to Escalante. Take your time: the remoteness and silence is epic, plus a half-day canyoning tour is unmissable. The sheer pleasure of navigating your way through sinewy slot canyons is intense.

>>>>

The westward drive to Bryce Canyon National Park will pack out the next two days, before Zion National Park fills the windscreen and offers an almost transcendent experience. Here your superlative hiking destinations are Angels Landing and the Narrows.

MORE TIME? South of Utah, another of the USA's other most compelling destinations lies in wait in Arizona: the Grand Canyon.

PRACTICALITIES

GETTING THERE AND AROUND

Salt Lake City is Utah's international gateway and by far the smartest option for starting this trip. Moab, served by Canyonlands Regional Airport, has domestic connections, but round-trip car hire is more economical from the Utah state capital. And you will need a car. Not only is driving around half the fun but, as is the case in most of the US, public transport options are limited.

WHEN TO GO

To avoid the crowds, visit between November and March when temperatures are cooler and snow lingers. In recent years, timed-entry reservations have been introduced at both Arches and Zion national parks from 1 April to 31 October, with reservations released three months in advance. If travelling in the heat of summer, prepare to hike in high temperatures.

THINGS TO NOTE

This is wild country, meaning that if you do head off road, you'll need to pack for all eventualities – in the national parks, water is always your most precious resource.
For more information visit visitutah.com

USA

Treat Yourself *in* New York City

NEW YORK IS AN infinity of cities, all layered on top of each other. A city of artists, of immigrants, of scrappy strivers – but the one we're here for this weekend is the city of millionaires. Just two days of living the classic New York high life. The extravagant shops. The opulent hotels. The restaurants you have to book a year in advance. It's just a taste of the golden New York dream. Like a shaving of white truffle, a single glass of 1982 Lafite. After all, any more might make you sick.

New York doesn't lack upscale shopping districts, but the most iconic is no doubt Fifth Ave. Art Deco skyscrapers tower over block after block of glittering storefronts. Tiffany, with its diamonds and silver baby rattles tucked into robin's-egg-blue boxes. The futuristic glass box of the Apple store. Heritage department stores like Saks and Bergdorf Goodman, their perfumed aisles lined with silk scarves, crystal decanters and skin creams made from rare Swiss mountain flowers.

A Traveller's Tale

It was late when I checked in, and the hotel had just one room left. 'Would the penthouse suite be alright?' asked the clerk, with a smile I opened the door to the suite and dropped my bag in shock. The room was gorgeous, yes. But the view: the glittering skyline, the river gleaming in the moonlight beyond. Ohhhh. For just a night, I had the ultimate New York dream.

EMILY MATCHAR

AT A GLANCE

EAT
A tasting menu at a three-star Michelin restaurant, porterhouse and martinis at a luxe steakhouse.

DRINK
Linger over classic cocktails at hushed, low-lit bars; champagne on the dance floor at nightclubs.

STAY
Find old-school luxury in the Plaza, or cool new fashion-forward spots like the Refinery.

EXPERIENCE
Talk your way into a bar or shop that's so exclusive entry is by personal recommendation only.

Opposite: the Plaza Hotel offers old-school luxury in Manhattan; *This page:* New York City's iconic Times Square

For lunch, a well-heeled New Yorker might choose an *omakase* meal of fish-just-flown-from-Tokyo sushi, a high tea of tiny cakes and finger sandwiches at a five-star hotel or a multicourse tasting menu of jewel-like titbits. Ditto for dinner. In between, a stroll through a museum, one of the enormous palaces of culture endowed by Gilded Age millionaires whose mansions still line the Upper East Side. Or perhaps a trip to a spa – a hot-rock massage in a private suite overlooking Central Park, or a soak in a tub scented with lemongrass and rose petals.

In the evenings, it's see-and-be-seen at bars and nightspots: fancy hotel bars with cocktails decorated with gold leaf; velvet-rope clubs filled with musicians and models; modern-day speakeasies with hidden doors. To sleep, a classic New York hotel – the bellmen with shiny brass buttons, the lobby chandeliers, the perfectly crisp white sheets. In the morning, there's only one thing to do: order in. In the words of Eloise, the luxury-loving six-year-old who lives in the Plaza penthouse in the classic children's book, 'Ooooooooo I absolutely love room service'.

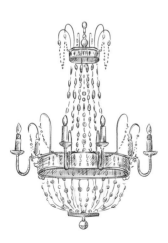

This page: the sun sets over Central Park and New York's famous skyline

PRACTICALITIES

GETTING THERE AND AROUND

New York's three main airports are LaGuardia (more domestic) and JFK (more international), both in Queens, and Newark (both international and domestic), in New Jersey. All are connected to Manhattan by public transportation or taxis/rideshares.

WHEN TO GO

New York has its charms year-round, but August is when many locals leave town to escape the heat. Spring sets Central Park abloom, autumn brings out the city's cosy side, and the holiday season is especially classic.

THINGS TO NOTE

This trip is set in a small, walkable area around the southern half of Central Park. You won't need taxis or the subway unless the weather's bad. Make restaurant bookings well in advance.

Further information is available at nyctourism.com

Two Day Itinerary

> In the afternoon of day one, check in at the Plaza. Cross the street and enjoy an hour-long stroll through Central Park before taking in a Broadway show – splash out on the best seats you can afford. Afterwards, grab drinks and global tapas at the St Cloud Rooftop Bar, with 'sky pods' overlooking Times Square. Walk or taxi back to the Plaza for a luxurious sleep.

>> Next morning, ease into the day with room service for breakfast, then wander Fifth Ave for a few hours of shopping (or window shopping). After a lunch of top-line beef at the Grill (in a dining room designed by starchitects Ludwig Mies van der Rohe and Philip Johnson), walk north to the Metropolitan Museum of Art for some culture. Head across the park for a late-afternoon massage at the Mandarin Oriental's spa, leaving relaxed and ready for your dinner reservation at Jean-Georges, the longtime temple of French cuisine. Nurse a nightcap at the wonderfully charming Bemelmens Bar.

MORE TIME?

Try avant-garde luxury shopping in Soho.

USA

Gaze at Geysers
in Yellowstone
National Park

THE OLDEST NATIONAL PARK in the US wears many crowns. No other place on Earth holds as many geothermal features as Yellowstone – a whopping 10,000 hot springs, mud pots and fumaroles, not to mention 500 geysers, about half the world's total. The park is also wildlife-watching heaven. Along with wolves, bears and bighorn sheep, there are more free-roaming bison (some 6000) than anywhere else in the country. Yellowstone is also massive – in the Lower 48 states only one other park (Death Valley) is larger.

With four distinct sectors and five far-flung entrances, it's hard to know where to begin. Most people head straight for the most famous attraction, Old Faithful, the geyser that earned its name for its regular eruptions, roughly 17 times a day. From the boardwalk, you can hear it roar to life as super-heated water blasts 180ft (55m) into the air. It lies near scores of other hydrothermal attractions, from sputtering mud pools to sulphur-spewing streams.

Opposite: Lower Falls in Yellowstone National Park; *This page:* bison in the Lamar Valley in the park's northeastern corner

On the other side of the park, the Grand Canyon of the Yellowstone has long captivated visitors. Viewpoints on both the north and south rims offer vantage points over the canyon and its two sets of waterfalls. After taking in the views, you can lose the crowds on trails through the surrounding forests, including a memorable walk along the south rim.

Although you can see wildlife anywhere in the park, the Lamar Valley is the epicentre of biodiversity with bison, elk, moose and pronghorn – along with the predators that hunt them. Wolves

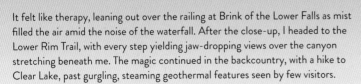

A Traveller's Tale

It felt like therapy, leaning out over the railing at Brink of the Lower Falls as mist filled the air amid the noise of the waterfall. After the close-up, I headed to the Lower Rim Trail, with every step yielding jaw-dropping views over the canyon stretching beneath me. The magic continued in the backcountry, with a hike to Clear Lake, past gurgling, steaming geothermal features seen by few visitors.

REGIS ST LOUIS

AT A GLANCE

EAT
A local 'delicacy' foisted on tourists is Rocky Mountain oysters, aka deep-fried bison testicles.

DRINK
Yellowstone lodges proudly serve Old Faithful ale, along with other local craft beers.

STAY
Park lodges are often grand reminders of a bygone era, but the rooms have been comfortably renovated.

EXPERIENCE
You can view apex predators up close at the nonprofit rescue Grizzly & Wolf Discovery Center.

This page: Yellowstone's spectacular West Thumb Geyser Basin

were driven to extinction in Yellowstone in the 1920s, but then reintroduced in 1995, and their return has been one of the great success stories of US conservation. At dawn or dusk (the best time to spot them), wildlife enthusiasts gather hoping to spot the packs on the move. Easier to find are the great herds of bison, which graze on open meadows like Madison Valley. As evidenced by the many repeat visitors, it's easy to fall in love with the magic of Yellowstone. One longtime park ranger explained, 'You could spend a lifetime here and still not see it all.'

PRACTICALITIES

GETTING THERE AND AROUND

You can fly into Jackson, Cody, Bozeman and Billings. At each of these airports, you can rent a car, which you'll need since there's no public transport in the park.

WHEN TO GO

Many roads close from November to April, and some sections of the park aren't accessible until late May. July and August are best for hiking, though they're also the busiest months. Several Yellowstone lodges open in winter, with special buses providing transport into the park and tours to the highlights.

THINGS TO NOTE

Purchase bear spray, learn how to use it and don't go hiking without it. More people, however, are injured by bison than grizzlies, so keep your distance and never approach wildlife.

Further information is available at nps.gov/yell

Four Day Itinerary

>

Spend the first day exploring the spouting geothermal wonders in the Upper Geyser Basin, including iconic Old Faithful. Nearby, visit the Grand Prismatic Spring with its brilliant hues and the smoke-spewing pools at Fountain Paint Pot.

>>

Next day, make the 30-minute drive to West Thumb. Stop for more geyser action from lakeside trails, then motor another hour to the Grand Canyon of the Yellowstone. Gaze out from the overlooks, hike the canyon rim trail and peruse the exhibits at the Canyon Visitor Education Center.

>>>

Day three starts with a challenging hike up Mt Washburn (a 20-minute drive from the Grand Canyon), rewarded with wide views over the park. In the afternoon, drive an hour to the Lamar Valley to look for wolves and other wildlife.

>>>>

On your last day, make the one-hour drive to Mammoth Hot Springs, home to steaming terraces and historic Fort Yellowstone.

MORE TIME?

Grand Teton National Park lies just south of Yellowstone, and you could spend several days hiking trails and boating on lakes against a backdrop of mountain peaks.

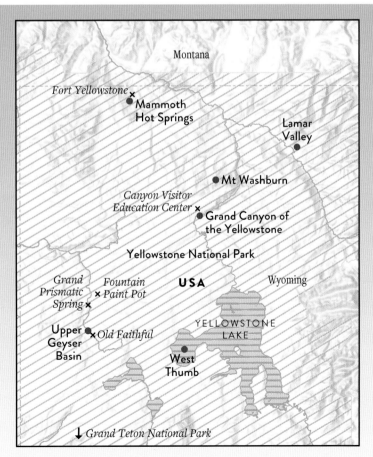

Montana

Fort Yellowstone ×
● Mammoth
Hot Springs

Lamar
Valley
●

● Mt Washburn

*Canyon Visitor
Education Center* ×
● Grand Canyon of
the Yellowstone

Yellowstone National Park

*Grand
Prismatic
Spring* ×
*Fountain
× Paint Pot*

USA   Wyoming

YELLOWSTONE
LAKE

Upper ● ×*Old Faithful*
**Geyser
Basin**

**West
Thumb**
●

↓ *Grand Teton National Park*

USA

Lose Yourself *in the* Big Skies *of* Texas

THE OLD WEST LIVES ON in the sunbaked streets of Fort Worth. Each morning, a handful of cowboys drive a herd of longhorn cattle along East Exchange Ave, in the heart of the historic Stockyards district. The intersections nearby offer old saloons, vintage steak restaurants and Western-wear stores that have been around for decades. By night, there are rodeos at Cowtown Coliseum and boot-scootin' dancing at Billy Bob's, the world's largest honky tonk. Yet, like other parts of Texas, Fort Worth – and Dallas, its near neighbour – is much more than a nostalgic relic of the past. The two cities have dynamic arts districts featuring world-class museums and concert halls, as well as botanic gardens and riverside greenways. And while you can certainly find good barbecue, the appetite here is much more wide-ranging, with burgeoning food halls and creative restaurants serving up dishes from around the globe.

A love for all things exotic extends to the state capital, where bumper stickers remind people to 'keep Austin weird'. Street art proliferates, along with curious galleries like the Cathedral of Junk, while the music scene brings live performances to a vast variety of venues.

A Traveller's Tale

While driving in the flatlands, suddenly Palo Duro Canyon opened before me, with eons of history etched in the rocks. One day I walked amid red-rock pillars up to windswept lookouts, and on the next I headed down to a riverside trail where I spotted wildlife including a sauntering coyote. Going outside of summer meant seeing only a handful of visitors, and it was easy to secure a prime camping spot.

REGIS ST LOUIS

AT A GLANCE

EAT

Texans fire up some of the world's best barbecue, including brisket.

DRINK

Local wines keep getting better, with outstanding Cabernet Sauvignon and Tempranillo.

STAY

Liz Lambert designs Texas' most stylish accommodations, including Austin's atmospheric oasis, Hotel San José.

EXPERIENCE

Learn about one of America's darkest days at the Sixth Floor Museum, set in the former book depository from where Lee Harvey Oswald shot President Kennedy.

Opposite: **Texas rodeo at Fort Worth Stockyards;** *This page:* **alfresco drinks alongside Lake Travis reservoir**

The old saying 'Everything is bigger in Texas' rings true when you hit the open highway – this is fabled terrain for road trips, and distances are vast as you motor beneath those big skies. You can work your way down the coast, exploring historic seaside towns, basking on the beach and learning about wildlife in the area – including the three species of sea turtles that nest on Texan shores. Or head west, where flatlands soon give way to undulating peaks in the state's age-old mountains, including the Chisos, a soaring range located entirely within Big Bend National Park. Here the wilderness encompasses three different ecosystems: desert, mountains and river (the park's name comes from its location along the sinewy curves of the Rio Grande). This makes for extraordinary wildlife-watching while hiking rugged mountain trails or rafting through smooth red-rock canyons. And once the sun sets the park reveals why it's the world's largest Dark Sky Reserve – the stargazing here has few rivals.

Opposite top: the stars align over Balanced Rock in Big Bend National Park; *bottom:* a street performer in Austin

One Week Itinerary

>

Start off in booming Dallas with a morning strolling the museums of the Arts District, then take in some Art Deco architecture and greenery at Fair Park. In the evening head to Bishop Ave for dining and drinking.

>>

On day two, make the one-hour train ride to neighbouring Fort Worth, where you can get a taste of cowboy culture in the Stockyards District.

>>>

Rent a car and make the three-hour drive to Austin, where you'll spend days three and four shopping, eating and catching live music in the state's most creative city.

>>>>

From there, it's a four-hour drive to Port Aransas, a laid-back place on the edge of serene, windswept beaches. Next up is the glorious wilderness of Big Bend National Park, a mere eight-hour drive west (this state is big). Spend your last two days hiking mountain trails, soaking in hot springs and enjoying clear nights of stargazing.

MORE TIME?

Add on a visit to Marfa, an arts-loving desert town known for its food trucks, dive bars and former army base turned sculpture gallery.

PRACTICALITIES

GETTING THERE
AND AROUND
Dallas-Fort Worth and Houston have the busiest gateway airports, with flights arriving from around the world. Once there, you'll want to rent a car as this car-loving state has limited public transport.

WHEN TO GO
The summer months (June to August) are sweltering in Texas and the winters (December to February) can get chilly, so plan a spring or autumn visit to enjoy the best weather and the widest range of activities.

THINGS TO NOTE
Pack the right footwear for outdoor adventures (hiking boots, water sandals), as well as a long-sleeved shirt for protection against the sun. You might also want to bring (or pick up some) cowboy boots – essential wear in Texan dancehalls. *For more information visit traveltexas.com*

USA

Road-Trip Coastal California

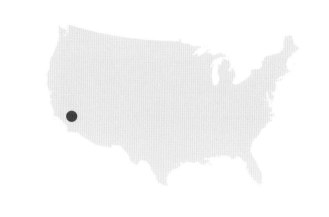

IF THERE'S A PLACE made to drive off into the sunset, it's California. Starry-eyed adventurers have flocked here ever since the 19th-century Gold Rush, all searching for their own piece of paradise. Even today, the very words 'California road trip' evoke freedom – the kind of freedom that wears movie-star sunglasses and drives a convertible.

The classic route is Hwy 1, which hugs California's west coast for 656 miles (1056km). Also known as the Pacific Coast Highway, it's a catwalk of the state's most famous sights – the Golden Gate Bridge, the Hollywood sign and the surf immortalised in songs by the Beach Boys. Along the way, you'll also encounter California's natural beauty, from the pin-drop silence of redwood forests to the deafening honks of sea lions.

Hwy 1 technically begins in northern California, snaking past lighthouses and the craggy Mendocino Headlands, but most travellers begin 180 miles (290km) south in San Francisco. Here, in the City by the Bay, centuries of boom-and-bust history are on show: there's colourful Chinatown, the

Opposite: sea lions battle on the Santa Barbara shore; *This page top:* Highway 1 hugs the coast; *Bottom:* California is world-famous for its surf

AT A GLANCE

EAT

What do you get when you combine local seafood with California's Mexican food obsession? Baja-style tacos, which fold deep-fried fish and crunchy cabbage into a warm tortilla. Squeeze lime generously.

DRINK

You're never far from wine country along Hwy 1, but one beverage reigns supreme: West Coast IPA. A go-to beer in surf towns, these ales are fragrant, floral and exuberantly hoppy.

STAY

Sleep in one of California's most eclectic buildings. The Madonna Inn in San Luis Obispo has themed rooms (for cavemen, romantics or nostalgics) and a bar-restaurant awash in neon pink.

EXPERIENCE

Surf's up! Book a lesson in Santa Cruz, watch locals hang ten at Steamer Lane, or head north to Mavericks Beach where pros ride monster waves.

SHOP

Browse like a health-conscious local at farmers markets, which focus on fruit, honey, gourmet jams and beauty products. Half Moon Bay and Santa Barbara both have delightful Saturday versions.

A Traveller's Tale

The shop owner presses an oar into my hands. 'Remember,' she warns, 'stay two kayak lengths away from wildlife – it's the law.' I set out towards the shore, dragging my kayak behind me. Moss Landing, north of Monterey, is one of California's best places to spot marine mammals. After only a few swishes of my oar I spot whiskery harbour seals on the banks of the estuary, snoozing in slick beds of kelp.

A furry head periscopes out of the water, only a few feet away – a sea otter. Remembering the edict to keep my distance, I gently steer away from this inquisitive new friend. The otter dives down and emerges on the other side of my kayak, now even closer. I paddle left, then right, but the otter only circles nearer, making a game of my attempts to evade him. After all, this is his playground. The rules only apply to humans.

ANITA ISALSKA

"The very words 'California road trip' evoke freedom – the kind of freedom that wears movie-star sunglasses and drives a convertible"

Right: vineyards in California Wine Country; *Opposite:* Bixby Creek Bridge on the Big Sur coast

Mission District's murals and margaritas, and Alamo Sq's Painted Ladies, century-old homes given a bright makeover in the Swinging 1960s.

South of San Francisco, the feeling of freedom truly kicks in. As you drive through Pacifica and Half Moon Bay, you'll see sandy beaches with specks atop the waves. Are they surfers, or dolphins? Pull over and see.

Next up is Santa Cruz, ideal for surfing lessons and rambling in state parks like Natural Bridges and Henry Cowell Redwoods. This is the tip of Monterey Bay, where kelp forests sway beneath the ocean surface, supporting dolphins, seals and sea otters. Whether in a kayak, snorkelling gear or on a bigger boat cruise, there are abundant opportunities to observe the bay's residents. Gray whales are a particularly special sight – they migrate 12,000 miles (19,312km) to reach Monterey Bay each winter.

Things get even wilder in Big Sur. Along this remarkably rugged stretch of coast, waterfalls tumble onto sandy beaches and white lilies blanket the hillsides each spring. And as you travel further south, the California lifestyle leans ever more laid-back. By the time you reach sweet, seaside Cambria and easy-going university town San Luis Obispo, you're practically horizontal. Once in Santa Barbara, a well-heeled haven for wellness and wine, your days are best spent in a haze of seaside vistas and buttery local Chardonnay.

Then, finally, there's Los Angeles, a sprawling city of excess, elegance and sleaze. The sensory overload is almost addictive – don't be surprised if you want to jump straight back in the car to extend your sun-kissed adventures.

Opposite: sundown on Santa Monica beach

10 Day Itinerary

>

Start with two days in the San Francisco Bay Area. Don't skip the rugged Marin Headlands, picturesque Sausalito and the mighty Golden Gate Bridge.

>>

On day three, it's two hours south on Hwy 1 to Santa Cruz, pausing along the way to watch surfers in Half Moon Bay. The next day, start with a surf lesson before driving an hour to Monterey's world-famous aquarium. Linger in Monterey on day five for whale watching and to admire 17-Mile Drive's cypress trees and golden beaches.

>>>

Devote day six to the soul-stirring drive through Big Sur, finishing up at the elephant seal haven of San Simeon.

>>>>

On day seven, tour Hearst Castle, grab lunch in Cambria, glimpse Morro Bay's volcanic rock and dine outdoors in San Luis Obispo. Next morning, head east along Hwy 246 through Santa Rita Hills wine country, then detour along Hwy 154, grabbing bottles of Syrah and Chardonnay before spending the night in Santa Barbara, two hours away.

>>>>>

On day nine, drive through superstar playground Malibu to Los Angeles, and spend your remaining time strolling Santa Monica pier, hot-stepping along the Walk of Fame and watching sunset over Griffith Observatory.

MORE TIME?

It's only 2½ hours to San Diego's live music and surf culture.

PRACTICALITIES

GETTING THERE AND AROUND

Begin the drive from either San Francisco or Los Angeles; international flights reach both cities. You'll need your own wheels for the full road-trip experience, but more ecofriendly options exist: the Coast Starlight train connects Oakland (near San Francisco) with Los Angeles, stopping at Salinas (for Monterey) and San Luis Obispo. You can also cycle 17-Mile Drive, a scenic detour around the Monterey Peninsula.

WHEN TO GO

California is beautiful year-round. Late spring and early summer (April to June) and early autumn (September and October) are sweet spots for wildflowers and sunshine without scorching temperatures, but listen out for local news about 'smoke season', when unpredictable wildfires can disrupt transport, cause air pollution and much worse.

THINGS TO NOTE

Distracted tourists and narrow coastal roads don't mix. Drive attentively, especially around serpentine Big Sur, and only stop to admire views from signposted pull-over areas. Round up your drive-time estimates to allow for sinuous roads, photo stops and to avoid driving after nightfall. *Further information is available at visitcalifornia.com*

USA

Raft *the* Grand Canyon

EARTH REVEALS ITS GEOGRAPHICAL secrets layer by dramatic layer along the Colorado River. After launching your raft from Lees Ferry – beneath the Vermilion Cliffs' red beauty, the graceful Navajo Bridges – you'll glide past Redwall Cavern, the Puebloan granaries and the blue waters of the Little Colorado River in quick succession, as monstrous rapids fling you ever deeper into the Colorado Plateau. Geological time becomes incomprehensible. And also quite real. Streaks of pink Zoroaster crack through black slabs of Vishnu Schist. The oldest exposed rocks on the planet, they squeeze against the river at the Granite Narrows. A short trail leads to the Great Unconformity, where two rock layers, separated by an age gap of one billion years, unexpectedly meet – a setting so unique it brings geologists to tears.

Sleeping under the stars is an unexpected gift. With canyon walls rising skyward, the Colorado River flowing past and an ancient stillness in the air, it's all quite wondrous here at night. The star-filled canopy is a sublime touch.

AT A GLANCE

EAT
River guides prepare delicious buffet-style meals beside the river.

DRINK
Nets thrown over the raft into the Colorado keep canned beers cold.

PRACTICALITIES

Trips run April to September and should be booked a year in advance. Grand Canyon National Park lists 15 approved whitewater outfitters (visit nps.gov/grca).

MEXICO

Greet Friendly Giants off Baja

AT A GLANCE

EAT
Tacos de pescado are corn tortillas
filled with fried, battered fish.

DRINK
Sample fruity reds along the Ruta
del Vino, south of Tijuana.

PRACTICALITIES

Breeding gray whales visit Laguna
San Ignacio roughly January to
April; many other marine giants
are resident in the Sea of Cortez
year-round.

AT THE RIGHT TIME, in the right place, even mortal
enemies can become friends. So it is in Laguna San Ignacio,
on Baja California's Pacific coast. A century and a half after
whalers decimated the population of gray whales that migrate
here to breed each winter, these mighty cetaceans are once
again thriving – and eager to greet visitors. Barnacled behe-
moths approach whale-watching boats, demanding to be tickled
and scratched. Countless other marine marvels throng the seas
off Mexico's 778-mile (1250km) finger. Cruises sailing south
from San Diego encounter mischievous seals and sea lions
around the San Benito Islands, thrill to the haunting songs of
breeding humpbacks off the Gordo Banks at Baja's southern
tip, and allow snorkelling alongside the world's biggest fish –
whale sharks – in La Paz Bay. And in the Sea of Cortez, hugged
between Baja and Mexico's mainland, sightings of diverse creatures including blue whales – the largest animals ever to roam
Earth, as long as three buses – are nigh on guaranteed.

MEXICO

Explore *the* Land *of the* Maya

OF MEXICO'S MANY HISTORIC monuments, none can match the dramatic setting of Tulum's ruins. Stretching along a rocky promontory on the Yucatán Peninsula's eastern edge, columned temples stretch toward the sky as the turquoise waters of the Caribbean pound the shores below. It's one of the rare places where you can see impressive carvings of the ancient world and then take a stroll along the beach – and not just any beach. With powdery white sand, swaying palms and balmy breezes, the so-called Riviera Maya is the stuff of dreams. It's also the gateway to myriad adventures on land and sea. Vibrant reefs draw snorkellers and divers, while closer to shore, places like Akumal are ideal for spotting sea turtles. In the interior, the jungle-clad terrain is pockmarked with hundreds of *cenotes* – sinkholes filled with crystal-clear water that make for dramatic swimming holes. Some are hidden in caves, with shafts of lights streaming through openings overhead; others are ringed by vine-shrouded rock formations deep in the jungle.

Opposite: swimming in Cenote Dzitnup near the Mexican city of Valladolid;
This page: Tulum ruins on the Yucatán

A Traveller's Tale

On my first trip to the Yucatán, all my notions of Mexican cuisine were redefined as I ate my way around Mérida, one of the nation's unsung culinary capitals. I deepened my knowledge (while expanding my waistline) devouring dishes like *papadzules* (similar to enchiladas but with a pumpkin-seed sauce), *relleno negro* (a black stew featuring charred peppers) and *queso relleno* (cheese balls stuffed with pork, boiled egg, almonds and spices).

REGIS ST LOUIS

AT A GLANCE

EAT
Used for centuries, achiote seeds give a rich flavor to *cochinita pibil*, a roast pork dish.

DRINK
Pox (pronounced posh) is a traditional spirit made from fermented corn, once used in Maya ceremonies.

STAY
Built in 1683, Hacienda Uxmal has hosted famous explorers, scientists and archaeologists.

EXPERIENCE
Southwest of Tulum, visit Muyil's ruins then snorkel through an ancient canal built by the Maya.

All across the Yucatán, you'll find awe-inspiring ruins from the Maya civilisation, which flourished for more than a thousand years, and Chichén Itzá is one of the most impressive.

Huge pyramids, elaborately carved temples and massive ball courts attest to the city's importance as both an urban centre and spiritual site during its peak, between 800 and 1200 CE. Mysteries abound, like the observatory with its doors facing cardinal directions, and windows in the dome aligned to stars that appear only on specific dates. Some Maya temples were lost to time or destroyed by the Spanish during their conquest. The striking city of Mérida was in fact built over a Maya settlement, and you can still see pre-Columbian carvings in some of the stones of the 16th-century cathedral. A tour of town reveals more elements from this hybridised past, including brilliant works of indigenous art at the Gran Museo del Mundo Maya and 400-year-old mansions where the city's first governors resided. Mérida is also within easy reach of celebrated Maya sites like Uxmal as well as the Ría Celestún Biosphere Reserve, where huge flocks of flamingos add another feather to the Yucatán's cap.

This page top: the Mayan pyramid of Kukulcan at Chichén Itzá; Yucatán-style tacos

PRACTICALITIES

GETTING THERE AND AROUND

Cancún has international flights from the US and Europe. From the airport, you can catch a bus directly to Tulum. Public transport is excellent in the region, and you can get around by bus or aboard the new Tren Maya railway.

WHEN TO GO

The Yucatán is a year-round destination, though temperatures are higher during the rainy season months of June to November (when hurricanes are also a possibility). April to August brings sargassum (brown seaweed) to the beaches.

THINGS TO NOTE

You can get deeper insights into the region on a guided tour. Estación Mexico leads free walking tours around Mérida, and Flavio's Tours help bring Chichén Itzá to life. *Further information is available at visitmexico.com/yucatan*

Six Day Itinerary

>

Spend your first two days in Tulum. Rise early for a morning visit to the ruins, then head up to Akumal to swim with sea turtles. Afterwards, enjoy some downtime on the beach.

>>

On day two, spend half the day exploring the ruins of Cobá (a 45-minute drive from Tulum), then stop off in one of the region's *cenotes* for a swim in crystal-clear water on the return.

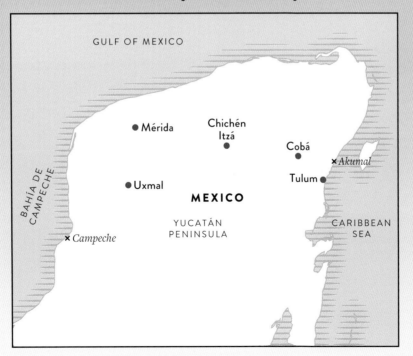

>>>

On the third day, make the three-hour bus ride to Chichén Itzá. Spend a full day wandering around the famed pyramids and stone carvings, then overnight at one of the nearby lodges. From there, it's a 90-minute ride by bus or train to Mérida.

>>>>

Spend your fourth and fifth days exploring the historic centre, visiting museums and indulging in outstanding Yucatecan cuisine.

>>>>>

On your last day, make the 75-minute bus trip to Uxmal for a look at yet another fabled Maya site.

MORE TIME? The Maya Train continues on to Campeche, a walled city with a lovely setting overlooking the Gulf of Mexico.

USA

Leaf Peep *in* New Hampshire

Opposite: driving New Hampshire's Kancamagus Highway during autumn;
This page: the Omni Mount Washington Resort

WHEN HIKERS ENVISION HEAVEN, they surely picture a place like Joe Dodge Lodge in early October. Hunkered at the base of Mt Washington in New Hampshire's White Mountains, this is a hub of camaraderie, weather talk and delicious anticipation. The lodge, together with the Highland Center in nearby Crawford Notch, anchors a network of hiking trails and high huts in an area that is prime territory for fall leaf peeping.

The rugged Whites are the epicentre of New England foliage country, with pops of red, yellow and orange painting the lower slopes of the Presidential Range, punctuated by evergreen conifers. And yes, the mountain byways get busy in autumn – the views are just too spectacular – but numerous adventures stand ready to whisk you away from the traffic to your own piece of fiery scenery and fun. Zip lining through Rosebrook Canyon is a 1000ft (305m) glide through a palette of autumnal colours as you drop into Bretton Woods. The centrepiece of the woods themselves is the Omni Mount Washington Resort, set brilliantly against the foliage and the mighty Presidential Range.

Jump aboard the 19th-century locomotive that heaves itself up the Mount Washington Cog Railway, belching steam as it approaches the summit of its namesake peak – at 6288ft (1917m), it's the highest mountain in New England, while the cog railway follows one of the steepest tracks in the world, climbing a 37% grade. The Cannon Mountain Aerial Tramway lifts passengers from the Franconia Notch pass to the top of Cannon Mountain. Carved by a glacier, the formidable notch looks tame from above, decorated with lakes, granite ridges and high cliffs softened by forests.

A Traveller's Tale

On a girls' trip in early October a few years back, we hiked from the Highland Center to the huts at Zealand Falls and Galehead. A rain-and-fog mix seemed to descend at every viewpoint, but I also remember the comradeship – a band of strangers linked by a common friend and shared adventure. At Zealand Falls, Mother Nature smiled: we had a clear view of the fall foliage for our hut-side happy hour.

AMY BALFOUR

AT A GLANCE

EAT
Clam chowder and lobster rolls, stuffed with seafood from the Atlantic, are a New England speciality.

DRINK
Order a Double Pig's Ear Brown Ale post-hike at Woodstock Inn Station & Brewery in Woodstock.

STAY
The Appalachian Mountain Club runs eight overnight huts, with bunks and family-style meals.

EXPERIENCE
The Extreme Mount Washington Museum, at the peak's summit, spotlights the mountain's wild weather.

This page: the Kancamagus Highway, a National Scenic Byway, runs through the White Mountain National Forest

Named for 17th-century Chief Kancamagus, the 34.5-mile (55km) Kancamagus Hwy is blissfully free of commercial development. Instead the Kanc, as it's known, is lined with trails, waterfalls and scenic overlooks just waiting for visitors to enjoy. Conclude with a drive to the summit of Cathedral Ledge in Cathedral Ledge State Park, where a short walk ends at a wide view of brilliant fall colours blazing across the Saco River Valley and the White Mountains.

PRACTICALITIES

GETTING THERE
AND AROUND

From Boston, follow I-93N and take any exit between Waterville Valley and Littleton to explore the east-to-west roads into the White Mountains. The Appalachian Mountain Club runs hiker shuttles to popular trailheads on weekends, late September to mid October.

WHEN TO GO

Foliage season runs from mid-September through mid-October, with peak leaf peeping usually from the last week of September to early October.

THINGS TO NOTE

Higher elevations will be cold and windy, with the potential for snow, so prepare for winter conditions and pack layers. If exploring the summit of Mt Washington, bring a warm coat. Gear up at International Mountain Equipment in the Village, the downtown stretch of North Conway. *For further information see visitwhitemountains.com*

Four Day Itinerary

>

Kick off at Joe Dodge Lodge in the heart of the Presidential Range. After a hearty breakfast, gather information at the visitor centre then hit the trails. If time and weather allow, drive the Mt Washington Auto Road.

>>

Drive to Crawford Notch and Bretton Woods. Treat yourself to two nights at historic Omni Mount Washington Resort, where cocktails on the veranda come with views of the eponymous mountain. Guided nature walks depart the AMC Highland Center, or you can soar on the Bretton Woods zip line. If you didn't drive the Mt Washington Auto Road, take the cog railway to the summit.

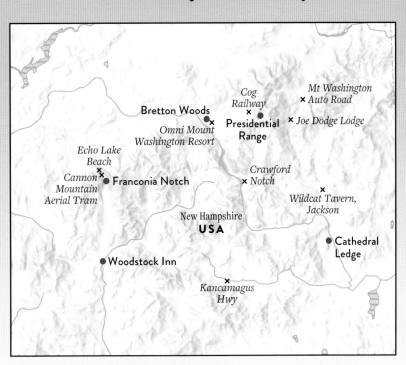

>>>

For a classic New England experience, get cosy at the Woodstock Inn for your last night. Spend the next day in Franconia Notch: hike or cycle through the forest, admire Echo Lake Beach or ride the Cannon Mountain Aerial Tram. From here, the Kancamagus Hwy awaits. End with sunset views at Cathedral Ledge.

MORE TIME?

Join locals on a Tuesday for open-mic performances at Wildcat Tavern Hoot Night in Jackson.

USA

Discover Kaua'i's Natural Wonders

IT'S EASY TO SEE why Kaua'i is a firm favourite as a movie location. Its fluted mountains, dramatic waterfalls, tropical rainforests and scenic coastline are photogenic in the extreme and have all landed starring roles on the silver screen. *Jurassic Park*, *Raiders of the Lost Ark* and *King Kong* were filmed on this Hawaiian island, to name just a few. The endless shades of green and dramatic natural features are even more impressive in real life. Kaua'i's good looks also encourage instant relaxation. The salty breeze puts travellers at ease as soon as they stroll out of the airport. Enthusiastic songbirds seem just as happy to be here as the humans do. It's undoubtedly an absolute haven for outdoorsy types, birders and beach bums.

About five million years ago, Kaua'i rose out of the ocean when an underwater volcano erupted. The result was a 552-sq-mile (1430-sq-km) paradise. Small, yes, but full of things to do. Take the west side, for example. It's home to Waimea Canyon, a mini Grand Canyon more than 3600ft (1097m) deep. Kaua'i's dry, sunny south side is ideal for snorkelling and easy coastal

A Traveller's Tale

It was a perfect, clear day off the Na Pali Coast. I was on a small boat. We'd spotted whale after whale breaching and even one slapping its fluke on the surface. As if that wasn't enough, one passed right beneath the vessel. The passenger next to me grabbed his snorkel mask and dipped his head underwater. When he came up for air he enthusiastically recounted his eyeball-to-giant-eyeball encounter.

SARAH SEKULA

AT A GLANCE

EAT
Hawaiian comfort foods include crab mac salad, paniolo pork chops and Spam Musubi (sushi Spam).

DRINK
POG is a delightful combo of passion, orange and guava juice.

STAY
Relax in a fancy hotel, book a beach bungalow or bring a tent and camp on the beach in designated areas (permit required).

EXPERIENCE
Chat with locals at the Kaua'i Culinary Market at The Shops at Kukui'ula.

Opposite: the apapane honeycreeper is endemic to Hawai'i;
This page: Waipo'o Falls in Waimea Canyon

strolls. The centre of the island is known for Mt Waiʻaleʻale and a superlative – the rainiest spot on earth. Also known for its rain is the north shore, home to verdant rainforests and the famous Na Pali (meaning 'many cliffs') Coast, where spinner dolphins perform aerial moves, sea caves abound and humpback whales stop by from December to April.

This rural island is the oldest of the major Hawaiian islands and the most isolated. While much of the Hawaiian archipelago has been over-commercialised, Kauaʻi has managed to hang on to its rural appeal; there are still plenty of wide-open spaces, red-dirt roads (leave any white shoes at home), wild chickens and no buildings taller than a coconut tree. Life here is simple and low-key – nightlife includes stargazing and hitting the sack by 9pm. That, plus the fact that it's the oldest inhabited Hawaiian island, is why locals lovingly refer to it as the 'Grandmother Island'.

Opposite top: Tunnels beach on Kauaʻi's north shore;
Bottom: a local vendor serving shave ice

Six Day Itinerary

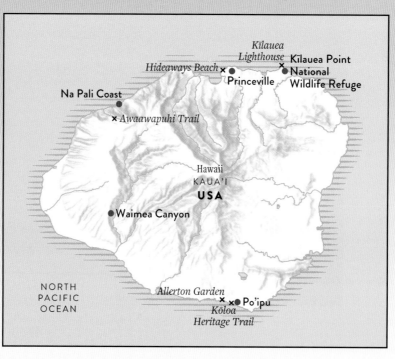

>

Make south-side beach town Poʻipu your home base so that on day one you can head straight to the airport for a doors-off helicopter excursion – much of Kauaʻi is inaccessible by car, so it's worth the splurge. Explore the 10-mile (16km) Kōloa Heritage Trail by bike or on foot, then commune with hundred-year-old banyan trees at Allerton Garden.

>>

See a different perspective of the Na Pali Coast's huge sea cliffs with Blue Ocean Adventures, venturing beneath waterfalls and through sea caves.

>>>

Back on land, a drive to Waimea Canyon is a must. You can hike to the bottom, lounge on boulders and swim in the cool waters.

>>>>

Next it's the north shore, making Princeville your first stop. Grab lunch and enjoy it at Hideaways Beach, followed by a dip in the ocean. Continue to Kīlauea Point National Wildlife Refuge, where the Kīlauea Lighthouse stands, and see if you can spot a nene (Hawaiʻi's state bird).

MORE TIME?

The views on the six-mile (10km) Awaʻawapuhi Trail are worth an extra day.

Map labels:
Kīlauea Lighthouse
Hideaways Beach
Kīlauea Point National Wildlife Refuge
Princeville
Na Pali Coast
Awaawapuhi Trail
Hawaii
KAUAʻI
USA
Waimea Canyon
NORTH PACIFIC OCEAN
Allerton Garden
Poʻipu
Kōloa Heritage Trail

PRACTICALITIES

GETTING THERE AND AROUND

Fly into Lihue Airport; there are plenty of direct flights to Lihue from the US mainland and rental companies to pick up a car.

WHEN TO GO

May to mid-June and September to mid-December are considered off season and airfares and accommodation options are typically lower. Avoid US holidays like spring break, Thanksgiving and Christmas.

THINGS TO NOTE

It's smart to bring a rain jacket and a light layer for cooler nights. Mosquitoes can be found year-round in this tropical climate, with June through August being peak season, so be sure to pack bug spray. Ocean conditions in Kaua'i can often be dangerous so only swim at beaches that have lifeguards.
Further information is available at gohawaii.com

CANADA

Go Off-Grid *in the* Great Bear Rainforest

LISTEN FOR WHISPERS in the trees. That's the insider advice for a trip into British Columbia's Great Bear Rainforest, the world's largest coastal temperate rainforest and a labyrinthine maze of deep fjords and island archipelagos. The sound you're listening out for is the spirit or kermode bear, a white-coated black bear with a single recessive gene; bald eagle, deer, coastal wolf and grizzly also make their home in the rainforest. On both sides, as you sail upstream or down inlet from the town of Klemtu, hemlock and Douglas fir, some as old as 1500 years, rise to the heavens and the deluged estuaries are dotted with fallen, half-submerged trees the size of totem poles. Beyond that, out in the bays, sea lions mosh and spray from humpbacks lingers in the air like smoke. This is a place of emotive wildlife. Seemingly limitless forest. Isolated archipelagos weaving First Nation legends of the Kitasoo/Xai'xais with reality. Its story is one of an encounter with the seldom-seen wild – and oneself.

AT A GLANCE

EAT
The local speciality is sockeye salmon barbecued on cedar wood.

EXPERIENCE
Learn first-hand the folklore of the Kitasoo/Xai'xais people who live in Klemtu.

PRACTICALITIES
Visit from April to October. Gulf Island Seaplanes and Harbour Air fly from Vancouver to Klemtu and Hartley Bay. Maple Leaf Adventures runs immersive cruises from Vancouver Island.

CANADA

Find Joie de Vivre in Québec

AT A GLANCE

EAT
Poutine, a mix of fries, cheese curds and gravy, is Québec's classic comfort food.

DRINK
Tree sap is elevated to cocktail stardom in the maple martini.

PRACTICALITIES

Most people travel in the summer, but winter brings its own rewards, including big festivals like the Carnaval de Québec.

QUÉBEC IS A VIBRANT blend of the old world and the new. Montréal, Canada's second largest city, has Parisian-style bakeries, traditional *auberges* (inns) and grand churches dating back to the 18th century. But there's also eye-catching street art, delicious eating options celebrating the bounty of Canadian fields, and riotous sports bars where everyone gathers to watch that beloved Canadian invention – ice hockey. Québec City has much the same mashup of North America and Europe. Fortifications ring the historic centre, and the parliament building is a case study in Second Empire architecture. Bilingualism is deeply imbedded in the culture. 'Bonjour, hello' is the standard greeting – a visitor's reply indicating whether talk will continue in French or English. Beyond these two cities, there's much to explore, from the charming villages of Île d'Orléans to the sea cliffs of the Gaspé Peninsula. The province also has a serious love for winter, with skiing on the slopes of Mt Tremblant and ice skating on frozen lakes.

CANADA

Touch *the* Roof *of the* Rockies

Opposite: canoeing on Emerald Lake at the Yoho National Park; *This page:* a snow coach carries visitors to Athabasca Glacier

BANFF AND ITS SURROUNDING national parks saw the genesis of Canada's environmental movement. As you hike around the sky-scraping peaks that guard the border of Alberta and British Columbia, you won't just be walking on the rooftop of the Rockies, you'll be delving into the early history of Canada's vast national park network.

There are four conjoined parks in the region – Banff, Jasper, Yoho and Kootenay – all protected within an expansive UNESCO World Heritage Site that was first designated in 1984. If you only come to Canada once in your life, this is where you should make your base, quietly absorbing a conveyor belt of quintessential Canadian scenery that no photograph or YouTube video can hope to replicate.

Picture sipping a revitalising cup of tea outside a backcountry chalet above Lake Louise; witnessing the gloriously unmani-cured wildflowers of Sunshine Meadows on the Continental Divide, or getting a fleeting glimpse of Banff's syrup-coloured larch trees before they shed their leaves in early October. For those willing to part with more money for their thrills, there are gondola rides, whitewater rafting trips and a spine-chilling

A Traveller's Tale

Summer or winter, I always get an expectant buzz when I roll into the town of Jasper, be it by car, bus or train. The excitement starts as soon as I arrive, usually at the historic railway station, from where I can survey the familiar shops and hotels of Connaught Dr, ringed by the national park's sentinel peaks – ice-crusted Mt Edith Cavell, the bald hump of Whistlers Peak and the triangular summit of Pyramid Mountain – practically imploring to me to dump my bag immediately and run directly for the slopes.

Of Canada's 48 incredibly diverse national parks, Jasper has always been a personal favourite. Rugged, challenging and more all-encompassing than its Rocky Mountain siblings, it acts as a yawning gateway to a vast but refreshingly accessible wilderness. I never tire of its undulating bike paths, spontaneous wildlife encounters and delicious bakeries.

BRENDAN SAINSBURY

AT A GLANCE

EAT
Alberta is Canada's beef capital so try a steak. Alternatively, opt for its other typical local meat dishes, namely bison short ribs and pulled elk.

DRINK
Maybe it's the fresh water from the mountain-fed streams, but the craft beer in these parts tastes exceedingly good.

STAY
Book an oTENTik, a pre-installed canvas tent with basic furnishings and heating. It's a step up from backcountry camping but not as plush as glamping. You'll find oTENTiks set up at campgrounds in all four national parks.

EXPERIENCE
Stop in the mountain town of Golden on the way to Yoho for a scary ride on its new canyon-drop swing, a kind of upright version of a bungee jump.

SHOP
Look out for Indigenous items, especially in the shops of Banff and Jasper where you can peruse a multitude of only-in-Canada souvenirs, including soapstone sculpture, *mukluks* (warm hide boots), prints, jewellery and blankets.

"If you only come to Canada once in your life, this is where you should make your base, quietly absorbing a conveyor belt of quintessential Canadian scenery"

Left: Bow River in the Canadian Rockies on a winter morning

via ferrata to quicken your pulse – plus a choice of three natural hot springs to bring it down again afterwards.

Although all four national parks are user-friendly, Banff is far and away the most accessible thanks, in part, to its railway history and early development as a tourist destination. Unusually for Canadian national parks, Banff also has a townsite with shops and restaurants, a spectacular chateau-style hotel and four bona fide ski resorts.

Roads in the area are wide, smooth and lined with dramatic scenery, meaning navigating between the parks is a pleasure rather than a pain. The finest – and arguably one of the most spectacular slices of asphalt in North America – is the 145-mile (233km) Icefields Parkway, between Lake Louise and Jasper, which has so many viewpoints and trailheads, you could con-

ceivably dedicate a whole month to exploring it. But that would mean missing out on the area's many nuances.

Jasper is a larger, less commercial version of Banff, with its own diminutive, blue-collar town. Yoho is famed for its ancient fossils and lofty Takakkaw Falls. And Kootenay is the most diverse, where you can encounter cacti and alpine tundra in the space of a few miles.

The region's wildlife is ubiquitous, and you're just as likely to see animals from your car as on a lonesome trail. If you return home from this adventure without having spotted a bear, elk *and* bighorn sheep, count yourself very unlucky.

Opposite: Fairmont Banff Springs resort in Banff National Park

Two Week Itinerary

>

Starting point Banff deserves three days: one to survey the townsite; one to tackle Sulphur Mountain and nearby Banff Springs Hotel; and a third to explore Lake Minnewanka with its hiking trails and narrated boat cruises.

>>

It's then a 90-minute drive to Radium Hot Springs on the edge of Kootenay National Park. Stop en route at roadside attractions like Marble Canyon. Spend an extra day soaking in the recuperative springs. Motor north on Hwy 95 to Yoho National Park, where in two busy days you can experience the spray of towering Takakkaw Falls, circumnavigate gorgeous Emerald Lake and organise a guided hike to the Burgess Shale fossil deposits.

>>>

Heading back east over Kicking Horse Pass, home in on Lake Louise with one day for the two teahouse treks, one for bear-watching from the summer gondola and a third for checking out Moraine Lake and Larch Valley.

>>>>

Drive slowly north on the Icefields Parkway, overnighting at the Columbia Icefield where you can jump on a Snowcoach and drive onto the Athabasca Glacier. Finish in Jasper with three days of single-track cycling, stargazing and contemplating the Rockies from Jasper SkyTram.

MORE TIME?

Diminutive Waterton Lakes National Park, three hours south of Calgary, is like a compact version of Banff.

PRACTICALITIES

GETTING THERE
AND AROUND

Calgary is the main gateway to the region and has an international airport and regular bus connections to Banff. Edmonton is another potential hub with an international airport and daily shuttles to Jasper. Although bus services run some routes within the parks, a car allows more spontaneity and flexibility. Local roads are excellent. Car rentals are available at Calgary and Edmonton airports.

WHEN TO GO

Most park facilities are open between Victoria Day (late May) and Labour Day (early September). Outside these times, activities and trail access may be limited. For snow-free mountain hiking, come between mid-July and late September. If you're planning to ski, make January and February your preferred months.

THINGS TO NOTE

The parks – especially Banff – get busy in the summer and accommodation is limited so book several months in advance. If hiking alone, always leave a route plan with a trusted contact. Wildlife is abundant in the parks – carry bear spray and know how to use it.
Further information is available on the Parks Canada website parks.canada.ca/pn-np

CANADA

Wrap Up *for a* Polar Bear Safari

SEEING POLAR BEARS from a distance is one thing. Seeing them approach your tundra vehicle is quite another. It happens often during polar bear season in Churchill, a small town on the southern edge of the Arctic that's known as the polar bear capital of the world, and for good reason – Canada is home to 60% of the world population. Starting in August each year, the bears leave the sea ice and roam Hudson Bay's three eco-zones: subarctic tundra, boreal forest and Arctic marine. If caught wandering into town, they land themselves in polar-bear jail where they are tagged and relocated. The bears aren't the only attraction, though. Churchill is also home to the largest beluga migration on Earth when, from June to September, the bright white whales show up in western Hudson Bay. It's also possible to see the Northern Lights up to 300 nights a year here – February to March is the best time.

AT A GLANCE

EAT
Sample elk meatloaf with garlic mashed potatoes.

DRINK
Trans Canada Brewing Company's BlueBeary Ale is the drink to try.

PRACTICALITIES

As the largest land predators, polar bears are dangerous. Guided tours in polar rovers are the only way to see them safely.

Europe

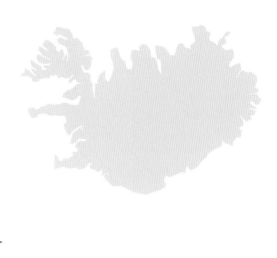

ICELAND

Drive Iceland's Epic Ring Road

WHO WOULD HAVE THOUGHT the road through hell would be such a pleasant drive? Iceland's Ring Road (Rte 1) passes blackened lava fields, scalding-hot pools and craters that belch sulphurous steam – but infernal landscapes are just part of this road trip's allure.

Rte 1 wraps around the entire coast of Iceland, so it's practically a showreel of the country's variety. In the space of an 821-mile (1322km) journey, the landscape transforms from monochrome to technicolour and back again. One stretch might appear unearthly and barren, then around the bend the scenery morphs into a fairy tale of lagoons, meadows and grass-roofed houses.

Considering the ever-changing landscape, the Ring Road is a surprisingly easy-going road trip. Rte 1 is fully paved and, unlike the interior roads criss-crossing Iceland, there's no need for a 4WD. You can drive it clockwise or anticlockwise, but most visitors start with a trio of celebrated sights: the Golden Circle. First, there's Þingvellir National Park, where early Icelanders formed their first parliament at the meeting point of two tectonic plates. Next is the Geysir geothermal area, where mud

Opposite: Námafjall geothermal area at Hverir, Lake Mývatn; *This page top:* Icelandic horses; *Bottom:* the blue church in Seyðisfjörður; *Previous page:* the skyline of Florence, Italy

AT A GLANCE

EAT

A steaming bowl of *kjötsúpa* (lamb soup). Potato, carrot and melt-in-the-mouth lamb bob in a salty broth, especially nourishing after a bracing hike in the wilderness.

DRINK

Icelanders pour Brennivín with knowing glee; it's strong, fiery and flavoured with caraway seeds. Shots are a rite of passage but it's best served as a martini, or muddled with berries and soda water.

STAY

Farmstays are found along the Ring Road. Expect simple but cosy rooms, and breakfast tables laden with eggs, cheese, yoghurt and *hangikjöt* (smoked lamb). Bonus activities include riding shaggy-haired Icelandic horses.

EXPERIENCE

Rent a kayak to paddle pristine fjords, or join a guided scuba tour: Iceland's waterways are crystal clear. At Silfra, you can even snorkel between two tectonic plates.

SHOP

Lopapeysa sweaters, made from unspun sheep's wool, have a semicircular geometric pattern radiating out from the collar. Look for 'handknitted in Iceland' labels to ensure you support local knitters.

A Traveller's Tale

I walk slowly over the frosty surface of Vatnajökull, my boots crunching with every step. The glacier sparkles under the midsummer sun but swirls of dark ash are contouring the surface, a reminder of the volcanic activity beneath.

Struck by the urge to take a photo, I fumble in my pocket for my phone. My guide calls out in a sing-song voice: 'If you drop your phone, it could be decades before the glacier gives it back!' With a gloved hand, she points to deep crevasses spidering across the ice and beckons me to join her. She's standing near the mouth of a small cave, sculpted by meltwater rushing through the ice sheet.

My breath forms a cloud as I step inside: the cave is bright blue, glowing like stained glass in a cathedral. Back out in the sunshine, I feel elated. Unlike with many phones, the glacier has agreed to give me back.

ANITA ISALSKA

"In the Geysir geothermal area, mud pots reach boiling point and fumaroles cough out subterranean steam"

Right: relaxing in the geothermally heated Mývatn Nature Baths; *Opposite:* Þingvellir National Park

pots reach boiling point and fumaroles cough out subterranean steam. And finally Gullfoss, where clouds of mist billow from a two-tier waterfall on the Hvítá River.

Once the Golden Circle is in the rear-view mirror, crowds drop away and the road trip begins in earnest. Shimmering waterfalls like Skógafoss require only brief turn-offs, while Jökulsárlón Glacier Lagoon needs no detour at all from Rte 1. In this glacial lake, bergs clink like ice cubes in a cocktail glass while grey seals somersault in the frigid water. The further east you drive, the more bucolic the scenery gets, culminating in Seyðis-fjörður's romantic wooden buildings and celestial-blue church.

The landscape grows darker as you continue north. Dettifoss, Europe's second most powerful waterfall, pummels silt over 144ft-high (44m) cliffs, turning the waters in Jökulsárgljúfur canyon a shadowy grey. At Lake Mývatn, summer clouds of biting midges can seem like a biblical plague. Nearby, the black lava towers of Dimmuborgir resemble unholy church spires, and volcanic stone arches look like portals to another realm. Along the drive, nature is bound to play tricks – rainstorms descend without warning, and sudden winds wreak havoc on roadside photo ops.

For the final third of the Ring Road back to Reykjavík, the route flies past bays and fjords that are teeming with life. Minke whales and dolphins dance in the waves, while Arctic terns wheel above. Around every bend there's another reminder that, in Iceland, nature is a force to be reckoned with.

This page: an Atlantic puffin watches over Iceland's Dyrhólaey Peninsula coast

PRACTICALITIES

GETTING THERE AND AROUND

Other than cruise ships and weekly summer ferries from Denmark to Seyðisfjörður, the main transport links to Iceland are by air: flights reach Reykjavík year-round. Many travellers rent a car, but if you plan well you can take buses all the way around the Ring Road and Snæfellsnes Peninsula (limited services in winter).

WHEN TO GO

Peak season is June to August, when days are long and there's plenty of sunshine. Summer crowds thin out beyond Reykjavík and the Golden Circle, but book accommodation and car rental well ahead. Shoulder season (April to May and September to October) brings unpredictable weather but it's relatively quiet. November to March are bitterly cold and daylight hours are short, but with snow sports, stargazing and the Northern Lights, winter can be magic.

THINGS TO NOTE

High mountain passes close from September to May and, even in summer, conditions can change dramatically; keep up to date at safetravel.is. Advance accommodation bookings are always wise, but southern Iceland is especially popular and options are limited in the southeast.
Further information is available at visiticeland.com

Two Week Itinerary

> First, get acquainted with Reykjavík's coffee and cocktail scene. On day two, drive the Golden Circle before joining Rte 1 heading east to Landeyjahöfn (3½ hours' drive total). In the morning, catch the ferry to Vestmannaeyjabær for a puffin-spotting day trip before driving one hour to Vík's black-sand beach.

>> On day four, continue 50 minutes east to Kirkjubæjarklaustur's basalt columns and base yourself near Skaftafell for two nights – glacier hikes and Jökulsárlón's icebergs await.

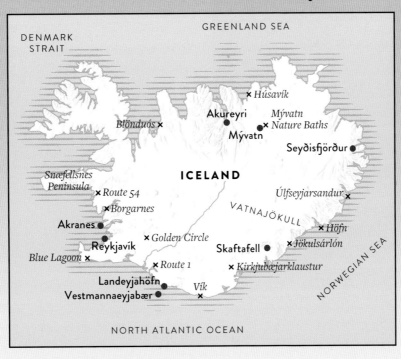

>>> Grab lunch at fishing town Höfn (2½ hours) on day six, then it's north along fjordside roads, stopping at black-sand Úlfseyjarsandur. Arrive at colourful Seyðisfjörður on day seven, then head northwest to smelly but soothing Mývatn Nature Baths on day eight.

>>>> Spend day nine rambling around Lake Mývatn's craggy shores, then drive to Akureyri (1¼ hours) by nightfall. Devote day 10 to Akureyri and stay another night for a whale-watching trip from Húsavík.

>>>>> Complete the circuit on days 12 to 13, stopping at sleepy Blönduós, Borgarnes and Akranes for burial mounds and rusty old ships. Finish by sliding into the Blue Lagoon's mineral-rich waters.

MORE TIME? Take Route 54 for a few days on the Snæfellsnes Peninsula for toothy mountains and shipwreck beaches.

IRELAND

Road Trip *the* Wild Atlantic Way

YOU SCOUR THE MIRROR-CALM sea on a wildlife-watching boat. A dolphin pod appears at starboard in the midst of a plankton-feeding frenzy. Excitement ensues. Then excitement turns to screams, with the emergence of a far larger creature. Now, closer to the vessel, is a marine leviathan – a bullet-headed Minke whale.

These are common sights on the Wild Atlantic Way, the uninterrupted drive that stretches 1615 miles (2600km) from the Inishowen Peninsula in County Donegal to Kinsale in County Cork along Ireland's west coast. Naturally, this weather-beaten route has always been there, sculpted over centuries by prevailing Atlantic wind and rain. But these wild, wonderful shores are now also the backdrop for a gigantic eco-tourism network promoting sea kayaking, hiking, fishing, surfing and foraging all along the full length of the West Irish mainland. The logic is this: Australia has the Great Ocean Road, South Africa the Garden Route, California the Pacific Coast Highway. Ireland's pitch is that its dream road trip is better.

Opposite: Classiebawn Castle on the cliffs of County Sligo; *This page:* a fisherman repairs his nets

More than just terrific, twisting tarmac, though, this is a drive full of heart-stealing diversions, from the sandy beaches and sea cliffs near Malin Head, Ireland's northernmost point, to the UNESCO-listed Skelligs of County Kerry. In the portrait-posing seaside villages between are myriad areas of outstanding natural beauty. Consider stops at Gola and Dowey Islands and the cliffs of Slieve League, and factor in a stay in historic County Sligo – poet Yeats' country – and a hike up stunning tabletop Benbulbin. Achill, Ireland's largest offshore island, recently a star turn in *The Banshees of Inisherin*, is also within easy reach from the road.

A Traveller's Tale

We had left Baltimore on a marine life safari, but I hadn't expected to meet a fin whale so soon – we were less than a mile off the coast. We had sailed west beyond Cape Clear and yet the captain was in buoyant mood: 'We may see one or two,' he said, 'but only if we've the luck of the Irish.' The twinkle in his eye should have warned us he knew something was already out there waiting.

MIKE MACEACHERAN

AT A GLANCE

EAT

Savour chowder and pint of stout at a classic pub on the Connemara Coast.

DRINK

Stick to a west coast stout like Murphy's or Galway Hooker.

STAY

There are cliff-hugging guesthouses and creaky pubs all along the route.

EXPERIENCE

Undertake a spirit-lifting hike up Croagh Patrick, Ireland's holiest mountain.

This page: the Cliffs of Moher along Ireland's Wild Atlantic Way

Further along the route, side-trip and go kayaking to the inland seas of Lough Hyne Nature Reserve. Or perhaps let a skipper do all the hard work on board a whale-watching vessel leaving from Baltimore's pint-sized harbour. And, of course, what would any Irish trip be without folk music, food and plenty of craic with some of the most welcoming people on the planet?

PRACTICALITIES

GETTING THERE AND AROUND

To drive north to south, fly into Belfast. Alternatively, Cork is your entry point to the West Cork Coast. A rental car is essential; opt to travel sustainably with an electric vehicle, as charging stations are now widespread along the entire route.

WHEN TO GO

Irish traditional music and food are highlights of the summer festival season. Cork Midsummer Festival happens in June and Galway International Arts Festival takes place in July. Alternatively, for the ultimate craic, visit on St Patrick's Day on 17 March.

THINGS TO NOTE

Driving in Ireland is on the left-hand side of the road — drive north if you really want to hug the coastline.
Further information at ireland.com

10 Day Itinerary

>

Begin by driving north to southwest, as if you're constantly chasing the sun, and start at Malin Head, where romance and rugged scenery collide on the Inishowen Peninsula.

>>

Days two and three then take you through County Donegal, from the lighthouse at Fanad Head, through Sligo and Wild Nephin National Park, home to Atlantic blanket bog — ideal for easy nature rambles or remote backpacking.

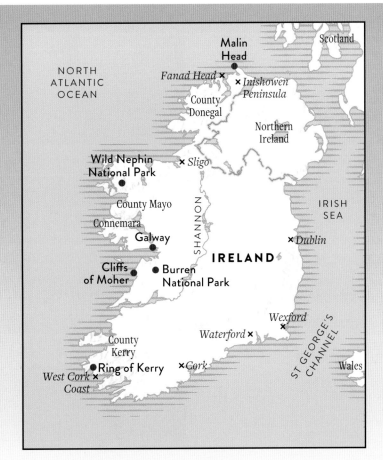

>>>

In County Mayo, the road winds westward through the scenic mountains and heaths of Connemarra on day four and, by day five and six, Galway and Burren National Park will be in the rearview; hiking the karst landscape is essential here. The soaring Cliffs of Moher are also unmissable, as is the 30-minute ferry ride across the Shannon into County Kerry.

>>>>

Fill your last days exploring the silvery sands of the Ring of Kerry and the inlets of West Cork Coast, where marine life competes for your attention alongside salty pubs and historic harbours.

MORE TIME?

The coastal route from Cork via Waterford and Wexford to Dublin is quieter, yet lays on an equal amount of roadside drama.

ENGLAND

Tread *the* Boards *with* Shakespeare

STRATFORD-UPON-AVON IS JUST the gateway to a theatrical world of sights linked to England's greatest playwright. In this atmospheric Midlands town, you can almost hear Shakespeare pacing about concocting similes at a string of Tudor-era houses linked to the Bard. Feel his spirit linger at his graveside and during rousing performances by the Royal Shakespeare Company, then head to nearby Kenilworth Castle to relive scenes from *A Midsummer Night's Dream* and *Henry VI*, ringed by moody toppled battlements. Onwards to King's Lynn, where you can walk time-polished boards that were trodden by Shakespeare the actor at the agreeably wonky Guildhall. Let the curtain fall in London, with a convincing recreation of Elizabethan drama at the reconstructed Globe; a moment of reflection at the nearby sites of the original Globe and Rose theatres; a face-to-face encounter with William's receding hairline at the National Portrait Gallery; and a gruesome circuit around murder scenes from *Richard III* in the Tower of London.

AT A GLANCE

EAT
Try modern takes on medieval pub grub in historic coaching inns.

DRINK
Down real ale at Stratford's Garrick Inn, reputedly Shakespeare's local.

PRACTICALITIES

Travel Shakespeare's England by train and book Royal Shakespeare Company and Globe Theatre shows well ahead.

NORWAY

See *the* Lights *on* Svalbard

AT A GLANCE

STAY
Try a trapper's life at Basecamp Hotel in Longyearbyen.

EXPERIENCE
Learn dogsledding as the Northern Lights flash overhead with greendog.no.

PRACTICALITIES
The Northern Lights shine from mid-September to March. Norwegian and SAS fly to Longyearbyen to Tromsø and Oslo. *More information at visitnorway.com*

NIGHT FALLS AND THE SKY sways in the most unnerving way, with wizard-wand flashes of green. The lights. The lights are here. And it's as if the Nordic gods are having a strobe party up in the heavens. Everyone turns their eyes upwards and holds their breath in the chill night, as if to speak would be a travesty. Frozen fingers fumble to set shutter speeds that can capture the greatest show on Earth. All around, snow-frosted mountains glow pearl white as if lit from within. Midway between Norway and the North Pole and home to more polar bears than people, Svalbard is the High Arctic proper, a place of rock, ice and mind-bending beauty. Beyond the rumbling snowmobiles and howling huskies awaits white wilderness, echoing silence and regular displays of the aurora borealis. During the darkest months of the Polar Night (mid-November to January), the odds of seeing the latter are excellent, providing skies are clear and activity is high.

ENGLAND

Have a Right Royal Time

THE INTRIGUE AND CONTROVERSY depicted in the *The Crown* is just the beginning. Unfolding across England's green and pleasant land, the story of the royals is a soap opera a millennium in the making. The English capital is the epicentre of regal razzmatazz, the seat of power for every king and queen since William the Conqueror. London royal experiences range from the cheesy – joining the hordes at the Changing of the Guard at Buckingham Palace and trying to coax a reaction out of the King's Guards – to the sublime, such as wandering the elegant gardens of Hampton Court Palace. Dominating the River Thames, the Tower of London is steeped in the history of feuding dynasties. The gleaming Crown Jewels impress less than the graffiti scrawled by unlucky souls who fell foul of the ruling royals. It's a palace, a prison, a monument to monarchy and a murder scene – where two princes, three ex-queens and a succession of earls, cardinals and chancellors came to a sticky end. West along the Thames, experience the breadth of the royal story at Westminster Abbey, where 39 English (and subsequently British) monarchs have been crowned, and 30 kings and queens lie buried (alongside Isaac Newton, Charles

A Traveller's Tale

I've visited royal sights great and small, but Sandringham House stands out for the picture it paints of an ordinary family doing their best with a complicated life. Sure, it's ostentatious, but also homely – a setting for sibling squabbles, bedtime stories, family fallings out and momentous personal moments, from the death of George V to the birth of George VI. Don't overlook the sweeping grounds, where an air of peaceful privacy pervades.

JOE BINDLOSS

AT A GLANCE

EAT
Indulge at favourite restaurants for the royals such as Bellamy's of Mayfair and Quaglino's of St James's.

DRINK
Try the Old Boot Inn in Stanford Dingley, a regular watering hole for William and Kate.

STAY
Book the head gardener's cottage at Sandringham House, available for overnights year-round.

EXPERIENCE
Relax over high tea at Littlecote House in Berkshire, where Jane Seymour was courted by Henry VIII.

Opposite: **Hampton Court Palace in London;** *This page:* **Westminster Abbey with Big Ben and the Houses of Parliament in the background**

Dickens and other deserving commoners). Then cross Hyde Park – via the memorial raised by a grieving Queen Victoria for her husband, Albert – to the Princess Diana Memorial Fountain, which performs an invaluable civic service for overheating inner-city toddlers every summer.

Then there are the royal homes, all filled to the rafters with Queen Anne furniture, surprised-looking stuffed wildlife and XL-sized armour handed down from Henry VIII. Make a house call at Kensington Palace or Windsor Castle, or take the train through Cambridge to elegant Sandringham House, where a sense of the Windsors as a normal family endures. To feel like a royal for the day, swap the palaces for the races. Every June, royals, hangers-on and highfliers from Britain's rich list gather in Ascot for a week of horses, champagne brunches and extraordinary hats. Why just watch *The Crown* when you can pretend that you're in it?

Opposite top: Windsor Castle, one of the Royal residences; *Bottom:* a guard on duty outside the Tower of London

One Week Itinerary

>

Start the royal rendezvous at Buckingham Palace. Within a few blocks, you can wander two royal parks and goggle at the king's carriages in the Royal Mews.

>>

On day two, make for Westminster Abbey and follow Whitehall to the Household Cavalry Museum, dedicated to the king's official bodyguard. Save day three for the Tower of London, to admire the Crown Jewels, the armoury and the cells that held Queen Elizabeth I, Sir Walter Raleigh and Anne Boleyn.

>>>

Set aside one day for the riverboat ride to Hampton Court Palace and deer-filled Richmond Park, the largest royal park, and devote another to Windsor and the king's most elegant castle.

>>>>

Take the train to Cambridge (one to two hours) and visit Trinity College, alma mater of King Charles, then use your last royal day to visit Sandringham House, where Queen Elizabeth II spent her childhood.

MORE TIME?

Head to Brighton to view the fantasy pavilion built for George, Prince Regent, stopping at Battle, where William the Conqueror seized control, and Hever Castle, childhood home of Anne Boleyn.

PRACTICALITIES

GETTING THERE AND AROUND

Four major airports bring the world to London, with easy connections to the centre by train, tube or taxi. Explore central London by bus and tube; overland trains are handy for trips out to Hampton Court Palace, Windsor and Sandringham.

WHEN TO GO

Come in summer – the weather is warm in London's royal parks, the State Rooms at Buckingham Palace are open to the public and it's race season at Royal Ascot.

THINGS TO NOTE

Royal tours are easy to find – consider something extravagant, such as Audley Travel's Royal Britain tour, or seek out irreverent options such as the tours of the Tower of London offered by the yeoman warders.

Further information is available at royal.uk

SCOTLAND

Take *the* Road *to* Skye

Opposite: Clachaig Inn in Glencoe; *This page:* a highly impressive Highland cow

THE ROAD TO THE ISLES winds through Britain's most spectacular scenery. As you drive towards the ferry crossing to the mystical island of Skye, you're in for a treat, crossing a region that offers the greatest hits of the Highlands in microcosm. The only route through the region, the 46-mile (74km) Road to the Isles (aka the A380) starts from Fort William, in the shadow of Ben Nevis, Britain's highest mountain, then races through a quintessential landscape of heather-dotted moorlands, steeply pitched hills and lonely glens populated by bellowing stags. This is where the Scotland you've seen on screen is at its most familiar and, from every angle, it offers up a wellspring of Gaelic-tinged culture.

Before you set off, though, it's worth a detour south, to Glen Coe, a star in its own right that rewards the diversion with a heart-in-mouth drive through Scotland's most famous glen, with pyramid-shaped Buachaille Etive Mòr and a glut of cinematic backdrops crowding the horizon. You may recognise some from the 007 film *Skyfall* or *Harry Potter* saga. Otherwise, you're here for a mix of summits and valleys that beg to be

explored by boot, bike, board or ski. Central to the experience is getting out of the car, no matter the weather.

Back on the A380, more *Harry Potter* movie lore awaits around Glenfinnan. Just outside the village, the West Highland Line (and the Jacobite Steam Train, aka the Hogwarts Express) chugs over a photogenic railway viaduct. Glenfinnan is also the true heart of Jacobite Scotland, and the story of defeated claimant to the throne, Bonnie Prince Charlie, is at its most evocative here. In 1745, on the shores of Loch Shiel, he raised his standard in an attempt to take the British crown.

A Traveller's Tale

The path led to moorland dominated by the Red and Black Cullin, Skye's brooding mountain ranges. I was hiking to Sgùrr na Strì, a modest spine of rock that many say offers the country's most spectacular view. And I'd agree. Looking from the scree-covered corries of Sgùrr Dubh Mòr and Sgùrr Alasdair across turquoise-green Loch Coruisk to the Small Isles was life-affirming – and the finish-line pint afterwards tasted like the best of my life.

MIKE MACEACHERAN

AT A GLANCE

EAT
Some of the Highlands' most memorable restaurants are on Skye, including Edinbane Lodge, the Three Chimneys, Loch Bay and Kinloch Lodge.

DRINK
Nothing beats a single malt whisky from one of Skye's two distilleries, Talisker or Torabhaig.

STAY
Glencoe's Clachaig Inn has history and ambience at every turn.

EXPERIENCE
Ride the historic Jacobite Steam Train over the Glenfinnan Viaduct.

This page: Glenfinnan Viaduct, much visited by Harry Potter fans hoping to see it crossed by the steam train that inspired the Hogwarts Express

The road then winds north to Arisaig and Mallaig and the unspoiled Silver Sands of Morar, a string of blue-on-gold beaches as Caribbean as any in Britain. Perhaps though, the ultimate reward is what awaits across the Sound of Sleat by ferry: the Isle of Skye, a place with enough experiences to last a lifetime. Chief among these are hikes into the famous Black Cuillin mountains, seafood feasts and coastal adventures from lighthouse hunting to beachcombing for coral.

PRACTICALITIES

GETTING THERE
AND AROUND

If arriving by air, Glasgow and Inverness are both convenient entry points; to avoid backtracking, start in one and finish in the other. Travel by train or bus is also possible, but there are limited services in the Highlands, particularly on Skye. A hire car will maximise your time.

WHEN TO GO

July and August bring with them the largest crowds, plus – surprising to many – the wettest weather. For golden days, late light-filled skies and quiet glens, travel from May to June or September to October.

THINGS TO NOTE

Clouds of voracious midges (tiny bloodsucking insects) descend on the Highlands every summer. Pack strong repellent and cover up at dusk.

Further information is available at visitscotland.com

10 Day Itinerary

>

Start in Glencoe – if you like stag-filled moors, ridge walks and pubs, your first two days are taken care of. There's macabre history too. The Massacre of Glencoe, one of the country's worst atrocities, took place here in 1692.

>>

Day three and the road to Fort William and beyond beckons. You'll need two days to savour it all – add a third if you're climbing Ben Nevis, or want a day of mountain biking or snow sports on Aonach Mòr. In summer, consider a day of paddleboarding or snorkelling the Arisaig skerries.

>>>

Three days is just enough for the lovely landscapes and lonely roads of the Isle of Skye. From Sleat to Trotternish and Uig, it can take more than two hours each way, so stay somewhere different each night. Make sure to factor in a memory-making hike around the Old Man of Storr or Quiraing.

MORE TIME?

With an extra 1-2 days, make the quick ferry hop to Isle of Raasay, home to a super-slick whisky distillery and guesthouse.

BELGIUM

Raise a Glass *on an* Urban Beer Tour

'**BEHIND THE HORSE!**' bartenders tell customers looking for the toilets. It's no joke. At Brasserie Surréaliste microbrewery, in the hipster Dansaert district of Brussels, salvaged church furniture fills a 1930s banana warehouse, drinkers enjoy 24 beers on tap beneath chandeliers – and a life-sized equine sculpture stands sentry over the basement facilities. Cosmic Rainbow, Beatific Ecstasy, Venus Effect: the list of sour ales, single-hop IPAs et al reads like a sorcerer's spell book. Around the corner, Brussels Beer Project collaborates with other disruptor breweries to co-create 40-odd pop-up beers a year. Belgian brewers have experimented since the Middle Ages, using local varieties of wild yeast, flavours and styles to create indigenous beers impossible to find elsewhere (lime and sea salt infuses Brasserie Surréaliste's Hands of Desire ale). In 2022, the country counted 430 breweries, including six in Trappist monasteries and dozens on farmsteads and in surprising urban spaces. Drink in the scene: Belgian beer culture is a UNESCO 'Intangible Cultural Heritage of Humanity' treasure.

AT A GLANCE

EAT
Fill up on *carbonnade flamande* (beef stew) and fries at the Nüetnigenough brasserie.

DRINK
Sip Gueuze, the 'champagne of Belgium beer', at Cantillon.

PRACTICALITIES
Read up on the history of Belgian beer in Brussels at Belgian Beer World, inside the capital's former stock exchange.

THE NETHERLANDS

Embrace Dutch Flower Fields

AT A GLANCE

EAT

Lunch on *bitterballen* (meatballs) and *stamppot* (veg mash) at Het Oude Dykhuys.

EXPERIENCE

Rent a bicycle or join a guided bike tour (tulipbicycletour.com).

PRACTICALITIES

Take a Keukenhof Express bus from Amsterdam's Schiphol Airport or from Europaplein in the city to Lisse's Keukenhof Gardens.

IT'S AS IF A SUPER-SIZED paint pallette has been emptied over the Dutch town of Lisse. Keukenhof Garden's seven million tulips, daffodils and hyacinths in eye-popping bloom have to be seen to be believed. The sweep of red, pink, scarlet and sunflower-yellow ribboning to the horizon and waltzing around trees in whimsical swirls assaults every sense. Knowing that the springtime show at these bulb fields and manicured gardens southwest of Amsterdam lasts just eight weeks each year makes it even more special. Arrive in April to pair the world's largest bulb-flower garden with southern Holland's Bloemencorso (flower parade) in Bollenstreek. Floats festooned with gigantic characters and creatures sculpted in blooms progress through the streets, from the North Sea sand dunes of Noordwijk Beach to quintessential Dutch town Haarlem. Inhale sweet floral perfumes and seek out Queens of the Night – these rare, velvet-indigo flowers are the closest Dutch breeders have got to a black tulip and, in the language of flowers, symbolise joy.

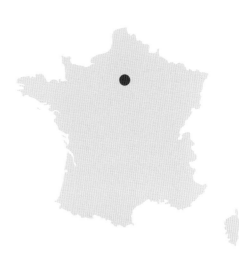

FRANCE

Find Romance
in Paris

OPERA BENEATH THE STARS. Champagne atop the Eiffel Tower. A sunset Seine cruise. Coffee on a pavement terrace or a rainbow of macarons devoured on a park bench in the company of marble centaurs, Trojan princesses and ripped Greek gods. There is simply no escaping the romance of Paris. This graceful city of classic landmarks and manicured parks has inspired love and desire since time immemorial. The Parisian art of seduction permeates every one of its 20 *arrondissements* (districts), each with different mood boards and foibles to entice, intrigue, excite and woo.

Take hilltop Montmartre. This storybook 'village' of steeply pitched lanes and never-ending staircases is a brazen heart-stealer with its captivating stories (bloody St Denis crossing Montmartre on foot, head in hand, after being beheaded by Roman priests in the 3rd century) and timeless theatrical thrills (can-can dancers at cabaret club Le Moulin Rouge). Rattling up the hillside in a vintage funicular to the landmark pearl domes of Basilique du Sacré-Cœur, then climbing 300 steps inside the church to take in panoramic views of one of the world's most

A Traveller's Tale

Paris is awash with serendipitous encounters. Île aux Cygnes (Island of Swans) is one of them, a whimsical sliver of an islet created in the Seine in 1827 to buffer Paris' Left Bank river port. How could I have possibly known, on that sunny day in spring, that my afternoon stroll along the island's alley of 60 tree types would unveil a quarter-scale *Statue of Liberty* and blossom-framed Eiffel Tower views?

NICOLA WILLIAMS

AT A GLANCE

EAT
You can't beat traditional French onion soup and Grand Marnier soufflé in a bistro.

DRINK
Nurse a glass of red Burgundy in a candlelit wine bar.

STAY
The 1er *arrondissement* has romantic River Seine views and elegant parks on your doorstep.

EXPERIENCE
Glide past famous landmarks on a hop-on-hop-off water bus by day or a romantic cruise after dark.

Opposite: multicoloured macarons; *This page:* the domes of Paris's Sacré Coeur de Montmartre rise above cobbled streets

beautiful cities, is intoxicating. Back down on main square Place des Abbesses, learning how to say '*Je t'aime!*' in 350 languages at the enamel-tiled I Love You Wall in a bijou Montmartre garden couldn't be more apt.

It's no coincidence that the Romanticism movement which swept through Western Europe in the early decades of the 19th century had its epicentre in the French capital. The city's illustrious artistic pedigree found further expression in Renoir, Rodin, Picasso, Monet, Manet, Dalí and Van Gogh – just some of the masters who lived and worked in Paris, contributing to its reputation as one of the world's mightiest art repositories. The blockbuster Louvre and Musée d'Orsay are inspiring and brilliant, but it's the smaller house- and studio-museums peppering the elegant streets and boulevards that evoke a more privileged intimacy between artist and audience. Indulging in tea and cake in the flower-scented summer garden of the house in Montmartre where George Sand, Chopin and Delacroix among others attended literary salons is the epitome of old-school romance.

This page: table service at Bar du Marché in St Germain; the sculpture hall in the Louvre, the world's most visited museum

PRACTICALITIES

GETTING THERE AND AROUND

International flights land at Paris Charles de Gaulle and Orly airports, both connected to the city centre by public transport. Many central Paris sights are walkable. A straightforward mix of shared Vélib bikes, metro, RER train and buses cover longer distances.

WHEN TO GO

April, May, September and October are pleasantly warm and dry. Greyer November and January are the quietest months, with fewer crowds and lower accommodation rates.

THINGS TO NOTE

Plan ahead: buy tickets for major sight and theatre shows in advance online and make restaurant reservations. State museums, including the Louvre and Musée Rodin, are free the first Sunday of each month.

Further information is available on the Paris tourist office website parisjetaime.com

Three Day Itinerary

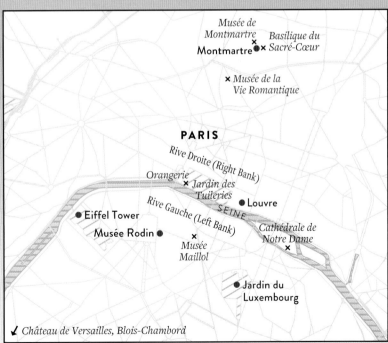

> Admire the skyline from Montmartre's Basilique du Sacré-Cœur – lofty views orientate Paris first-timers. Spend the morning exploring this artistic neighbourhood, diving into can-can culture at Musée de Montmartre and literary-salon life at Musée de la Vie Romantique. Walk south to Jardin des Tuileries, Monet's lily-filled Orangerie and the Louvre. Drink in sunset's golden glow with the gargoyles of Cathédrale de Notre Dame.

>> Day two is a *Rive Gauche* (Left Bank) affair. Meander south from the Seine to sculptor Aristide Maillol's studio-museum and beyond to Auguste Rodin's 1732 mansion; embrace *The Kiss*. Walk 30 minutes, either east to the Eiffel Tower or west to Jardin du Luxembourg to chase 1920s toy boats around the lake. Come dusk, sail along the Seine.

>>> Head out of town on day three to Château de Versailles, gawping at the interiors, strolling the gardens and indulging in an exceedingly grand afternoon tea at Le Grand Contrôle.

MORE TIME? Take a train to Blois-Chambord (1½ hours) then shuttle or taxi to Château de Chambord, France's finest Renaissance castle.

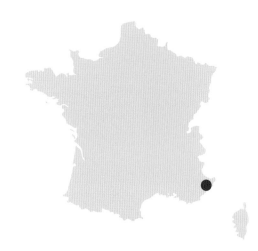

FRANCE

Glam Up *on the* Côte d'Azur

ANYTHING GOES ON FRANCE'S most mythical coastline. Flaming cocktails, entertainers on stilts, sun butlers facilitating every last swim whim and sunbathing desire – all this and more is available on the Côte d'Azur in the country's hot, sun-soaked south. And it has been for quite a long time. Artists, aristocrats and an era-defining British queen were the first to embrace this Mediterranean strip as their go-to destination in the 19th century, and an inimitable, old-school glamour still drips off every last cushioned sun bed and seductive dot of soft golden sand.

No place says vintage cool quite like Nice, the party-loving seaside town where high season – originally winter – on the Côte d'Azur (or French Riviera) was born. By 1822, wealthy British visitors were already flocking to the new Promenade des Anglais seafront to be seen, and in 1864 the first overnight train pulled into the city from Paris. The alluring mix of medieval hilltop villages, snowcapped Alps, secluded turquoise coves and flame-red rocks of the Massif de l'Estérel mesmerised passengers as the blue-and-gold carriages of the luxurious Train

Opposite: Nice's pink-domed Negresco hotel on the Promenade des Anglais;
This page: Billionaire's Bay at Cap d'Antibes

A Traveller's Tale

The dogs in handbags, bottle-tops as nipple sun-shades and prima donnas dusting sand from their toes with shaving brushes can feel surreal in sexy St-Tropez, Riviera centre of madcap acts and hedonist pleasures. The first time I visited this jetset central, I made the rookie error of driving, getting stuck in traffic on the approach to town and cursing the place even before I parked. Years later, I glided into the honey-hued port by boat from St-Raphaël. I steered clear of the crowds gawping at millionaire yachts in the Vieux Port, dedicating my time instead to early morning runs along golden Plage de Pampelonne, market shopping on Place des Lices and long walks along the coastal path. Only then did I finally understand why French pointillist painter Paul Signac, arriving by sailboat in 1892, fell so hard for this fishing village, with a quality of light sufficiently soul-piercing to inspire 20th-century fauvism.

NICOLA WILLIAMS

AT A GLANCE

EAT

Laze over a fish lunch on the sand at a restaurant on Plage de la Garoupe, the Cap d'Antibes beach created by the Murphys.

DRINK

Before a flutter in Monaco's casino sip a glass of Rosé Piscine wine on the rocks accompanied by dress-circle views of Monte Carlo at Café de Paris, hobnobbing hot spot since 1882.

STAY

Enjoy sweet dreams in a belle époque folly facing the sea: Nice's pink-domed Hôtel Negresco (1912), Cap d'Antibes' Hôtel du Cap Eden Roc (1870) and Cannes' Carlton (1911) are the height of prestige.

EXPERIENCE

Drive or e-bike the three corniches (coastal roads), bookended by Nice and Monaco. Hypnotic sea views glitter from the vertiginous Grande and Moyenne Corniches, and the sinuous Basse Corniche.

SHOP

In Vieux Nice, seek out Provençal olives, spices, olive oils and artisan soaps to take home at the food, flower and flea markets on old-world Cours Saleya.

© PHILIP LEE HARVEY / LONELY PLANET

"An inimitable, old-school glamour still drips off every last cushioned sun bed and seductive dot of soft golden sand"

Left: the Plage du Midi in Cannes at sunset

Bleu wound slowly south to the sea. And these charms remain equally appealing for those arriving by sleeper train from the French capital today. Ditto for the Côte d'Azur's year-round restorative warmth, sunshine and captivating beauty.

Jazz Age jetsetters created the summer season. Drink in their intoxicating vibe on Cap d'Antibes, an hour south of Nice. In 1923, American socialites Sara and Gerald Murphy (the inspiration for F Scott Fitzgerald's Nicole and Dick Diver in *Tender is the Night*) cleared the shore of seaweed and persuaded the hotelier at Hôtel du Cap-Eden Roc to stay open for the summer to host their friends. Rosé-fuelled picnics, sea swimming, sunbathing and frolicking on the sand in the Riviera's summer sun have been fashionable ever since.

Scandalous tales from the carefree belle époque period (1860–1914) and post-war Roaring '20s are linked to the old beach clubs, historical gardens and grand hotels on the Côte d'Azur. Wacky, wicked and occasionally downright ludicrous, it's the stories of mimosa flower cuttings being smuggled in on steamships from America, cleavage-inspired architecture and luckless gamblers dying at Monte Carlo's gaming tables that delight, shock and keep the coast's glamour alive. Be it following in Queen Victoria's royal footsteps in Nice, those of Matisse, Picasso and innumerable other modern artists around Vence and Antibes, or hand imprints of Hollywood stars in film-fest-famous Cannes, a journey along this coastline evokes the wanton abandon, unfettered creativity and unapologetic decadence of the most hedonistic period in French history. Indulge.

This page top: Monaco's old town, otherwise known as Le Rocher (the rock)

PRACTICALITIES

GETTING THERE
AND AROUND

Arriving by overnight train from Paris evokes the belle époque rail experience aboard Le Train Bleu. Nice-Côte d'Azur airport, with abundant international flights, is 4.5 miles (7km) west of town; tramline 2 to Port Lympia connects the airport with the Jean Médecin stop (for the city centre and train station) and bus 12 goes to Promenade des Anglais and Jardin Albert 1er (for Vieux Nice). Efficient regional buses and trains make travelling along this traffic-busy stretch of coast easy. In summer, sail to over-touristed St-Tropez from St-Raphaël, Ste-Maxime or Cannes.

WHEN TO GO

September ushers in near-perfect sea swimming conditions, thinner crowds, lower prices and the wine harvest. July and August are usually sizzling hot and insanely busy.

THINGS TO NOTE

Avoid *autoroutes* on Saturdays in August when seemingly half of France is on the move. Many beaches have lifeguards mid-June to mid-September. Expect to pay around €25/day to rent a sun-lounger and parasol; bathing topless is routine.

Further information is available at nice-tourism.com and explorenicecotedazur.com

Two Week Itinerary

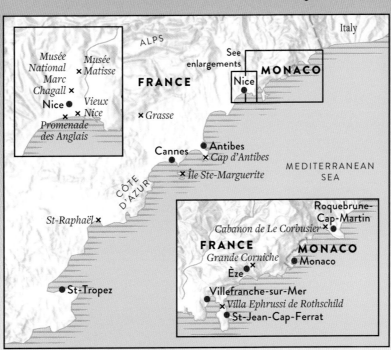

> Base yourself in Nice for a week and explore this vibrant Riviera capital along people-busy Promenade des Anglais and the back alleys, squares and markets of Vieux Nice. By day, visit the Musée Matisse and Musée National Marc Chagall, then party all night in Vieux Nice bars.

>> Day three or four, catch bus 82 along the coast to Villefranche-sur-Mer, for its sandy beach and fishermen's chapel decorated by Jean Cocteau. Continue to St-Jean-Cap-Ferrat, home to eucalyptus-scented footpaths and palatial Villa Ephrussi de Rothschild. On day five, bus it to hilltop Éze on the Grande Corniche for spectacular Med views.

>>> Next day, blow your mind in Grace Kelly's Monaco or, for architecture fans, revel in Le Corbusier's seaside cabin and Irish architect Eileen Gray's modernist tour de force next door in Roquebrune-Cap-Martin.

>>>> The following week, head southwest along the coast from Nice, enjoying a couple of days in Antibes and Cap d'Antibes. In glitzy red-carpet Cannes, pair a seafront stroll along La Croisette with oysters at the covered market. Sail to Île Ste-Marguerite, then catch a train to St-Raphaël and sail to St-Tropez.

MORE TIME? Rent a convertible and head for the hills to trace three millennia of perfume-making in Grasse.

FRANCE

Celebrate Champagne

MARRIAGE PROPOSALS, BIRTHDAYS, cork-popping F1 victories. No tipple is so celebratory or desired as champagne, unwittingly conceived by 17th-century monk Dom Pierre Pérignon in a Benedictine abbey in northern France. 'Come quickly, I am tasting the stars!' the God-loving wine aficionado purportedly cried upon tasting his accidental bubbles in 1693. Centuries later, Marilyn Monroe took a bath in 350 bottles of France's famous fizz. Forget the silver-screen glamour, though, and enjoy champagne's grassroots heritage and savoir-faire in the countryside where 16,200 *vignerons* nurture Pinot Noir, Meunier and Chardonnay grapes. It's an intoxicating journey. Motor or e-bike through vineyards to villages where alchemist cellar-masters blend vintages to create the perfect toast. In cathedral-clad Reims, where 34 French kings and queens were crowned, learn how the effervescent magic unfurls in chalk cellars hewn 130ft (40m) underground by Gallo-Romans. And in celebrity Épernay, no single street evokes the promise of a sparkling occasion quite like Ave de Champagne.

AT A GLANCE

EAT
Pair rosewater-infused *biscuits roses de Reims* with champagne.

DRINK
Book tastings at champagne houses and with producers along the Champagne Route.

PRACTICALITIES

Trains link Reims and Épernay, but to unearth smaller producers in rural Champagne, you'll need your own wheels.

GERMANY

Unplug *in the* Black Forest

AT A GLANCE

EAT

Schwarzwälder Kirschtorte is a cherry, chocolate and whipped-cream dream.

STAY

Pitch up at a back-to-nature trekking camp or hole up in a rustic farmstead.

PRACTICALITIES

Arrive by train or fly to Stuttgart, Karlsruhe Baden-Baden or Basel-Mulhouse. Come in summer to hike, or winter for markets and snow. *For more information see schwarzwald-tourismus.info*

HAZY LIGHT STREAMS THROUGH the spruce canopy in the piney freshness of morning. A woodpecker hammers out a lonely tune. But otherwise, only footfall on rock and the crackle of branches interrupt the silence in the Black Forest, which throws a fir blanket across Germany's southwest. Summers bring bracing walks to gather berries and mushrooms, and starlit nights at remote trekking camps. Winters bring the glitter of snow. When the Grimm brothers were dreaming up fairy tales, they surely had the Black Forest in mind. Its plaitwork of hills and valleys, rambling farms and deep, dark woods are, after all, bedtime story stuff. While the region is most famous for cherry gateau and giant cuckoo clocks, both of which can be found in Triberg, where the country's highest waterfall roars, nature is the scene-stealer here. Corkscrewing into the national park, the Black Forest High Road from Baden-Baden to Freudenstadt is a terrific starting point for backcountry road trips and crowd-dodging hikes.

GERMANY

Roam *the* Romantic East

EASTERN GERMANY RADIATES ROMANCE of a very distinct flavour. Wanderers gazing across mist-swathed crags, ancient stones standing in forested mountains, shattered Gothic monasteries bathed in moonlight. The romance here is richer, stranger, more melancholy than the west's fairy-tale brand. This is the world of Caspar David Friedrich and others, who transformed art two centuries ago. Put yourself in the picture on a rail journey through the former GDR to discover the dramatic scenery that inspired the Romantic Movement.

Long the divided capital of a divided country, Berlin's multiple personalities clash and complement. Among its street art, hip nightlife and monuments to 20th-century tumult – Holocaust Memorial, Checkpoint Charlie, Stasi Museum – rise relics of past glories: graceful squares and boulevards, the wedding-cake confections of Charlottenburg and Sanssouci palaces, and world-class museums showcasing art, archaeology and more.

To the south lies Saxony, the industrial heartland of former East Germany. Away from the smokestacks and Stalinist blocks, though, the state boasts stirring landscapes littered with medieval castles and monumental rock formations, along with cities

A Traveller's Tale

Sweat streamed from my brow as I huffed up the Papststein, a sheer-sided sandstone monolith rising from lush forest in the heart of Saxon Switzerland. Chimes of laughter and chinking glasses lured me through a lost world of ferns and improbable rock stacks to surely Germany's most dramatic crag-top cafe terrace, perched alongside a historic mountain pub. Drinking in the verdant vista, each gulp of ice-cold Weissbeer sparked dopamine fireworks.

PAUL BLOOMFIELD

AT A GLANCE

EAT

The famous Dresdner Eierschecke is a luscious, three-layered, egg-heavy cheesecake from the Saxon capital.

DRINK

Sip crisp Weissburgunder (Pinot Blanc) and Grauburgunder (Pinot Grigio) on the 37-mile (60km) Saxon Wine Route along the Elbe Valley.

STAY

Numerous Schlosshotels (castle hotels) offer stately stays: Burg Hohnstein, overlooking Saxon Switzerland, even incorporates a hostel.

EXPERIENCE

Cruise along the Elbe aboard a 19th-century paddle-steamer of the Sächsische Dampfschifffahrt.

Opposite: **Berlin's Brandenburg Gate;** *This page:* giant figures guard Dresden's partly rebuilt royal palace, with the dome of the Frauenkirche behind

adorned with opulent architecture. Today, Leipzig – dubbed 'little Paris' by Goethe – is a creative powerhouse, celebrated as the 'City of Heroes' for its role in bringing down the Communist regime. Mendelssohn, Wagner, the Schumanns and JS Bach lived and composed here, but irreverence trumps tradition in the city where Mephistopheles caroused with Faust, its cabarets and clubs fizzing into the small hours.

To the east, the resurrection of Dresden's magnificent old core – flattened by Allied bombing during WWII – is nothing short of miraculous. The bombastic Residenzschloss (Royal Palace), the soaring baroque dome of the Frauenkirche (Church of Our Lady), the palace-garden complex of the Zwinger – all dazzle again on the River Elbe's south bank, while to the north, counterculture thrives in the Äussere Neustadt (Outer New Town).

No artist's imagination could conjure landscapes more fantastical than the Elbe Sandstone Mountains, or Saxon Switzerland. This forest of pinnacles, looming east of Dresden, is studded with ruined bastions and rock-top fortresses such as colossal Königstein. Hike among these curious crags on the 72-mile (116km) Malerweg (Painter's Way), delving into scenes that fired those Romantic artists' passions.

Opposite top: the Bastei Bridge above the River Elbe; *Bottom:* street art in Berlin

Two Week Itinerary

> Begin with three days exploring Berlin's rollercoaster story. Stroll from the Reichstag and Brandenburg Gate along tree-lined Unter den Linden to Museumsinsel for world-class art, including masterpieces by Romantic artists such as Friedrich. Gawp at over-the-top Schloss Charlottenburg, and make the half-hour hop to Potsdam for a day trip wandering Frederick the Great's fabulous Schloss Sanssouci.

>> Ride 75 minutes south from Berlin to Leipzig for two days' revelry, bingeing on Bach at the Thomaskirche and Bach Museum.

>>> Dresden, 70 minutes to the east, demands at least a couple of days. Admire art in the Albertinum, the extravagant Residenzschloss and the sprawling Zwinger complex, but also dive into the grittier post-Communist street art and nightlife of the Äussere Neustadt, and sample crisp whites among the vineyards surrounding Pillnitz's extravagant palace and gardens.

>>>> Finally, take the train 30 minutes southeast to Bad Schandau to hike the Malerweg among Saxon Switzerland's otherworldly rock outcrops.

MORE TIME?

Cross the border into Bohemian Switzerland then discover Czechia's share of scenic spectacles, then continue to Prague for more medieval marvels.

PRACTICALITIES

GETTING THERE
AND AROUND
European Sleeper rail services
operate three times a week from
Brussels and Amsterdam to Berlin
and Dresden – arriving in the
morning – and continue to Bad
Schandau and Czech capital Prague.
Deutsche Bahn trains link all
destinations in this itinerary.

WHEN TO GO
Spring and autumn – March to June,
September and October – are perfect
for exploring the east, dodging the
biggest crowds and avoiding the
sometimes stifling heat of high
summer in Saxon Switzerland.

THINGS TO NOTE
Deutsche Bahn's Deutschland-Ticket
is a great-value monthly option
covering travel on most local and
regional public transport (not
private services or some intercity
trains though).
Further information on the region is
available at germany.travel/en

EUROPE

Visit Great Capitals *by* Rail

TRAVEL BY RAIL in Europe and you won't waste a single moment. As soon as you step aboard a train, you can admire the scenery as it morphs from industrial smokestacks to farmland to steeple-dotted towns. On sleeper services, you can wake up in an entirely new country and disembark in the heart of a city – no waiting at the baggage carousel and not an airport bus in sight.

The tricky part is choosing where to start, but Amsterdam is a well-connected springboard to Central and Eastern Europe. Within moments of renting a bike from Centraal station, you can cycle past the canalside *grachtenpanden* (narrow historic houses) en route to the poignant Anne Frank House and awesome Rijksmuseum, which houses artwork by Dutch master painters. That night, you'll board the European Sleeper and dream of Van Gogh's sunflower fields.

Your alarm clock is the sound of the train clattering into Berlin Hauptbahnhof. Public transport makes it easy to zip around the teeming German capital (the most populous in the European Union), so take it all in: WWII and Cold War sights; the

Opposite: cycling alongside the Amstel in Amsterdam; *This page top:* the U-Bahn runs through Berlin's Friedrichshain-Kreuzberg; *Bottom:* pouring beer at a Prague brewery

AT A GLANCE

EAT

Chocolate sponge, chocolate coating and apricot jam, Sachertorte is a cake connoisseur's dream. Nibble it in Vienna's Hotel Sacher where it was created by chef Franz Sacher in 1832.

DRINK

Since Benedictine monks began brewing in 993 CE, gallons of pilsner have been gulped at venues around Prague. Try the vaults of 15th-century beer hall U Fleků.

STAY

Budapest has distinct Art Nouveau flourishes and many of its hotels have conserved this opulent style, including Gresham Palace, complete with original ironwork and stained glass.

EXPERIENCE

The East Side Gallery, a mile-long section of the Berlin Wall, stands witness to the city's past division. Its murals are darkly funny, often political and brimming with hope. Go early to beat the crowds.

SHOP

For over 300 years, De Negen Straatjes (the Nine Streets) of Amsterdam have been alive with arts and crafts, and today they're also filled with cafes and vintage boutiques.

A Traveller's Tale

'I want to introduce you to Trabi, the authentic Czechoslovak car!' grins Brano, my guide. We're meeting just outside Bratislava's pastel-coloured Old Town, and our transportation is definitely offbeat – Trabi is a Trabant, a vintage Škoda from the Communist era.

'Accelerate, and a little prayer', mutters Brano as he fires up Trabi. The whole car vibrates as the engine groans to life. I can feel every bump in the road as we leave behind steeples and fountains and start our tour of Brutalist buildings, architectural relics of the mid-20th century. We snap pictures of the Slovak Radio Building, an upturned pyramid, and gaze up at the Petržalka neighbourhood's Lego-like tower blocks.

By the end of our tour, my phone isn't full of charming churches and quaint streets; instead, it's all scowling statues and architectural eyesores. They end up being my most treasured pictures.

ANITA ISALSKA

144

Right: The Museum of Natural History, one of the many cultural attractions in Vienna's MuseumsQuartier; *Opposite:* Charles Bridge in Prague

monumental Brandenburg Gate; flea markets; modern-art galleries; and nightlife you won't be telling mum about.

Onward, to Prague. The train journey passes in a pleasant blur of forests and fields along the Elbe and Vltava Rivers. When you leave Prague Hlavni station, it's only a short walk to the twin-spired Church of Our Lady before Týn and tourist favourite Charles Bridge – and you're even closer to a thirst-quenching half-litre of beer (likely your first of many).

By now, your brain is brimming with quaint canals, baroque buildings and modernist art. Then you reach Vienna, adding even more to your crowded photo library – palaces, royal gardens and the MuseumsQuartier, where 60 world-class galleries vie for attention in a former imperial stables.

A brisk train ride away is Bratislava. With fewer big-ticket sights, the scrappy Slovakian capital is a palate-cleanser for frazzled travellers. Meander around the Old Town's candy-coloured streets, and make time for local curiosities, from humorous statues to Brutalist architecture to dinner inside a UFO.

After a week of navigating cobblestone streets and laby-rinthine museums, Hungary's capital is a fitting last stop – travellers have been resting their weary feet in Budapest's thermal springs for centuries. The views are just as restor-ative. Gaze out from the turrets of Fisherman's Bastion or from Batthyány Sq across the Danube toward the Gothic Revival–style parliament building. Or you could head behind the grand facade of Budapest Keleti station – who says your train-hopping adventure needs to end here?

Opposite: Groenburgwal canal in Amsterdam

10 Day Itinerary

>

Spend a full day exploring galleries and cycling canalside in Amsterdam. After dinner, board the European Sleeper to Berlin.

>>

On day two, your train arrives in time for breakfast in Germany's capital, before you set out to discover eclectic galleries and sobering historic sights.

>>>

After two nights in Berlin, get a morning train to Prague (four hours) to arrive for lunch, perhaps pork knuckle or *smažený sýr* (fried cheese), washed down with malty Kozel beer. Spend the afternoon and following day exploring the Old Town and enjoying the nightlife.

>>>>

On day six, board a train to Vienna (four hours) and devote 36 hours to strolling the Ringstrasse and feasting your eyes on the MuseumsQuartier's collections.

>>>>>

On day eight, jump on the train to Bratislava (one hour); dawdle around the historic centre, take a Trabant tour or visit nearby Devin Castle. The next day, take the high-speed service to Budapest (2½ hours) and close out the trip simmering in Széchenyi Baths and carousing in ruin bars.

MORE TIME?

Start in London and take the Eurostar to Brussels, where you can join the European Sleeper train. Bonus: add a night in gorgeously Gothic Dresden, between Berlin and Prague.

PRACTICALITIES

GETTING THERE
AND AROUND

Reach Amsterdam or Budapest by
train from around Europe or, from
the UK, catch a ferry to Amsterdam.
From further afield, international
flights reach Amsterdam.

WHEN TO GO

Summer (June to August) is peak
season, with the best chance of
sunny skies and 100% chance of
crowds. Avoid them by travelling in
spring (March to May) or autumn
(September to November). If
you don't mind short, cold days,
Christmas markets fill city squares in
December – grab a *Glühwein* (spiced
hot wine) and shop. Book well ahead
for Christmas and New Year.

THINGS TO NOTE

Book in advance, especially sleepers,
to guarantee your chosen trains and
lower prices: advance tickets can be
a quarter of the cost of flexible fares.
Under-26 discounts apply to many
journeys, and some countries offer
cheaper fares (or free travel) for
over-65s. Print out tickets or show
them on your phone. Follow local
news to be aware of train strikes,
which can throw out journeys by
multiple days.
*Further information on travelling
Europe by train is available at
seat61.com and bahn.de.*

FINLAND

Find *the* Magic *of* Lapland

LAPLAND IS A REAL-LIFE snow globe in winter. Swirling flakes blanket forests in white, with sparks of colour provided by reindeer. Finland's Arctic North has Christmas in its bones, with the icing on the festive cake being Santa's HQ in Rovaniemi. You are forever five years old when you whisper your wish list into the attentive ear of the one-and-only St Nick in his twinkly grotto. Rudolph and his flying friends, glittery train rides, elves baking gingerbread and decorating trees – the gateway to Finnish Lapland delivers the whole shebang with (jingle) bells and whistles on.

But there's so much more to Lapland than the jolly red-robed dude. Just a snowball-throw from Rovaniemi and you're in the Arctic proper. Unwrap the region and you'll find the winter wonderland of your wildest childhood dreams, whether you're dashing through the snow on a reindeer-driven sleigh, mushing a team of yelping, run-hungry huskies across the frozen tundra, ice fishing on a lonely frozen lake as temperatures dive below -20C (-4F) or padding out into the night on snowshoes as the Northern Lights ripple overhead.

Opposite: visitors riding snowmobiles in Lapland; *This page:* more traditional means of transport are also available

Cold? Forget it. The Finns don't let several feet of snow stop them getting out there. Bundle up, grab a thermos and throw yourself into the winter fantasy, skiing in resorts like Levi and Ylläs, where the powder is deep and the crowds are few; whizzing down Lapland's longest toboggan run in Saariselkä; or gliding on cross-country skis through snow-daubed pine, spruce and birch forest in the wondrously silent Urho Kek-konen National Park, home to the mythical 1594ft-high (486m) fell of Korvatunturi, Santa's spiritual home.

A Traveller's Tale

Up in the snowbound forest in Finland's far north near Utsjoki, day takes its leave with the pink flare of a would-be sunset. Night falls instantly and reindeer graze on lichen in the darkness. In the *lavvu* tent, faces are lit by a campfire's glow. We eat reindeer stew and drink *glögi* as our Sámi hosts tell stories and sing hairs-on-end *joik* (rhythmic poems) that remember the souls and spirits of long-lost ancestors.

KERRY WALKER

AT A GLANCE

EAT
Warm up with *poronkäristys*, sautéed reindeer served with mashed potatoes and lingonberry jam.

DRINK
Glögi is a hot spiced wine flavoured with berry juice, cinnamon, cloves and cardamom.

STAY
Sleep in a traditional Sámi log cabin, an igloo or a glass-roofed dome with views of the Northern Lights.

EXPERIENCE
Feel the Christmas magic with a ride through a frozen forest on a reindeer-driven sleigh.

This page: the Northern Lights over Saariselkä, Finland

For a true sense of Lapland beyond the Christmas hype, hole up in a log cabin and tune into the culture of the indigenous Sámi, who have been herding their reindeer across Arctic tundra and hills for millennia. You'll feel their heartbeat in the western wilds of Pallas-Yllästunturi National Park, in remote northern villages like Utsjoki and Nuorgam, nudging the Norwegian border, and in lakefront Inari, Finland's Sámi capital, where you can visit a reindeer farm and zoom in on their one-of-a-kind culture in the Siida museum.

PRACTICALITIES

GETTING THERE
AND AROUND

Rovaniemi links Lapland to the rest of the world. From Helsinki, Finnair fly to Kittilä (for Levi and Ylläs). Public transport is thin on the ground, but transfers can usually bearranged; or, you can drive (rental cars should be equipped with winter tyres and snow chains).

WHEN TO GO

While you can visit Lapland year-round, it's most magical in winter. You'll pay a premium for flights and accommodation in December (blame Santa). For snow fun and Northern Lights, go from November to April.

THINGS TO NOTE

Pack thermals and full-on cold weather gear. In peak season, advance reservations are highly recommended – Santa trips in December book up months in advance.

Further information is available at visitfinland.com

One Week Itinerary

>

Get your Santa groove on atop the Arctic Circle with two days in Rovaniemi, enjoying elf encounters, grottoes and reindeer rides. Don't rush off: you'll find snowy wilderness on the doorstep, explorable by snowmobile, husky- or reindeer-driven sleigh.

>>

Factor in a night in a glass-roofed aurora igloo at Apukka Resort before driving a couple of hours north to Ylläs, a cute, uncrowded resort with a great snow record, seven fells to ski, cosy log cabins to hide away in and the world's only sauna gondola for a sky-high steam.

>>>

From Ylläs, it's a three-hour push to Saariselkä, where you can take a sled to Lapland's longest toboggan run and tiptoe off the radar cross-country skiing in Urho Kekkonen National Park.

>>>>

A pretty hour's drive further north, feel the true pulse of Sámi culture in Inari, home to the Sámi parliament and the enlightening Siida museum. For more insights, snowmobile out to the farm of reindeer herder Petri Mattus.

MORE TIME?

Head into the silent white wilds in Finland's northernmost village, Nuorgam.

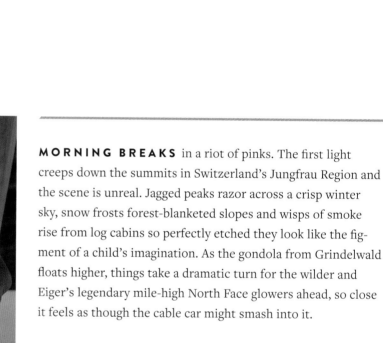

SWITZERLAND

Hit Alpine Highs
in the Jungfrau

MORNING BREAKS in a riot of pinks. The first light creeps down the summits in Switzerland's Jungfrau Region and the scene is unreal. Jagged peaks razor across a crisp winter sky, snow frosts forest-blanketed slopes and wisps of smoke rise from log cabins so perfectly etched they look like the figment of a child's imagination. As the gondola from Grindelwald floats higher, things take a dramatic turn for the wilder and Eiger's legendary mile-high North Face glowers ahead, so close it feels as though the cable car might smash into it.

At Eiger Glacier, it's time to switch to the Jungfraubahn, a little red train that, since 1912, has been chugging over ice and rock to 11,332ft (3454m) Jungfraujoch, Europe's highest train station. Here the Sphinx observation deck elicits gasps with its top-of-the-beanstalk view of the Swiss Alps, reaching over a wavy sea of summits and the 14-mile (23km) swirl of the Aletsch Glacier, the longest in the Alps. It's beautiful, and even more so when you give the madding crowds the slip to crunch through the snow to the Mönchsjochhütte for a bowl of goulash or a night in a bunk next to early-rising climbers scaling the big ones.

This page: **serving the regional delicacy raclette, atop a croissant**

A Traveller's Tale

As the cable car climbs above Grindelwald, flakes spiral down, blotting out the view of Eiger in the whiteout. I pick out the knobbly peak of Faulhorn as I walk for more than two hours through fresh snow, breaking a sweat as I haul my sled behind me. But it's worth it for the chance to whoop and whoosh old-school-style through the forest on 9-mile (15km) 'Big Pintenfritz', one of the world's longest tobogganing runs.

KERRY WALKER

AT A GLANCE

EAT
Devour your weight in cheese with fondue or raclette in the rosy-cheeked warmth of a mountain hut.

DRINK
Farm-distilled Heuschnaps is a sweet, floral liqueur with aromas of hay and Alpine herbs.

STAY
Bed down in a *Berghütte* (mountain hut) at eye level with Eiger and rock-leaping ibex.

EXPERIENCE
Take a wobbly ride down the snowy slopes on an old-fashioned *Velogemel*.

This page: preparing to sled at Grindelwald, at the foot of the Eiger

Overshadowed by Eiger (Ogre), Mönch (Monk) and Jungfrau (Virgin), the Jungfrau Region is an insanely lovely slice of Switzerland. Mother Nature pulled out all the stops here, with mountains of myth, glacier-capped peaks, 72 waterfalls nose-diving over cliffs in the Lauterbrunnen Valley and wildflower-freckled meadows full of bell-swinging cows that make you want to yodel out loud and break into a Heidi-like skip. Locals complement nature's loveliness in villages like cliff-perched Wengen, Mürren and Grindelwald, full of good looks and rustic charm.

All of this forms the most sensational backdrop for outdoor adventures, come snow or shine. Hut-to-hut hiking, mountain biking, zip lining, skydiving, ice climbing, glacier hiking, off-piste skiing, tobogganing, whizzing downhill on a bonkers *Velogemel* (a traditional wooden ski-sledge-bike hybrid) – choose your thrill and the Jungfrau Region will have a location with your name on it

This page: Grindelwald's Cliff Walk offers stunning Alpine views in every season

PRACTICALITIES

GETTING THERE AND AROUND

Interlaken, a two-hour train ride from the nearest airport, Zürich, is the main rail hub, with frequent connections to the rest of the Jungfrau Region. If you're travelling around, invest in the money-saving Jungfrau Travel Pass, offering unlimited travel for three to eight days, plus a discount on the trip to Jungfraujoch. Various passes cover the region's ski area in winter.

WHEN TO GO

Come when the flakes fall in winter (December to March) for snow sports like skiing, sledding and snowshoeing, or in summer (mid-June to mid-September) for hiking, biking and adventure sports.

THINGS TO NOTE

Pack sturdy boots and layers for high-Alpine terrain. In peak season, book activities and gear in advance. *Further information is available at jungfrau.ch*

One Week Itinerary

>

All trains pull into Interlaken, the springboard for the Jungfrau Region, which has enough film-set looks and adventure-loving soul to warrant a day's pause. Try heart-pumping pursuits from white-water rafting to canyon skydiving and bungee jumping, or give chocolate-making a whirl at the Funky Chocolate Club.

>>

A 30-minute train ride brings you to Grindelwald, a village with plenty of sparkle and front-row Eiger views. Enjoy three days here, hiking, skiing, zip lining, go-carting and scootering, and make sure to sled 'Big Pintenfritz'. The Eiger Express gives you a headstart to Jungfraujoch for stupendous views of the Swiss Alps and Aletsch Glacier.

>>

From Grindelwald, take a half-hour train ride to Lauterbrunnen and spend a day watching waterfalls gush over sheer cliff faces. Top billing goes to the mist-dashed, 974ft (297m) Staubbach Falls extolled by Lord Byron and Goethe. A cable car floats from Lauterbrunnen up to Grütschalp, where a train continues 20 minutes along a ridge to final stop, pinch-yourself beautiful Mürren.

MORE TIME?

Squeeze in a day trip to Bond mountain, Schilthorn, and its revolving restaurant, which starred in the movie *Her Majesty's Secret Service*.

CROATIA

Undertake *an* Adriatic Adventure

NOTHING DEFINES CROATIA like its long Adriatic coast and dizzying number of islands. There are over 1100 of them in total, stretching across the glittering blue-green of the Adriatic Sea like strings of pearls. Each has its own character, its own proud traditions and folk culture, its own peculiarities of landscape. Some are home to patches of verdant Mediterranean forest, others look more like the surface of the moon. All are surrounded by a fabulous coastline of rocky coves, sea cliffs, stony bays and the occasional arc of golden sand, where you can sit and watch a sunset so mesmerisingly beautiful it might make you cry.

Croatia's islands are dotted with rural villages, fishing ports and small, historic towns, where Romanesque churches and Venetian *palazzi* jostle with Habsburg facades and stout medieval walls. Olive groves alternate with vineyards, lavender fields and areas of ferociously jagged rock, and there are places where the agricultural landscape has hardly changed since it was laid out by the Greeks some two and a half millennia ago. There's

Opposite: walking on Dubrovnik's city walls with views of the old town;
This page: another Croatian old town, this time in the city of Rovinj

A Traveller's Tale

I first visited the Croatian coast and islands in the late 1990s, and despite countless visits since, they've lost none of their appeal. An early trip to Zadar is still particularly vivid. After mooching about the Old Town, I remember just stopping in awe and watching an insanely beautiful sunset from the waterfront, as waves sloshed against limestone steps and islands were silhouetted against a sky and sea of liquid gold.

RUDOLF ABRAHAM

AT A GLANCE

EAT
Try a dish cooked *ispod peka*-style (roasted under an iron dome in hot coals).

DRINK
Sip wines from Istria, which are among the very best in Croatia; Malvazija is especially good.

STAY
Look for boutique, design and heritage hotels, some newly built, some within restored medieval palaces.

EXPERIENCE
Chartering a yacht isn't within everyone's budget, so kayaking makes a fantastic alternative for exploring the islands' rocky coastlines.

wonderful food, plenty of local wine, stacks of history, several UNESCO sites and fantastic hiking among the islands' rocky hills. Down on the shores are windsurfing hotspots and swimming in water that is among the clearest you'll find anywhere in Europe.

Of the islands in the north, Rab has its beautiful Old Town bristling with bell towers, while Pag has its salt pans and lunar landscape. In central Dalmatia, you'll find Brač with its iconic beach, Zlatni rat, and Hvar with its atmospheric old squares and splintering of smaller islands. Vis charms with its ancient port, founded by the Greeks, while Korčula is home to a magnificent walled town. On the mainland, Italianate Rovinj has narrow streets and brightly painted facades rising to a soaring Venetian bell tower. Poreč boasts celebrated Byzantine mosaics and Pula has one of the largest Roman amphitheatres in the world. Diocletian's Palace in Split is an unforgettable place, so thoroughly integrated into the fabric of the city that it's like wandering a living ruin. And no-intro-needed Dubrovnik is arguably the most exquisitely preserved medieval city in the Mediterranean.

Opposite top: the courtyard of Diocletian's Palace in Split; *Bottom*: wine tasting in Istria's Benvenuti Winery

Two Week Itinerary

> Spend a couple of days in Rovinj, taking a bus to Poreč to visit its Euphrasian Basilica, then to Pula for awesome Roman ruins.

>> Continue by bus to Rijeka, take a catamaran to Rab and Pag, then a bus to Zadar. (Alternatively, take a catamaran from Pula to Zadar via Lošinj.) Wander Zadar's Old Town, then take a bus to Split for a couple of days exploring Diocletian's Palace – don't forget nearby Trogir with its UNESCO-listed cathedral.

>>> Next, travel by ferry or catamaran to Brač, Vis, Hvar and Korčula – there are several route options.

>> From Korčula, take a boat to Pelješac, then a bus to Dubrovnik. Stop in Ston for some of the most extensive medieval walls in Europe – and Croatia's best oysters. You need at least two days to really do Dubrovnik justice – head up onto the city walls early in the morning, before it gets too hot and crowded.

MORE TIME?

For some of Croatia's most beautiful landscapes, head to Paklenica and Krka National Parks near Zadar.

PRACTICALITIES

GETTING THERE AND AROUND

Airports can be found at Pula, Rijeka (actually on the island of Krk), Zadar, Split and Dubrovnik. Trains run from Zagreb to Rijeka and Split. Frequent buses travel along the coast and to some islands. The state-run ferry company Jadrolinija has services to most main islands from Rijeka, Zadar, Split and other ports, as well as between islands. Local buses operate on the islands, or consider renting bikes.

WHEN TO GO

Spring and autumn are the best times to visit. The coast and islands are at their busiest (and hottest) in August.

THINGS TO NOTE

Take a refillable bottle rather than buying bottled water – recycling is limited on the islands and plastic may end up in landfill.
Further information is available at croatia.hr

SLOVENIA

Hike *the* Juliana Trail

THEY SAY EVERY TRUE SLOVENIAN should climb Mt Triglav at least once – but the Juliana Trail deliberately avoids it. This award-winning route – stretching 205 miles (330km) through Slovenia's stunningly beautiful Julian Alps, and making a circuit of Triglav, the country's highest mountain – opts for the low road instead of the high road, with an emphasis on slow travel and sustainability – encouraging people to explore further and stay longer, rather than just climbing one mountain and heading home. It takes in a whole slew of spectacular landscapes – ridges and passes offering breathtaking panoramas of the surrounding mountains, exquisite river valleys and thrilling gorges, roaring waterfalls, lush green pastures and rolling vineyards – with overnight stops in small towns and villages. The Juliana Trail still takes in some must-see places like Lake Bled and Lake Bohinj, but it also makes a point of exploring less-frequented valleys, passes and plateaus – which, you'll find, are equally beautiful.

AT A GLANCE

EAT
Experience Slovenian cuisine at its finest at three-Michelin-starred Hiša Franko in Kobarid.

DRINK
Taste outstanding wines in the Goriška Brda region.

PRACTICALITIES

Download maps from the Juliana Trail app to use offline. Trailheads are easily reached by public transport. Hiking season is May to October.

GREECE

Hop Around
the Ionian Islands

AT A GLANCE

EAT
Try *pastitsada*, beef braised in spices
and red wine with bucatini pasta.

DRINK
Sweet, amber-hued kumquat liqueur,
a Corfu speciality.

PRACTICALITIES

Seasonal (April to September) ferries
connect the islands with companies
like Kerkyra Lines and Levante Ferries.
Further information at visitgreece.gr

THE FERRY GLIDES IN and makes a gentle ripple in a sea as still and blue as stained glass. Pine-clad mountains stagger above scalloped bays. A happy burble rises from *kafenio* terraces and tavernas in harbours lined with pastel-painted Venetian houses, each one prettier than the next. Up in the hills, monastery bells ring, goats hop from rock to rock and time slows. There are 6000 islands and islets in Greece, but the Ionians – closer to Italy's heel than Athens – are special. These lushly green, cypress-studded places, ruled by the Venetians for centuries and swirling in Homeric lore, have a pull that is irresistible. Go for a week. Go for two. Go by boat, drifting from the fortress-topped old town of Corfu to sleepy Paxos, with its white-pebble coves and cicada-filled olive groves, then move gradually south to the likes of Lefkas; legend-steeped Ithaka with its forgotten mule trails; wild and mountainous Kefalonia; and rugged, cliff-rimmed Zakynthos.

TÜRKIYE

Take *an* Aegean Odyssey

Opposite: ferries shuttle through the Golden Horn in İstanbul; *This page:* spices for sale at a local market stall

İSTANBUL'S GRAND MONUMENTS from ancient empires are just the start of an epic Homeric journey. Seagulls soar as the call to prayer sounds from the Ottoman mosques crowning the city's hills. Sellers wave carpets in the Grand Bazaar, ferries dot the Bosphorus and crowds stream down İstiklal Caddesi, the city's main thoroughfare. Despite millennia of history, the former capital keeps visitors grounded in the present with a stream of sensory stimuli, from the glittering gold of a Byzantine mosaic to the yellow blur of a honking taxi. There are pockets of calm – Aya Sofya's upstairs galleries, the cool depths of Emperor Justinian's subterranean Basilica Cistern, a hammam, breakfast on a rooftop – but after a few days you might be ready to leave town.

Famously swum by Lord Byron and fought over by Atatürk and the Allies in 1915, the Dardanelles connects the Sea of Marmara, south of İstanbul, to the Aegean. Tours from the fishing town of Eceabat and Çanakkale, a university city on the Asian side, take in the Gallipoli beaches where half a million troops perished during WWI, creating a pilgrimage site for Australians, New Zealanders and Turks. Continuing, an unspoilt coastline

A Traveller's Tale

My first visit to Türkiye was 25 years ago, when I finished a European rail odyssey in İstanbul. I'll never forget drinking çay (tea) on my hostel's terrace, scribbling in my notebook and watching the ferries cross to Asia. I was down to my last travellers' cheque, but I wanted to visit somewhere between the continents as a conclusive end to my trans-European adventure.

Spying some promising-looking dots in the Sea of Marmara on a map, I jumped on a ferry to the Princes' Islands, once a place of exile for troublesome Ottoman heirs. It was a hot day and I'd reached the far side of the island with little more than some baklava and water, when an old man gave me a lift in his horse-drawn *fayton* carriage. He didn't request payment, but seemed satisfied to roll into the town square with a *yabancı* (foreigner) on board – my first experience of Turkish hospitality.

JAMES BAINBRIDGE

AT A GLANCE

EAT
Join the locals for a slow-paced evening of hot and cold *meze* dishes from a circulating trolley; vegetables *zeytinyağlı* (sautéed in olive oil) or *dolma* (stuffed with rice or meat) are favourites.

DRINK
Sweet black *çay* (tea), served in a tulip-shaped glass, will propel you through the busiest day of sightseeing; avoid the *alma* (apple) brew, which locals spurn.

STAY
Experience Turkish hospitality and a generous *kahvaltı* (breakfast) in a family-run *pansiyon* (pension), with options ranging from simple guesthouses to boutique hotels.

EXPERIENCE
For more insight into the Aegean coast during Ephesus' heyday, tour the ancient sites of Priene and Miletus, both now ruined, silted-up port cities, and the vast Temple of Apollo at Didyma (Didim).

SHOP
The ocular blue glass amulets you'll see in every hotel reception are lucky charms known as *nazar boncuk* (evil eye), designed to thwart precisely that.

"Despite millennia of history, Türkiye's former capital, İstanbul, keeps visitors grounded in the present with a stream of sensory stimuli"

Left: the prayer hall inside İstanbul's Blue Mosque

and olive-farming hinterland characterise the journey south to Behramkale, a rustic village split between a hilltop and harbour, where the ancient Greek city of Assos hosted Aristotle, Alexander the Great and St Paul. Linger over sunset views of Lesbos from the Temple of Athena, before exploring a more recent chapter of history in Ayvalık's old quarter, built by Ottoman Greeks, who were forced to swap places with Muslim families from Lesbos during the population exchanges of the 1920s.

Buying olive oil on cobbled lanes, pairing aniseed-flavoured *rakı* and fish dishes on waterfront terraces and day-tripping to road-connected Cunda (or Alibey) island add up to a quint-essentially Aegean experience. The journey returns to classical history in the laid-back market town of Bergama, where

everyday life dawdles between teahouse and bazaar in the shadow of a sky-high acropolis, complete with a vertigo-inducing theatre built into a hillside.

Another site that vividly brings the past to life is the ancient port of Ephesus, once the Roman Empire's fourth-largest city and capital of Asia Minor. Descend Curetes Way, where Anthony and Cleopatra once walked, from the 4th-century Hercules Gate, installed to bar chariots from the pedestrianised street, to the two-storey facade of the Library of Celsus. With its marble flagstones and pillars, it's easy to appreciate that this street was the İstiklal Caddesi of its day – especially if you imagine the other sightseers wearing togas.

Opposite: Roman ruins of the Library of Celsius in the ancient port of Ephesus

15 Day Itinerary

> Spend a week exploring Byzantine and Ottoman history through İstanbul's grand monuments – the Aya Sofya, Grand Bazaar, Blue Mosque and Topkapı Palace alone could take two days. Cruise the Bosphorus Strait that divides the continents of Europe and Asia, wonder about the contents of Turkish Viagra in the Spice Bazaar, enjoy views across the Golden Horn from the Galata Tower and dine on *meze* (small plates) in modern Beyoğlu.

>> Drive or join a tour to the WWI battlefields on the Gallipoli Peninsula, a four-hour journey along the Sea of Marmara.

>>> It's a further two hours south, across the Dardanelles and down the Aegean coast, to Behramkale and its hilltop 6th-century BCE Temple of Athena. Budget a couple of days in the tumbledown village's lanes and the same in Ayvalık's old Greek Quarter, then overnight in Bergama to see the UNESCO-protected acropolis and Asklepion medical centre.

>>>> It's about three hours around the Bay of Edremit from Behramkale to Bergama, and two past urban İzmir to the ruin-dotted town of Selçuk, where you should leave at least two days for ancient Ephesus and other sights.

MORE TIME?

Three hours south is the mountainside haven of Akyaka, where you could spend a few days exploring the Datça and Bozburun Peninsulas.

PRACTICALITIES

GETTING THERE
AND AROUND

Major carriers serve İstanbul
International Airport; budget
flights often use Sabiha Gökçen
International Airport on the city's
Asian side. Airports at İzmir,
Bodrum-Milas and Dalaman offer
frequent connections between the
Turkish coast and İstanbul.
Public transport, taxis and guided
tours are plentiful in İstanbul, while
hiring a car or joining a bus tour is
the best way to travel out of town.
The well-maintained road network
is reasonably safe and recommended
if you drive defensively.
There's a good intercity transport
network, including coaches, rural
dolmuş minibuses and trains
from İstanbul to Selçuk via İzmir.
Fast ferries across the Sea of
Marmara from İstanbul Yenikapı to
Bandırma are another route to the
Aegean region.

WHEN TO GO

Avoid summer crowds by visiting in
spring (April and May) or autumn
(September and October). Ramazan
(Ramadan) disrupts services as
Muslims fast during the day.

THINGS TO NOTE

Many tour operators offer
Aegean itineraries from İstanbul,
including the Gallipoli Peninsula
and optionally continuing south
to Ephesus.
*Further information is available at
goturkiye.com*

ITALY

Trace *the* Renaissance

IN *INFERNO*, A GROTESQUE Lucifer, encircled by dancing ape-like demons, greedily devours sinners. In *Triumph of Death*, you can practically hear the damned screaming as they're roasted alive on spits. These provocative illustrations of hell (1336–41), frescoed by Italian painter Buonamico Buffalmacco on the walls of a cloistered cemetery in the Tuscan city of Pisa, are hauntingly unsettling – and beautiful. The cemetery's location on Pisa's landmark Piazza dei Miracoli, built on soil shipped from the Holy Land during the Crusades, only heightens the thrill. This is one of the focuses of the Renaissance, a period of intense artistic creativity and curiosity that, from the 14th century, bewitched artists and intellectuals, kings and queens, dreamers and cynics alike with its frenetic quest for rebirth and discovery.

Its epicentre was the Tuscan capital of Florence, 52 miles (85km) east of Pisa. From the 15th to 18th centuries, the powerful Medici banking dynasty dominated Florentine civic life. The family controlled the *signoria* (city government); their bank was Europe's most powerful; and under the enlightened patronage of de facto rulers Cosimo the Elder (1389-1464) and Lorenzo the

Opposite: blame unstable foundations for Pisa's leaning tower; *This page top:* Piazza del Duomo and cathedral of Santa Maria del Fiore in Florence.; *Bottom:* bite-sized treats at Venice's Cantina do Spade

AT A GLANCE

EAT

Devour a succulent *bistecca alla fiorentina* (blue and bloody, chargrilled T-bone steak) in a trattoria in Florence.

DRINK

Linger over a coffee or spritz at historic Vasari Caffè, beneath cinematic porticos overlooking Arezzo's famously sloping central square, Piazza Grande.

STAY

In Florence's *centro storico* (historical centre) several uber-chic boutique hotels lie within the walls of atmospheric Renaissance *palazzi* (palaces).

EXPERIENCE

Join Florentines for a *passeggiata* (early evening stroll) along Florence's poshest shopping strip, Via de' Tornabuoni, lined with grand Renaissance mansions, ending with a bite-sized truffle panini and prosecco at 19th-century Procacci.

SHOP

Look out for traditional Sienese *panforte* (spiced fruit-and-nut cake) at Il Magnifico, an old-world bakery with the city's best baker, Lorenzo Rossi, at the helm.

A Traveller's Tale

If I'd been told that a staircase would reduce me to tears, I would have emphatically disagreed. A Botticelli painting in Florence's Uffizi, perhaps. The heart-wrenching sculpture of bodies entwined in Gianbologna's *Rape of the Sabine Women* in Piazza della Signoria, certainly. But a functional flight of steps?

Said staircase, sculpted by Michelangelo in 1524 for the Medici's private library, is not regularly open to the public, so I was thrilled to get an audience with this unsung masterpiece. The approach on foot, beneath orange trees in Basilica di San Lorenzo's hushed cloister, reduced me to silence. And then there was that first giddying glance at the simple, stunning sweep of grey Pietra Serena stone, filling the vestibule, the sober prelude to the Reading Room. Imagining the 11,000 ancient manuscripts beyond, with magnificent illuminations inspired by Botticelli, Cimabue and other masters, the magnitude of this Renaissance wellspring of ideas and emotion hit home. And the tears welled.

NICOLA WILLIAMS

"Visitors swoon over the world's greatest collection of Renaissance art at the Gallerie degli Uffizi in a palace overlooking the Arno river"

Right: artistic masterpieces at the Galerie degli Uffizi in Florence; *Opposite:* medieval Ponte Vecchio spans the River Arno

Magnificent (1449-92), the arts flourished. Expressing a renewed interest in classical arts, Tuscan painters and sculptors such as Michelangelo, Botticelli and Domenico Ghirlandaio were invited to Florence to work. Visitors ever since have followed them to the city, admiring the awe-inspiring cupola designed by groundbreaking architect Brunelleschi to crown Florence's Duomo; swooning over the world's greatest collection of Renaissance art at the Gallerie degli Uffizi in a monumental palace overlooking the Arno river; and marvelling at a treasure chest of frescoes which provided a powerful social commentary as well as religious inspiration in the 15th and 16th centuries. The peak of Florence's Renaissance riches, though, is arguably Michelangelo's *David* – the era's enduring icon that ensures a permanent queue outside its home, the Galleria dell'Accademia.

The unparalleled flowering of art, music and poetry spread beyond Florence and Pisa to other cities in Tuscany. In Arezzo, homegrown architect, painter and art historian Giorgio Vasari (1511–74) popularised the Italian term *Rinascimento* (rebirth) to describe this artistic golden age. His home, now the Museo di Casa Vasari, provides insight into the man whose tome *The Lives of the Artists* (1550) is deemed the 'bible of the Italian Renaissance'. And in Siena, the Renaissance saw a sweep of marble mosaics adorn the floor of its Duomo – drink in bird's-eye views of the cathedral interior on Porta del Cielo (Gate of Heaven) tours up, inside and around the roof and dome. Expect frissons galore.

This page: Piazza del Campo in the heart of the Tuscan town of Siena

PRACTICALITIES

GETTING THERE AND AROUND

International flights land at both Florence and Pisa airports, each linked to their city centres by public transport. Direct intercity rail services operate from Florence to major Italian cities and other points in Europe. Pisa, Siena and Arezzo are easy day trips from the Tuscan capital by local train or bus. In the cities, walking is the best way to experience local life and happen upon spontaneous, chance discoveries.

WHEN TO GO

Consider December or January when festive illuminations, lower accommodation rates and smaller crowds add to the appeal. From April to October, food markets overflow with fresh produce, cafe life and dining moves outside – and the crowds can be insane. July and August are sizzlingly hot and torturously busy.

THINGS TO NOTE

Advance ticket reservations – weeks in advance during high season – are essential for major sights; only buy tickets from official websites. For further information see firenzemusei.it and musefirenze.it (Florence) and *turismo.pisa.it* (Pisa).

One Week Itinerary

> Begin in Florence with unrivalled paintings at the Uffizi, frescoes at Cappella Brancacci, and views of Europe's most beautiful Renaissance city at sundown from Piazzale Michelangelo.

>> Day two, explore the cathedral ensemble on Piazza del Duomo, not missing the 463-step climb inside the dome and an intimate guided tour of the baptistery's mosaic restoration site.

>>> Next day, bask in a 360-degree admiration of the world's most famous naked man in Galleria dell'Accademia, and view earlier *Davids* by Donatello in the Museo del Bargello. End on Piazza della Signoria with Medici stronghold Palazzo Vecchio and Loggia dei Lanzi's free, open-air collection of Renaissance sculptures.

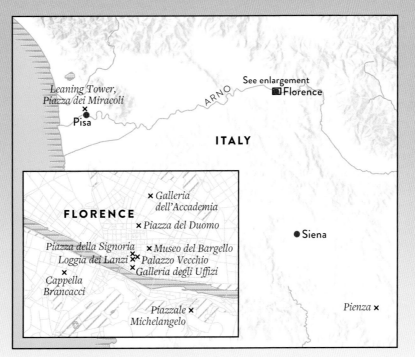

>> Devote the latter half of the week to day trips. The short train journey to Pisa rewards with the iconic Leaning Tower and sublime aerial views of celebrity Piazza dei Miracoli from atop the city's ancient walls. While in Siena, Old Testament tales painstakingly created in mosaics over the course of five centuries carpet the floor of the cathedral.

MORE TIME?

Stay longer in Florence. This notoriously overcrowded city merits so much more than a quick flit. From Siena continue to Pienza, the 'ideal Renaissance city', built between 1459 and 1462 under the patronage of Pope Pius II.

ITALY

Harvest Dolce Vita
in Cinque Terre

VINEYARDS SOAR VERTIGINOUSLY TO the sky.
Teasing the heavens, they accompany every walker lucky enough
to cross such an improbable landscape. Dry-stone walls hold back
the sun-soaked earth, defying gravity with a majesty and scope
likened only to that of the Great Wall of China. Autumn's soft
golden light spins an unmatched luminosity across grape pickers
working in the vines, and the toy-like *trenino* (cogwheel monorail)
that lurches up the hillside, piled high with honey-sweet Bosco,
Albarola and Vermentino grapes that will be dried, pressed and
aged in pear- and cherry-wood barrels to make prized Sciacchetrà
dessert wine. September's *vendemmia* (grape harvest) is the
essence of *la dolce vita* (the sweet life) in over-touristed Cinque
Terre. With the summer crowds gone, train journeys along the
cliff-chiselled coastline to these five pastel-hued gem villages
– Monterosso, Vernazza, Corniglia, Manarola and Riomaggiorie –
resume a yesteryear languor. Hiking trails hidden in the heights
offer privileged encounters with the bedrock of this ancient
hallowed land: passionate, tenacious winegrowers. *Saluti!*

AT A GLANCE

EAT
Sample local anchovies in a
medieval tower at Monterosso's
Torre Aurora.

DRINK
Sip wine with a sommelier at A Piè
de Campu in Manarola.

PRACTICALITIES

By train, boat or on foot is the only
access. Views from the Alta Via delle
Cinque trail between Porto Venere
and Levanto are epic.

ITALY

Walk Through History
in Ancient Rome

THANK HEAVENS FOR the Trevi Fountain. Its promise of a return to Rome in exchange for a tossed coin into its elegant pool of water is welcome news to travellers – because this city, the heart and soul of the ancient world, is too Herculean, too beautiful, too full of must-sees to cover in a single trip. The Italian capital is haunted by ghosts eager to tell their stories. From the smallest of the city's seven hills, the Capitoline, gaze over the Roman Forum where emperors celebrated and everyday citizens went about their daily lives. Follow in Julius Caesar's footsteps to the *domus* where he lived as Pontifex Maximus, and to the Area Sacra where he was assassinated in 44 BCE. Time-travel 120 years ahead to the spellbinding Colosseum, stage for gladiator fights and mock sea battles. Marvel at the acoustics in the Pantheon and remember the crucified enslaved people on the cobbled Appian Way. And don't forget to toss that coin.

ITALY

Feel *the* Heat *with* Sicilian Fire *and* Water

Opposite: the colourful slopes of Mt Etna; *This page:* looking out on the Sicilian coastline from the ancient Greek theatre in Taormina

IT NEEDED AN EXPLODING volcano in 1669 to fire up beautiful Catania. Sicily's charismatic second city was rebuilt after Mt Etna erupted that year, and as elegant *palazzi* (palaces) and grandiose churches rose from the ashes, so a flamboyant baroque architectural style took form, pairing creamy limestone with grey lava stone – the very rock that had rained down on the city. Such creative resilience and ingenuity forged by fire is the bedrock of Sicily. Wed this with water – the other omnipresent element on this island – and you have the essence of a Sicilian dream trip.

This gorgeous Mediterranean island has seduced travellers since the earliest times. Remnants of temples, baths and amphitheatres built by Phoenicians, Carthaginians, Romans and Greeks dot the island. And, of course, water is never far away. Catania's rooftops and terraces reveal jaw-dropping panoramas of the city's UNESCO-listed heart, Mt Etna's smoking hulk – and the iridescent blue sea. Similarly dreamy views form the backdrop to open-air performances at the ancient Greek theatre in Taormina, a cobblestone village suspended between sky and water on the Ionian coast.

Feeling the heat of the island's life-defining volcano up close is a tourist rite of passage. One-fifth of the population lives around Etna (11,014ft/3357m) – Europe's largest active volcano – and the steep ascent up its slopes by 4WD and foot helps unravel what makes this island tick. Arabs planted citrus groves in the fertile volcanic soil. Medieval locals stored snow in its high-altitude caves to make traditional *granita* (crushed ice flavoured with fruit syrups). And today's vineyards, producing DOC reds and whites, are an economic lifeline for many.

AT A GLANCE

EAT
No one makes *cannoli* (crunchy, deep-fried pastry tubes filled with ricotta cream) like Sicilians.

DRINK
Pair island capers with Salina's sweet Malvasia wine at a tasting.

STAY
Overnight at an Etna winery, with B&B rooms in a *masserie* (traditional farmhouse).

EXPERIENCE
Splash, snorkel and dive like a 1960s movie star in Med-lapped beaches on Isola Bella, a speck of an island below Taormina.

A Traveller's Tale

Having spent the day hiking along pumice-dust trails on an isthmus of land spewed out by a volcanic eruption in 183 BCE, dinner at Ristorante Il Cappero on Vulcano's northeast coast was welcome. The 10-course menu celebrating island produce was sublime. But it was the restaurant's vantage point – a rare spot in the Aeolian archipelago where you can admire every island in a single view – that made my heart sing.

NICOLA WILLIAMS

This page: a typical street scene in Syracuse's old quarter of Ortygia

After Etna's sparks and hissing, the seven-island Aeolian archipelago in the soothing cobalt waters of the Tyrrhenian Sea off Sicily's northeastern coast beckons. Legend has it that wind god Aeolus, fire god Vulcano and other mythological deities had a hand in the chain's creation. In reality, these islands were submarine volcanoes that emerged from the sea some 700,000 years ago. With gin-clear waters, whitewashed villages and honey-sweet Malvasia wine, Sicilian life doesn't get much sweeter or sun-spangled than this.

PRACTICALITIES

GETTING THERE AND AROUND
International flights serve Palermo and Catania airports, and car/passenger ferries sail to Messina from several towns on the Italian mainland, including Villa San Giovanni, Reggio di Calabria, Genoa, Livorno and Naples. Getting around Sicily is a combination - chaotic at times - of bus, train, boat, car and bicycle.

WHEN TO GO
April to June, and September and October are best: temperatures are comfortably warm, and beaches, coastal roads and tourist hotspots are less crowded. Offshore islands and coastal resorts largely shut down November to March, when accommodation rates in towns and cities drop by 30% or more.

THINGS TO NOTE
Whatever the month, bring something to cover up in churches, a sun hat, and warm clothes if hiking Etna.
For further information go to visitsicily.info

10 Day Itinerary

>
Begin in Catania, springboard for day expeditions up Mt Etna. Spend another day exploring the volcano's vineyards. Head north along the Riviera dei Ciclopi – dizzying cliffs and black-rock towers ensure you never forget the coastline's volcanic origins. Lap up history, geology and spectacular Etna views – preferably during a performance – at Taormina's Teatro Greco.

>>
If you have wheels, drive 50 minutes to Gole dell'Alcantara to swim or canyon in the icy waters of ancient lava gorges.

>>
It's four hours by bus to Milazzo, then 65 minutes by speedy hydrofoil to Lipari, the largest Aeolian island. Island-hop for five days. Don't miss walks on the archipelago's highest peaks on lush green Salina, Stromboli's black-sand beaches and hikes up the island's eponymous active volcano to watch its nightly eruptions, and Vulcano with its smoking crater and paddle-friendly shoreline.

MORE TIME?
Bus south from Catania to Syracuse, or take a epicurean train ride around Mt Etna's scenic western flanks to Bronte, famous for its 'green gold' pistachios, grown in lava soil and hand-harvested every two years.

SPAIN

Discover Andalucía's Magical Cities

FOR CENTURIES A CRUCIBLE of different peoples and cultures, Andalucía offers a deep dive into Spain's history. And there's no more rewarding place to jump in than its monument-rich cities, each evocatively ancient and thoroughly contemporary all at once. You could plan an entire trip around Andalucía based entirely on its thriving urban food scene, as many Spaniards do. With every bite, you're instantly immersed in the region's long story, too. Savour some *tortillitas de camarones* (shrimp fritters) in Cádiz, a chilled *salmorejo* (soup) in Seville, a rich *flamenquín* (serrano ham wrapped in pork loin and deep-fried) in Córdoba or a plate of *berenjenas con miel* (fried aubergines with honey) in Granada and the region's unique historical mix of influences emerges.

Founded over 2000 years ago, Andalucía's elegant capital, Seville, is a thrilling place, with countless tapas bars, a clutch of buzzing *barrios* (neighbourhoods), one of Spain's greatest flamenco scenes, and a stash of unparalleled sights that includes the Islamic-origin Real Alcázar and the world's largest Gothic cathedral. More dazzling architecture awaits in nearby

Opposite: a tapas bar in Seville; *This page top:* the whitewashed hillside village of Zahara de la Sierra; *Bottom:* dancing the flamenco in Seville

AT A GLANCE

EAT

There's nothing like cramming into a busy tapas bar and devouring the house speciality, whether that's a wedge of tortilla, crispy aubergines drizzled with honey or a few slices of *ibérico* ham.

DRINK

From fresh *fino* to deliciously sweet Pedro Ximénez, local sherries encapsulate what drinking in Andalucía is all about.

STAY

Spectacular historical buildings converted into boutique-style hotels, many of them with a design-forward touch, are likely to be a highlight of your trip.

EXPERIENCE

Hit the beautiful Andalucian coast for watersports adventures: kitesurfing along Cádiz's Costa de la Luz; kayaking beneath cliffs on Granada's Costa Tropical; diving in the Mediterranean around Cabo de Gata.

SHOP

Olive trees have been grown across Andalucía since Roman times and the region now produces some of the world's finest olive oil, particularly in the inland provinces of Jaén, Granada, Córdoba and Seville. Zesty Jaén *picual* ranks among the most prized varieties.

A Traveller's Tale

Granada's Alhambra has always been one of my favourite places in Andalucía. No matter how many times I visit, there's a newly uncovered layer of its story to learn about, a freshly restored corner to marvel at or something special blooming in the fragrant gardens. One sizzling summer evening, I escaped into the 14th-century Palacios Nazaríes for a cool, after-dark visit. Without the daytime crowds, these lavishly decorated Islamic-era palaces took on a whole new beauty, with shimmering pools reflecting the moonlight, intricately carved arches illuminated in a warm glow and the tinkle of the Patio de los Leones' fountain echoing all around. It's also possible to explore the Generalife – the Alhambra's summer palace and gardens – on a nocturnal visit. After the Alhambra, I love to drop down into the Realejo for tapas at beloved neighbourhood spots like Taberna La Tana, Rosario Varela, Picoteca 3 Maneras and Bar Candela.

ISABELLA NOBLE

"Andalucía offers a deep dive into Spain's history. And there's no more rewarding place to jump in than its monument-rich cities"

Left: the intricate arches and pillars of the Mezquita in Córdoba

Córdoba, where the UNESCO-listed mosque-cathedral on the banks of the Guadalquivir River – with its hundreds of distinctively striped arches – is another remarkable example of Spain's Islamic and Christian past.

Venturing towards Andalucía's windswept Atlantic coast, sunny Cádiz is a Phoenician-founded port city that helped nurture the birth of flamenco and has now grown into one of the country's most-loved gastronomic destinations – you'll catch wafts of *pescaíto frito* (fried fish) and other seafood staples as you wander its lively *barrios*. Few moments in Andalucía, however, can rival that first glimpse of the Alhambra palace-fortress looming over Granada. Built by the peninsula's last Moorish rulers in the 13th and 14th centuries, it's the culmination of their sophisticated, timeless architectural style. But as anyone who loves Granada will tell you, there's much more worth lingering for in this energetic city, starting with the tradition of a free *tapa* with every drink and the legacy of the great poet Federico García Lorca.

Andalucía's rural expanses offer a counterpart to these urban delights. Cádiz Province has some of southern Spain's loveliest countryside, with peaks rising beyond mountain lakes, undulating olive groves and traditional whitewashed villages, particularly around the Parque Natural Sierra de Grazalema. Hiking down the Garganta Verde trail here, with griffon vultures calling as they circle high above a gorge, is an unforgettable walk. Over in Granada Province, the peaks of the Alpujarras and Sierra Nevada have inspired creative souls for centuries and provide a dramatic backdrop for hiking among some of the country's tallest peaks, including mainland Spain's highest, Mulhacén.

Opposite: there's great hiking to be had in Parque Natural Sierra de Grazalema

Two Week Itinerary

A fortnight is plenty for combining Andalucía's cities with a rural escape. Start with three nights in Seville, where maze-like *barrios*, Islamic-era palaces and an unbeatable local tapas scene are just a taster.

>>

Head south (1¾ hours by train) to seaside Cádiz for two nights of flamenco, beaches and superb seafood. Time permitting, en route you could stop in ancient Jerez, known for its raw flamenco and earthy sherry *bodegas*.

>>>

Pick up a hire car in Cádiz and drive 1½ hours east into the mountainous Parque Natural Sierra de Grazalema, a haven for outdoor lovers with wonderful hiking, cycling and adventure sports.

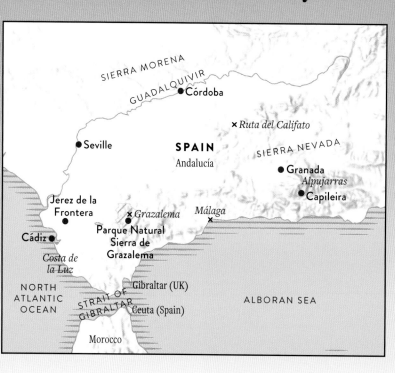

>>>>

After a two-night break in Grazalema village, a 2½-hour drive north leads to Córdoba, where one night is perfect for exploring the great mosque-cathedral, the flower-filled patios and the fired-up food scene.

>>>>>

From Córdoba, follow the Ruta del Califato for two hours, retracing a major medieval trading route, to Granada, where three nights of cultural exploration, fabulous food and flamenco await. Wrap up with a couple of nights in the rugged Alpujarras for hiking, staying in 4711ft-high (1436m) Capileira village, 1½ hours' drive from Granada.

MORE TIME? Add on art-loving Málaga or Cádiz's beautiful Costa de la Luz.

PRACTICALITIES

GETTING THERE
AND AROUND

Seville's airport is served by flights
from across Europe, and the city
has train links to Cádiz, Córdoba
and Granada. Málaga-Costa del
Sol airport is a good alternative
arrival point. If including time in the
Grazalema mountains, it's best to
have your own wheels.

WHEN TO GO

The loveliest seasons in Andalucía's
cities are spring (March to May) and
autumn (September to October),
which is also the best time for hiking
in Grazalema. A winter visit can be
rewarding too, with fewer crowds,
accommodation deals and plenty
of sunshine. Avoid July and August,
when inland Andalucía swelters
in the summer heat. Seville's Feria
de Abril festival kicks off each
April, with accommodation costs
soaring but with plenty of fun to get
involved in.

THINGS TO NOTE

A guided tour with a local expert is
the ideal way to explore Andalucía's
dynamic cities, whether you're keen
to unpack centuries of history on an
urban walk or go bar-hopping with
someone who knows their tapas.
For further information on the
region visit andalucia.org

SPAIN

Eat Well *in the* Basque Country

IT'S ALL ABOUT THE FOOD (and drink) on a journey through Euskadi (Basque Country), one of the world's most famous culinary destinations. Michelin-starred dining options sprout like wildflowers in San Sebastián, a historic seaside city, but you don't need a restaurant to eat well here. The narrow, lamp-lit lanes of the old quarter heave with tiny stand-up places turning out tender morsels of perfection known as *pintxos*. A slow, scenic train ride leads west to Bilbao, where you can work up an appetite exploring the architectural masterpiece of the Guggenheim Museum before diving into the gastronomic epicenter, the Casco Viejo (old quarter), with *pintxos* bars serving melt-in-the-mouth *jamón ibérico* (Iberian ham) sheep's milk cheese and countless other temptations. Beyond Bilbao, there's much more to experience, from legendary seafood in fishing village Getaria to the park-fringed eateries of Vitoria-Gasteiz, Euskadi's underrated capital. Further south, Laguardia is a great place to try award-winning La Rioja wines, with rolling vineyards surrounding the 13th-century town.

AT A GLANCE

EAT
San Sebastián's convivial Txepetxa is famous for its anchovies, served many different ways.

DRINK
Pintxos go perfectly with lightly sparkling *txakolí* wine.

PRACTICALITIES

Some places offer made-to-order *pintxos*. When in doubt, ask for 'la especialidad de la casa' (the house speciality).

PORTUGAL

Embrace Adventure
in the Azores

AT A GLANCE

EAT
Cozido is a rich meat-and-vegetable stew slow-cooked underground using geothermal heat.

EXPERIENCE
Climb Mt Pico, Portugal's highest (7713ft/2351m), with a guide.

PRACTICALITIES

Azores Airlines, easyJet and Ryanair are among airlines operating flights to the Azores. Ferries link up the islands. *Further information at visitazores.com*

THE AZORES PROVIDE ONE of Europe's last great island adventures. Whether it's watching the sunrise creep up Pico's cloud-shredding cone or tearing around an ink-blue crater lake by mountain bike on São Miguel, past spluttering *caldeiras* (hot springs) and smouldering fumaroles, there's plenty to do here. These isles are a place of natural wonders too, which you'll sense when walking through botanical gardens that are a fragrant mass of azaleas, camellias and hydrangeas on Flores, or holding your breath as sperm whales and humpbacks surface from the ocean on Faial. Asking someone to pin the archipelago on a map would have drawn a blank look until quite recently. But this chain of nine islands, sprinkled like stepping stones across the mid-Atlantic, is finally getting its moment as an outdoor activities travel hub with impeccable sustainable credentials. Where else can you hike from volcano to vineyard, kayak across a vivid-blue caldera lake and roam tea plantations all in one action-packed day?

PORTUGAL

Explore *the* Shores *of the* Algarve

Opposite: Benagil Cave's hidden beach on the Algarve coast; *This page:* the old lifeguard station in Fuseta, Ria Formosa Natural Park

WAVES CRASH AGAINST the cliffs and the Atlantic ocean blurs into the horizon. At your back stretches the Algarve region of Portugal – and an entire continent. This is Cabo de São Vicente, the southwesternmost point in mainland Europe. Nearby, a fortress guards the town of Sagres, where according to legend Prince Henry the Navigator founded a 15th-century school for mariners and cartographers. These days, the region draws different types of explorers – surfers tracking Portugal's renowned waves, and seafood fans seeking culinary delicacies like *percebes*, a rare mollusk that thrives on this stretch of coastline.

Some 19 miles (30km) east, famous expeditions once set sail from Lagos, where it's easy to conjure the past while strolling the cobblestone lanes enclosed by 16th-century walls. Visiting historic sites – including a fortification with an exhibition on the Portuguese Age of Discovery – makes a fine prelude to a feast at one of the city's lively terrace restaurants. Even more alluring are the wide sandy beaches and golden-hued cliffs arcing out into the water beyond the town.

The Algarve's dramatic coastal backdrop sets the scene for a wide range of adventures. Near Carvoeiro, kayakers paddle into the Benagil Cave, a striking rock formation containing a hidden beach only accessible by water. On land, fabled walks skirt the sea, including the Seven Hanging Valleys Trail, which winds past tiny coves and lofty promontories overlooking the sun-drenched shores.

A Traveller's Tale

Needing a break from busy Albufeira, I drove west, not sure where I'd end up. It was late afternoon when I passed Sagres and turned onto a dirt road. A few bumpy minutes later I was on a gorgeous beach, with crashing waves and rugged cliffs – Praia do Telheiro, I later discovered. Alone on the sand, I watched a magical sunset, struck by such beauty within easy reach but hidden just out of view.

REGIS ST LOUIS

AT A GLANCE

EAT
Of many outstanding seafood dishes, *amêijoas à bulhão pato* (clams, garlic, lemon and white wine) is a classic.

DRINK
The Algarve has excellent wines – look for the rich red blends sustainably produced by Monte da Casteleja.

SLEEP
Portugal's *pousadas* occupy former palaces, convents and other historic properties, with four in the Algarve.

EXPERIENCE
Watch magnificent sunsets at the Ponta da Piedade headland, just south of Lagos.

Nature plays a starring role near Faro, where the barrier islands of the Parque Natural da Ria Formosa draw tens of thousands of migratory birds each year. This is also a prime spot for seeing dolphins and other marine life. Boat tours glide through the park and head out to the uninhabited islands, with pristine beaches ideal for spending a leisurely day. More islands and beaches lie further east – on Tavira Island, a small train trundles out to picturesque Praia do Barril. If the sun gets too much, the nearby city of Tavira offers diverse attractions, from pre-Roman ruins to Renaissance churches, not to mention innovative restaurants and wine bars – memorable spots to toast the day's adventures on one of Europe's sunniest coastlines.

Opposite: the golden cliffs of Ponta da Piedade

Five Day Itinerary

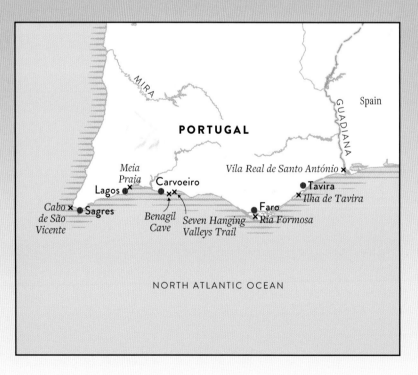

>

Start off in Sagres. Spend the day visiting the fortress and the windswept headland of Cabo de S.o Vicente. On day two, make the two-hour bus ride to Lagos. There, explore the cobbled lanes of the historic centre followed by some beach time at nearby Meia Praia.

>>

From Lagos, hop on the bus for the 75-minute journey to Carvoeiro, where you'll spend the third day hiking the Seven Hanging Valleys Trail, boating to the Benagil Cave and relaxing on the sand.

>>>

On day four, continue by bus (two hours) to Faro for a dose of history at the town's fine museums, coupled with wildlife-watching on a boat tour along the Ria Formosa.

>>>>

On your fifth day, ride the train (45 minutes) to Tavira, for a final day out on the pretty beaches of Ilha de Tavira and riverside dining in the evening.

MORE TIME?

Keep going to Vila Real de Santo António (a 30-minute train ride from Tavira), and take a scenic boat trip up the Rio Guadiana.

PRACTICALITIES

GETTING THERE AND AROUND

Faro has direct flights from several European cities including London and Cork. You can also fly to Lisbon and reach the Algarve by rail. Once in the region, trains run from Lagos to the Spanish border; there's also a good bus service with Vamus Algarve.

WHEN TO GO

With 300 days of sunshine, there's really no bad time to visit the Algarve. For swimming and other aquatic activities, the warmer summer months (June through September) are best, but it's also very crowded then, with high hotel prices.

THINGS TO NOTE

Mercados (markets) are a great way to sample the region's culinary bounty of breads, cheeses, olives, smoked meats, fruits and vegetables. Do as locals and grab a picnic to enjoy at the beach.

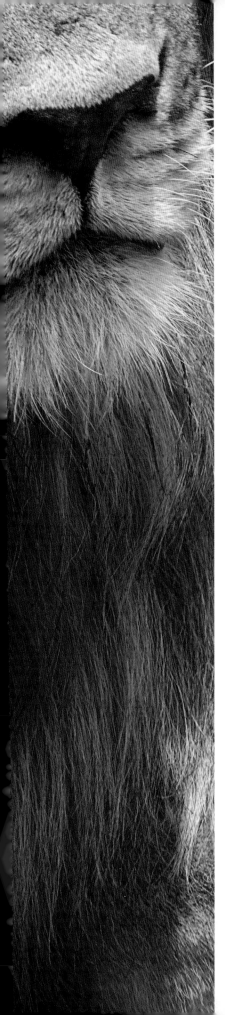

Africa *& the* Middle East

EGYPT

Sail *with the* Gods *on the* Nile

ALL THE HISTORICAL ROMANCE and melancholy of ancient Egypt can be found on a journey down the Nile. From the rock-cut temples of Abu Simbel and the high dams of Aswan and Lake Nasser in Upper Egypt to the ancient cities of the dead and burial place of former rulers at Kom Ombo, Edfu and Luxor further north, travel here takes on a poetic rhythm unmatched by any other river expedition.

Indeed, it's almost impossible to think of Egypt without the Nile. In ancient Egyptian culture, the river was the lifeblood of the pharaohs, interpreted as a gift from the heavens, helping cultivate the myths and ideologies of the cults of Isis, Horus and the crocodile god, Seth. In modern Egypt, the waters are the catalyst for harvests that transform the Nile Valley, via deep-cut irrigation channels, into a daisy-chain of flowering oases, where date palms and hibiscus flourish. For most travellers, meanwhile, the Nile is simply a passport to a darn good adventure.

A Traveller's Tale

We travelled north to Luxor, at a lulling, somnambulant pace. The banks I'd expected to look arid and empty were instead lush with palm trees and evergreen reeds. Now and then, relics of temples appeared, standing as ragged silhouettes in the hot sun. The sense was of travelling back in time – and, with such profuse history on the banks, I realised how excited the first Egyptologists must have felt.

MIKE MACEACHERAN

AT A GLANCE

EAT
Don't miss Egypt's national dish, *koshary*, a mix of rice, pasta, lentils, garlicky tomato sauce, chickpeas and onions.

DRINK
Karkadeh, made from boiling dried red hibiscus, is the tourist crowd-pleaser.

STAY
The Old Cataract Aswan hotel has charmed visitors for decades; Agatha Christie wrote *Death on the Nile* here.

EXPERIENCE
Be wowed at the sound and light shows at Karnak or Temple of Philae.

Opposite: traditional feluccas on the River Nile; *This page:* walking among the pillars of Karnak's towering temple complex

That adventure can take several forms – be it on the deck of a white-sailed *felucca*, the traditional Egyptian sailing pontoon, or on board a more elaborate cruise ship equipped with swimming pool and on-call Egyptologists ready to unpick every riddle and notoriously difficult hieroglyph. In such company, you'll be left with a sense of what the likes of King Farouk and Sir Winston Churchill experienced on their voyages along the waterway. Whichever way you choose, you'll feel close to the bulrushes and water buffaloes, the river-lapped shoreline, swaying date-palms and legendary architecture. Close your eyes, and you'll hear the squeak of sails and creak of the past.

Thanks to the ebb and flow of modern history, however, Egypt has largely been abandoned by the record numbers of tourists it used to welcome. This means prices are competitive and it's not uncommon to have some of the world's most astonishing temples and tombs to yourself.

This page top: Ramesseum memorial temple in Luxor; kicking back in the shade

PRACTICALITIES

GETTING THERE
AND AROUND

The gateway for northbound Nile trips is Aswan, well-connected to main hubs Cairo and Luxor by air, rail and road. Then it's onto your desert ship – there's no need to sail all the way to Cairo, as most operators only cover the stretch between Aswan and Luxor.

WHEN TO GO

Summer can be unbearably hot, so plan for a cooler trip either side of June to August – both April and October are ideal. A single lifetime wouldn't be enough to understand the wall-to-wall hieroglyphs on display, so if history is your currency, bookend your cruise with a day or two extra for further exploration.

THINGS TO NOTE

Egypt's main tourist areas are generally considered safe for travellers, but check your government's travel advice for up-to-date news. Further information at *experienceegypt.eg*

One Week Itinerary

>

Begin with two days in Aswan where the terrific Temple of Philae on Lake Nasser awaits. Before departing on your river trip proper, tour the botanical garden on El Nabatat (Kitchener's) Island, overgrown with oleander and sycamore trees, and fly south to see Abu Simbel's monumental temples on a day trip.

>>

Once on your boat, spend a couple of days sailing slowly north, with desert towns painting a vivid picture of Egypt today. At Kom Ombo, learn about the ancient Egyptian calendar and the early days of medicine (even the pharaohs went in for cosmetic surgery), before rural life takes over by the time you reach Edfu, home to the great Temple of Horus.

>>

The Nile then widens, leading you to Luxor for days five to seven. Karnak, the most storied temple of the lot, is arguably ancient Egypt's crowning glory, while the Valley of the Kings is where modern life and ancient death live in perfect harmony.

MORE TIME?

Add as many extra days as you can in Cairo for the Pyramids, Sphinx and new Grand Egyptian Museum.

MOROCCO

Visit Mountains
and Medinas

STARS SHINE BEHIND the mountains as the first call to prayer breaks the pre-dawn quiet. Camped on a village rooftop below the ruins of a crumbling kasbah, up in Morocco's High Atlas, you're entirely removed from the chaos and bustle of the city *souqs* (markets), the tight alleys of the medina traded for wide valleys and high peaked ridges that define the centre of the country.

In M'Goun UNESCO Geopark, the Aït Bougmez Valley blends traditional rural lifestyles and numerous trekking trailheads, including the three-day traverse of the M'Goun massif to Aït Ali N'Ito, crossing high shepherds' pastures and camping or overnighting with village families along the way.

En route to Imlil afterwards, stop for the Sunday *souq* in Demnate to pick up freshly ground spices, farm-to-market olive oil from the city's orchards and an inexplicably vast array of slippers. If the timing is right, weekly *souqs* in the Atlas villages that surround Toubkal are also a timeless scene

Opposite: the winding Tizi n'Tichka pass through the High Atlas mountains;
This page: mint tea in Marrakesh

of socialising and shopping. Imlil is no stranger to tourism, mostly in the form of trekkers who come for the two-day ascent of Jebel Toubkal, and visitors already missing fancy lodges and a strong post-hike drink will find both here. But push further into surrounding villages, such as Aroumd and Matat, and you find narrow lanes between traditional stone houses, the clicking and creaking of carpet looms and clopping donkey hooves keeping the time of a more traditional pace of life.

A Traveller's Tale

Scrambling the last, loose stretch to Tizi n'Toubkal Pass, I finally see Toubkal Peak (13671ft/4167m), the highest in North Africa, with the lights of Marrakesh far on the horizon. Crunching the final few gravelly steps of the summit trail, after six days of trekking through High Atlas hamlets, the light begins to burn on the peaks and valleys of what must be one of North Africa's most memorable sunrises.

STEPHEN LIOY

AT A GLANCE

EAT

Savour bubbling flavorful *tajine* stews, a go-to treat no matter where you travel in Morocco.

DRINK

You'll be unlucky to pass a single day without an offer of sugary mint tea.

STAY

Look for restored *riads* (traditional mansions) in historic cities and cosy *gîtes d'étape* (lodges) in trekking regions.

EXPERIENCE

Push into the Sahara for Ouarzazate's cinematic landscapes or the nearby oasis of Fint.

This page: experiencing the myriad sights and sounds of Marrakesh

Legs rested and supplies restocked, turn east away from the main ascent of Toubkal for a seven-day loop of the mountain, topping out at Morocco's highest peak before descending to Imlil via the thundering Cascades d'Irhoulidene and the rock-built homes of the hamlet of Azib Tamsoult. Finally, like caravans of old, descend from the Atlas to the Haouz Plain and Marrakesh. After so long in the mountains, the wide boulevards of Ville Nouvelle and busy alleys of the Medina may feel shocking – but after a few days bargaining on the Djemaa El Fna by day and soaking in historic hammams by night, it'll already be time for the next adventure.

PRACTICALITIES

GETTING THERE AND AROUND

Marrakesh Menara Airport (RAK) is an obvious entry point to the country. From the city, limited public transport traverses the High Atlas, often via Azilal, though private transfers save considerable time.

WHEN TO GO

March to June are the best months to visit - temperatures are still low in late spring but carpets of wildflowers in the high mountains will distract you from the chill. May into June are ideal hiking weather and still not scorching in the plains and Marrakesh.

THINGS TO NOTE

While officially mandatory only for treks in the Toubkal region, seeing the High Andes with a local guide will facilitate a deeper cultural experience, particularly in the villages where Amazigh languages are spoken.
Further information at visitmorocco.com

Two Week Itinerary

>

From Marrakesh, head straight to Aït Bougmez, a half-day drive or two days via Azilal on shared transportation. Visit the Sunday souq in Tabant, and spend a day or two experiencing village life or hiking to seasonal Lac Izoughar on the east end of the valley.

>>

Split the 35-mile (57km) M'Goun Traverse trek over three days, overnighting at Aït Ali N'Ito to finish, or continuing directly to the High Atlas village of Imlil – a half-day drive or a two-day journey via Demnate and Marrakesh on public transport.

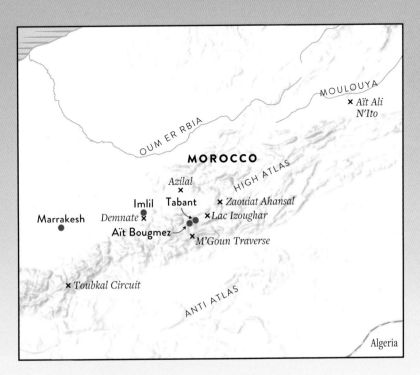

>>>

After a rest day in Imlil, hike from your guesthouse directly into the seven-day Toubkal Circuit – a 49-mile (79km) loop around the massif that begins and ends in the village. Finally, make the short drive back to Marrakesh to trade in your backpack for a shopping bag and dive into the chaos of the medina and souqs.

MORE TIME?

Detour to Zaouiat Ahansal for day hiking, climbing and the country's most spectacular *ighirmin* (collective granaries), continuing onwards to the Aït Bougmez Valley.

MADAGASCAR

Walk *on the* Wild Side

MADAGASCAR IS AN EVOLUTIONARY snapshot. Snipped off from Africa by plate tectonics, it's a Garden of Eden where wildlife found nowhere else on Earth endures. A circuit around the island's national parks is a trip worthy of a David Attenborough documentary. Your first encounter with a wild lemur will be something else – they'll look you up and down like they're aware you're distantly related, before scrambling for a closer inspection. For lemurs of the ring-tailed variety, head to Parc National Isalo and watch them bouncing theatrically across the park's canyons. You might then find yourself climbing breathlessly through the mountain forests of Réserve Spéciale d'Anjanaharibe-Sud, listening for the rhythmic wail of the wild *indri*. Wildlife experiences can be big, like spotting breaching humpback whales at Anakao or sea turtles frolicking off the Nosy Be's beaches; or small, like combing the leaf litter of Parc National Montagne d'Ambre for the tiny Brookesia chameleon. Whatever size the wildlife, you're in for an adventure.

AT A GLANCE

EAT
Try leafy, lip-numbing *romazava* stew with hunks of zebu meat.

DRINK
Rhum arrange is cane rum infused with Madagascan spices.

PRACTICALITIES

Fly to capital Antananarivo and arrange a car and driver. Visit from June to September to avoid the rains and meet the whales.

CABO VERDE

Cruise *an* Island Nation off Africa's West Coast

AT A GLANCE

EAT
National dish *cachupa* is a filling meat, bean and vegetable stew.

DRINK
Rum-like *grogue* (made from distilled sugarcane) goes well in cocktails like caipirinhas.

PRACTICALITIES

Various ferry companies, including CV Interilhas, connect neighbouring islands – and, less frequently, distant islands. BestFly Cabo Verde flies between islands.

EVERY ISLAND IS A WORLD unto its own in Cabo Verde. On Fogo, signs of the island's active volcano are everywhere: on black-sand beaches, in lava fields surrounding abandoned villages and in the farmlands where the rich soil nurtures the archipelago's best vineyards. Boa Vista, by contrast, resembles a strange collision of Sahara and Caribbean – a parched interior, home to the wind-whipped dunes of the Viana Desert, and golden beaches lapped by turquoise seas. Once you've set foot on its soft sands you'll agree that Praia de Santa Mónica ranks among the world's most beautiful beaches. Though formed by the same volcanic forces, Santo Antão feels far removed from Boa Vista's sunbaked flatlands, with craggy peaks rising above lush canyons and meandering river valleys. Trekking here is epic, with challenging hikes amid waterfalls, hillside villages and dramatic viewpoints. Cabo Verde's other inhabited islands (nine in all) are sprinkled with equally diverse landscapes – along with enchanting music-filled cities like Mindelo, adding another reason to make this trip.

SOUTH AFRICA

Drive Cape Town *to the* Garden Route

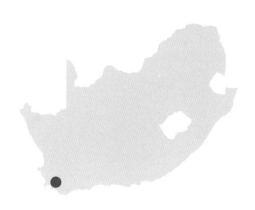

Opposite: Table Mountain Aerial Cableway in Cape Town; *This page*: African jackass penguins at Boulders Beach on the Cape Peninsula

CABLE CARS GLINT in the sunlight. Climbing the soaring face of Table Mountain, their passengers look down on hikers, cyclists and surfers on the slopes and beaches below, and to South Africa's 'Mother City', Cape Town. The country's pin-up city has added culinary and artistic kudos to its outdoor appeal in recent years, and now offers an unexpected dose of sophisticated charm at the southern tip of Africa, best seen in fascinating neighbourhoods such as pastel-painted Bo-Kaap, home to its Cape Muslim community. A city stay is often combined with a visit to the nearby winelands and a journey along the famous Garden Route, a wonderful road trip east of Cape Town through the region's diverse landscapes, a beloved holiday strip of beaches, lagoons and forests around the town of Knysna.

This classic urban-rural trip follows in the footsteps of the Dutch East India Company, Brits, Trekboers and others who ventured out of the maritime refreshment station turned colony at the Cape. It's tourists who lead the charge to Knysna these days, especially during December, to enjoy the town and island marina that gaze across a boat-dotted estuary at the sandstone cliffs of The Heads. Between breakfast at île de pain

A Traveller's Tale

Having read *Circles in a Forest* and *Fiela's Child* by Dalene Matthee, I was keen to experience the world evoked by these historical novels of hardy woodcutters and gold panners dodging wild elephants in the Knysna Forests. Matthee set her 'Forest Novels' during the area's 19th-century boom, when ships carried yellowwood and stinkwood to the burgeoning Cape Colony, which needed timber for European settlers' homes and furniture, shipbuilding and railways to the diamond mines. In the Wilderness section of Garden Route National Park, I followed the rustling footsteps of the books' protagonists among old-growth trees, strange fungi, towering tree ferns and rust-coloured streams on the Circles in a Forest trails. As I dipped my feet in a babbling brook, I heard the 'kow kow' call of a rare Knysna loerie, and I ended my woodland wander at the 880-year-old, 130ft-high (40m) Outeniqua yellowwood named after the writer herself.

JAMES BAINBRIDGE

AT A GLANCE

EAT
Try *bobotie*, a delicious Cape Malay dish of curried mince and raisins, topped with an eggy crust and served with saffron rice. The dish shows influences brought from Southeast Asia by Cape Muslim people.

DRINK
For a local take on Baileys Irish cream, order a sweet glass of Amarula, a liqueur made with the fruit of the marula trees that dot the African plains.

STAY
Immerse yourself in the African bush with a stay on a private wildlife reserve, such as Sanbona in the Little Karoo and Gondwana on the Garden Route.

EXPERIENCE
Enjoy the views across Cape Town's Kirstenbosch National Botanical Garden from the Boomslang ('tree snake') canopy walkway, which soars through the Arboretum.

SHOP
Visit the Old Biscuit Mill in arty Woodstock, Cape Town, for local craftwork and homewares, as well as the Neighbourgoods food and design market on weekends.

"The Garden Route is a wonderful road trip through the region's diverse landscapes, a beloved holiday strip of beaches, lagoons and forests"

Right: the chef's special washed down with a glass of white; *Opposite:* a Stellenbosch vineyard

artisan bakery and a sunset cruise, there are trails to follow and peaty lagoons to paddle in in the Afromontane forests beneath the Outeniqua and Tsitsikamma ranges. With the world's second-mildest climate (after Hawai'i) and activities such as the Tsitsikamma Canopy Tour, walking the Storms River Suspension Bridge and exploring a gorge by kayak and lilo, a few days on the Garden Route is more appealing than a platter of Knysna oysters. Stay on Thesen Island or find tranquility deep in the forest. Popular alternative bases include stylish Plettenberg Bay, beachfront Wilderness and rustic Nature's Valley or Stormsrivier.

After taking in the Garden Route's many delights, most visitors zip back to the city along the N2, but crossing the Outeniqua Pass to the ostrich-farming Oudtshoorn area offers a slower return through the semi-arid Little Karoo, where a bucolic mix of fruit orchards and vineyards unfurls between the Swartberg and Langeberg Mountains. Pick up some dried peaches from a roadside farmstall and join the dusty *bakkies* (pick-up trucks) on Route 62, which leads 240km (150 miles) west from Oudtshoorn to the town of Montagu. Toast the trip beneath a twinkling night sky at a farmstay in the peaceful town, where Cogmanskloof Pass is a dramatic portal from the Little Karoo to the Breede River Valley, marking a return to the fertile wine-farming area surrounding Cape Town.

Opposite: on the Garden Route coastal road towards Table Mountain

Two Week Itinerary

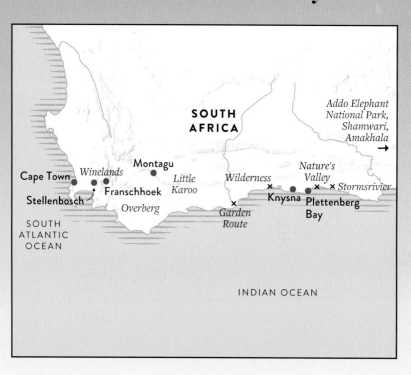

> Spend a week in Cape Town exploring food and craft markets, and walking trails and mountain-backed beaches in this ravishing African-European melting pot.

>> Drag yourself away from the vibrant restaurant, nightlife and art scenes to seek more gastronomic pleasures an hour's drive away in the Winelands. Franschhoek and Stellenbosch make pretty bases for a few days of wine-tasting tours. Continue between the Overberg region's rolling fields and coastal mountains to the Garden Route, where you'll reach the activity centre of Knysna after six scenic hours on the N2.

>>> Walks, cruises, surfing, shark-cage diving and bungee jumping await in the forests, lagoons and Indian Ocean coastline around Wilderness, Plettenberg Bay, Nature's Valley and Stormsrivier. After at least a long weekend, take the road less travelled. Rte 62 leads between the wrinkly mountain ranges and fruit farms of the Little Karoo, where sleepy Montagu is five hours' drive from Knysna and three from Cape Town International Airport.

MORE TIME?

Three hours' east of the Garden Route, spend a couple of nights in a safari tent or thatched cottage at Addo Elephant National Park, where more than 600 elephants roam the Sundays River Valley, or experience a private wildlife reserve, such as Shamwari or Amakhala.

PRACTICALITIES

GETTING THERE
AND AROUND
Many airlines fly to Cape Town
International Airport, but it
can work out cheaper to travel
via Johannesburg's OR Tambo
International Airport. The latter
is good if you'd like to include
northern highlights such as Kruger
National Park or neighbouring
countries in your itinerary. South
African roads are hair-raising,

but renting a car is still the most
convenient option. Drive on the
left. Having a car in Cape Town is
recommended, but Uber taxis are
widespread, MyCiTi buses serve the
city centre and guided tours explore
everywhere from the Winelands to
Cape Point. Hop-on, hop-off Bazbus
offers 13 stops between Cape Town
and Gqeberha (Port Elizabeth),
including Stellenbosch and Knysna.

WHEN TO GO
Avoid December, when roads are
busy and South Africans descend on
the Garden Route. Otherwise the
summer months between November
and February have reliably hot,
dry weather.

THINGS TO NOTE
If you'd like to overnight in a
wildlife reserve, book well ahead,
as safaris are popular among locals
and international visitors alike.
*For further information see
capetown.travel and southafrica.net*

Road Trip through Namibia

NAMIBIA MIGHT JUST BE the safest and most surprising driving encounter with the wild anywhere in Africa. Often called 'Africa for beginners', the country is the perfect place for a road-trip safari. Its low-density human population, low crime rate, excellent wildlife viewing, dramatic landscapes and highly developed road network all add up to a safe yet exhilarating adventure.

To see Namibia at its best requires careful planning. In part, that's because it's vast – if it were a US state, it would be second in size only to Alaska. Put another way, you could fit Texas within Namibia's borders with room to spare. But it's also because there's so much to see.

Yes, there's wildlife in abundance. Etosha National Park, in the north, ranks among the most wildlife-abundant parks in the continent, while elsewhere, in the barren mountains of Damaraland, desert-adapted animals – lions, elephants, rhinos – are

Opposite: tourists climb the giant sand dunes of Sossusvlei; *This page*: elephant in the slow lane at Etosha National Park

major drawcards. Increasingly, private reserves like Erindi and Okonjima combine conservation with the thrill of a wildlife-filled safari. But animals tell only part of the story. This is a world of dramatic natural beauty, and of unique juxtapositions. Sand dunes hundreds of feet high and part of the Namib Desert, the oldest on Earth, press up against the crashing waves of the Southern Atlantic shore. Inland, Fish River Canyon – which is known as the Grand Canyon of Africa – contrasts sharply with the vast plains of the Kalahari.

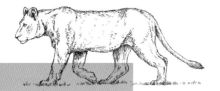

A Traveller's Tale

The first time I visited Etosha National Park, it was like landing on another planet. Elephants emerged out of the dust, springboks swarmed the waterholes, and horizons merged with the sky. And then I saw her. The lioness was feeding on a kill while gemsbok antelopes, wildebeests and giraffes milled around nervously nearby. Every creature, myself included, had eyes only for this superb creature. Here was Africa, in high definition.

ANTHONY HAM

Namibia's human story, too, is a stirring tale. It begins with the San of the Kalahari, one of the oldest extant human civilisations on the planet, and moves through time in stories told by millennia-old rock art at Twyfelfontein and elsewhere. In the far north, the Himba maintain deeply traditional lives which couldn't be more different from the frenetic pace of adrenaline-fuelled Swakopmund, southern Africa's adventure-sports capital.

But more than any particular site, national park or human encounter, it's this that you'll remember about a visit here: imagine yourself driving along an empty road, as deserts and mountains unfurl around you, with the prospect of seeing some very big animals up ahead. Namibia is the place to make that happen.

Opposite: camping under clear night skies in Namibia

Two Week Itinerary

>

Pick up a vehicle in Windhoek and drive north. Break up the journey with some wildlife-watching in Erindi Private Game Reserve (two days) and Okonjima Nature Reserve (one day), on your way to Etosha National Park (three days), which belongs among the elite of African parks.

>>

Once you've explored Etosha, wind southwest to the coast for a couple of days rhino-tracking and looking for elephants amid Damaraland's mountains; add an extra day to visit the UNESCO-listed rock art of Twyfelfontein.

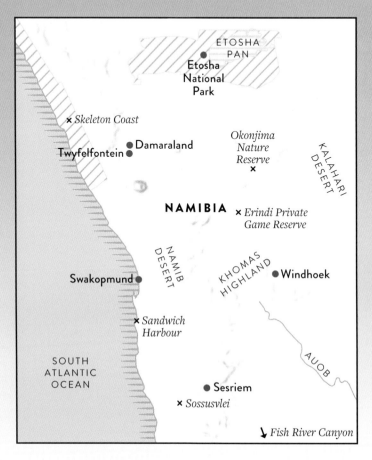

>>>

From Damaraland, it's a long day's drive down to the Skeleton Coast, where you'll find shipwrecks and a vast seal colony on your way to Swakopmund. This fun town has all sorts of excursions to choose from, including to the desert-meets-the-sea magnificence of Sandwich Harbour.

>>>>

It's a half-day drive into the Namib Desert to the town of Sesriem, launchpad for two days of sand dunes at Sossusvlei and surrounding valleys, before heading back to Windhoek.

MORE TIME?

For a three-day add-on, consider an excursion south to drama-filled Fish River Canyon.

PRACTICALITIES

GETTING THERE AND AROUND

Namibia's only international airport is in the capital, Windhoek, and it receives only a handful of international flights. It may work out cheaper or more convenient to fly into Johannesburg or Cape Town (South Africa), or Maun or Kasane (Botswana), which have better connections, and drive into Namibia from there. The best way to get around is in a rented 4WD.

WHEN TO GO

Although you can visit Namibia year-round, the best time for a trip is during the June-to-October dry season, when you can expect the best weather (clear skies, mild days), road conditions are optimal and the wildlife is easiest to see.

THINGS TO NOTE

Book your 4WD vehicle (and possibly your accommodation, although many 4WDs have rooftop tents) through Drive Botswana (drivebotswana.com).

RWANDA

Track Mountain Gorillas *in* Primate Paradise

NOTHING BEATS YOUR FIRST spine-tingling glimpse of mountain gorillas. Roaming their lush rainforest homelands, with gentle mums suckling their babies, mischievous toddlers tumbling around and a mighty silverback watching over them all, this is the ultimate wildlife encounter.

Volcanoes National Park in the tiny East African country of Rwanda, aptly known as the 'Land of a Thousand Hills', is home to 12 gorilla groups habituated to human visitors. From a population of just 400 in the 1980s, over 1000 are today thriving in the rainforests of Uganda, Democratic Republic of the Congo and northern Rwanda, thanks to astounding conservation efforts. Some gorilla families stay on the volcanoes' lower slopes, but others venture higher, wandering through the mists of Mt Karisimbi, sometimes taking visitors three to four hours to reach – prepare for an arduous trek through dense vegetation with vines, ferns and nettles the size of dinner plates. When your trackers find them, you'll have just one magical hour with these enigmatic animals, but it's worth every muddy, tiring footstep you've taken. Watch primate family life playing out in front

Opposite: tree canopy trail in the
Nyungwe rainforest; *This page top:*
downtown Kigali, Rwanda's capital;
Bottom: a gorilla enjoys a snack in
Volcanoes National Park

AT A GLANCE

EAT

Try a traditional cooking class at
the Nyamirambo Women's Centre
in Kigali's oldest neighbourhood.
Enjoy delicious *matoke* (fried green
bananas), *ibihaza* (pumpkin with
beans) and *dodo*, a garlicky, chilli-
infused spinach dish.

DRINK

Banana beer, or Urwagwa, is a
popular alcoholic beverage, made
with fermented banana juice and
sorghum. Make it yourself at Red
Rocks Rwanda in Musanze or at the
Heaven Restaurant in Kigali.

STAY

For sheer indulgence, stay at one of
Musanze's ultra-luxury lodges whilst
tracking the gorillas. Wilderness
Bisate, Singita Kwitonda, Virunga
Lodge and One&Only Gorilla's
Nest all have conservation and
community projects at their core.

EXPERIENCE

In Volcanoes National Park, don't
miss a (far simpler) trek to see
golden monkeys – they are both
endearing and entertaining,
swinging through the bamboo
forests like acrobats on overdrive.

SHOP

Kigali is fizzing with creative talent,
best seen at the Inema Arts Centre.
Home to 10 contemporary artists-
in-residence, it shines a light on
African talent in art, crafts, dance
and music.

A Traveller's Tale

Like a first love, you never forget the first gorilla you see. Mine was
called Kurira. The strapping 440lb (200kg) silverback, tall, dark and
handsome with hair as black as the night, swaggered casually in my
direction, oblivious to the excitement and trepidation soaring through
me. Every nerve in my body had zapped into life. As I backed nervously
into brambles, he stopped at the bush beside me, crouched quietly on
his haunches and studied the blackberries, contemplating which one
to pick as if choosing his favourite treat from a box of fine chocolates.
Kurira's gnarled leathery fingers delicately plucked off a single fruit,
tiny in hands the size of baseball gloves, and popped it into his mouth,
savouring every bit before choosing his next juicy morsel. Entranced by
his human-like expressions, his gentleness and strength, and his soulful
brown eyes, I was completely smitten.

SUE WATT

"Volcanoes National Park, aptly known as the 'Land of a Thousand Hills', is home to 12 gorilla groups habituated to human visitors"

Left: Volcanoes National Park

of you. Just like their human cousins, there'll be wise grown-ups, flirty or sulky teenagers, and youngsters smiling, laughing even, as they chase each other playing peek-a-boo and swinging through the trees.

Gorillas aren't the only primates in Rwanda, though. The fairy-tale rainforest of Nyungwe National Park in the south is home to masses of monkeys, and between the two national parks lies Lake Kivu, hugged by some of the country's myriad hills, draped in patchworks of greens. To reach Nyungwe, cruise the entire length of the lake on the luxury houseboat *Kivu Queen uBuranga*, exploring tiny islands en route and listening to the tuneful traditional singing of fishers at sunset. Then immerse yourself in Nyungwe's verdant nature, home to 13 of Africa's primates, including cheeky chimpanzees and black-and-white

colobus – with long white beards, they look like ageing hippies. Teeter across Uwinka Overlook, a gently swaying suspension bridge some 164ft (50m) above the national park's towering ebonies and mahoganies; all you'll hear is birdsong and the call of monkeys. Or try the new three-day Cyinzobe hiking trail, passing waterfalls and spectacular vistas and sleeping in eco-log cabins along the way, before heading to Kigali, Rwanda's dynamic capital.

The city is teeming with art galleries and craft markets, excellent restaurants and bars, gleaming skyscrapers and manicured gardens. Don't miss the Kigali Genocide Memorial, a surprisingly peaceful haven with sweet-scented rose gardens, where the history of the genocide that devastated the country in 1994 is sensitively told.

This page: rare mountain gorillas inhabit Volcanoes National Park in the Virunga mountains

PRACTICALITIES

GETTING THERE AND AROUND

Kigali International Airport is Rwanda's primary port of entry and home to RwandAir, with a network of routes around the world. National parks are all within easy reach of the capital by car and most visitors hire a driver/guide (through a tour operator) for that invaluable local perspective of Rwandan life.

WHEN TO GO

December to February and June to September are the best times for gorilla tracking, although it can rain at any time. Every September, baby gorillas are named at the Kwita Izina ceremony, a popular event that attracts thousands of people.

THINGS TO NOTE

On the last Saturday morning of every month, all Rwandans take part in Umuganda, working for their communities: shops and museums stay closed until 11am. Gorilla-tracking permits cost US$1500, with discounts if visiting Akagera and Nyungwe National Parks; book well in advance, ideally through a tour operator (or direct via visitrwandabookings.rdb.rw). Children under 15 are not allowed to track gorillas. You'll need to be able to hike for a few hours.
For further information see visitrwanda.com

Two Week Itinerary

>

Imagine Rwanda as a wheel, with its excellent road network like spokes emanating from the capital Kigali. Safe and spotlessly clean, the city merits a couple of days' easy exploration.

>>

On your third morning, drive two hours' north to Musanze (also known as Ruhengeri), the gateway to the mountain gorillas. Here and around the nearby village of Kinigi, home to Volcanoes National Park HQ, you'll find top-notch lodges, restaurants and art galleries. Many people visit the gorillas twice if the eye-watering permit cost isn't prohibitive – fees go towards conservation and community development – or you can go biking, hiking and canoeing. Spend at least three days here.

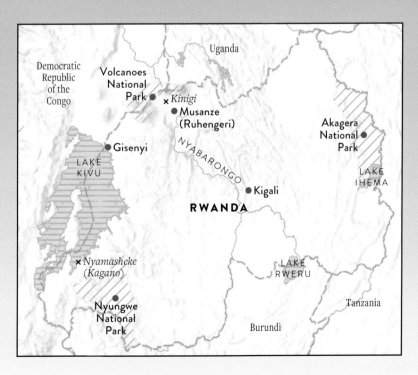

>>>

On day six, a two-hour drive takes you to Gisenyi on Lake Kivu's shore to meet your houseboat *Kivu Queen uBuranga*. Two relaxing days later, you'll disembark at Nyamasheke (also called Kagano) for Nyungwe National Park, thirty minutes' drive away. Spend five days here, spotting monkeys and chimpanzees, and immersing yourself in resplendent rainforest on a three-day hike, before driving back to Kigali.

MORE TIME?

Head east to Akagera National Park, a two-hour drive from Kigali. It's home to the Big Five wildlife, and its lakes, hills and savannahs make this one of Africa's prettiest parks.

ZIMBABWE

See Victoria Falls *and* Wondrous Wildlife

Opposite: elephants and baboons cross the savanna; *This page:* wildlife-spotting by canoe in Zimbabwe's Mana Pools National Park

ZIMBABWE IS ONE OF Africa's most underrated wildlife destinations. Come here and you can see thousands of elephants and voracious predators aplenty, including lions, cheetahs and wild dogs. Add to the mix the world's largest curtain of falling water, Victoria Falls, inspiring community conservation projects, excellent camps and lodges and some of the best guides on the continent, and it has all the ingredients for a dream safari. Yet few travellers visit Zimbabwe compared to Tanzania or South Africa – so bring a smile and an open mind and enjoy a magical trip without the crowds.

Hwange is the country's largest national park, spanning 5863 sq miles (14,650 sq km) of wilderness with teak woodlands, mopane forests and palm-dotted plains home to the prestigious Big Five: lions, buffalo, leopards, elephants and rhinos. On game drives and walking safaris, you'll spot some of the 100 mammal species roaming the park, from myriad antelopes to wildebeest and zebras. Or wait silently by one of Hwange's many waterholes for thirsty animals to come for a drink, including mesmerising herds of elephants slurping the water and rumbling contentedly. Away from the parks, browse

community craft markets and visit inspiring schools and women's projects that local lodges support.

Mana Pools National Park has a unique beauty, with atmospheric albida woodlands fringing the Zambezi River in the shadow of a purple-hued escarpment. Here you can kayak on the river, keeping a watchful eye out for hippos and crocs, or explore by vehicle or on foot, perhaps seeing the wild dogs that starred in David Attenborough's BBC series, *Dynasties*. Look out for Boswell and Fred Astaire as well, two bull elephants who unusually stand on their hind legs to reach for pods high up in the trees.

A Traveller's Tale

In 2022, I joined conservationists translocating two white rhinos – Thuza and Kusasa – on an exhausting 17-hour journey across Zimbabwe to Hwange's new Imvelo Ngamo Wildlife Sanctuary. Rhinos were extinct here and everyone was fizzing with excitement and pride: the community had given up land for their rare residents and protect them 24/7. Seeing their joy as they silently watched the rhinos emerging to explore their new home brought tears to my tired eyes.

SUE WATT

This page: Victoria Falls on the border between Zimbabwe and Zambia

The showstopping Victoria Falls are best seen by helicopter on the 'Flight of Angels' whirring above this natural Wonder of the World. The mile-wide (1.6km) cascades and the mighty Zambezi have plenty to offer adrenaline junkies, including bungee-jumping, zip lining, gorge-swinging and micro-lighting. For a calmer experience, walk the trail along the viewpoints, getting soaked and spying rainbows in the spray amid the roar of the raging water.

PRACTICALITIES

GETTING THERE
AND AROUND

Victoria Falls International Airport is the best port of entry. Companies such as Safari Logistics, Wilderness and Mack Air offer reliable light aircraft flights around Zimbabwe's national parks.

WHEN TO GO

The dry season from July to October is best for wildlife sightings. The rains from November to April make roads challenging and many lodges close. Views of Victoria Falls are at their best from June to September before the flow starts to diminish.

THINGS TO NOTE

Although safaris in Zimbabwe can be arranged independently, it's far easier (and not necessarily more expensive) to book everything through a specialist tour operator. Bring anti-malarials, binoculars, cool clothes and warm layers.

At Victoria Falls, protect your phones and cameras from the pervasive spray.
For further information visit zimbabwetourism.net

12 Day Itinerary

>

From Victoria Falls International Airport, head to Hwange either by road (four hours) or by a one-hour bush flight to the airstrip. Spend three to four days here on game drives and walking safaris, visiting the rhino sanctuary and local villages, and sipping sundowners in the bush, all offered by your lodge.

>>

It's a two- to three-hour light aircraft flight to Mana Pools for your next four days. Mana is ideal for walking safaris, when your senses become truly attuned to the sights and sounds of the bush. Many lodges also offer kayaking, birding and boat trips as well as game drives.

>>>

Your two-hour flight to Victoria Falls follows the Zambezi River and vast Lake Kariba. You'll easily fill a few days visiting the Falls, enjoying activities or taking things easy exploring the thriving eponymous town with its shops, curio markets and restaurants.

MORE TIME?

After Mana Pools, spend a couple of nights on a houseboat on Lake Kariba, where exquisite sunrises and sunsets enhance the lake's haunting beauty.

BOTSWANA

Take a Boat Safari
through the Okavango

YOU WISH THE EXPERIENCE will never end. You're drifting, gondola-style, through the watery channels of Botswana's Okavango Delta in a wooden dugout canoe, accompanied only by the gentle slap of wooden paddle on water, the screech of a fish eagle, or by the sudden silence that descends whenever a predator is nearby. This is sustainable travel at its most ancient and attractive. Moving at the whim of quiet currents, steering clear of hippos, you might encounter an elephant swimming or drinking quietly by the reeds. Birds known as skimmers make the barest ripple as they pluck insects from the surface. If you're lucky, you'll hear a lion roaring off in the distance. So magical are such moments that here in the world's largest inland delta, you could be forgiven for wondering if you've found Eden. And at the end of your watery adventure, you'll return to where you began, to a cluster of safari tents on an island accessible only by boat.

AT A GLANCE

EAT
Nibble on *biltong* (jerky) on a sunset picnic.

DRINK
Indulge in a iced G&T after a day of wildlife watching.

PRACTICALITIES

Plan on visiting from May to September, when water levels are ideal for boat safaris. *Book your safari through safaribookings.com*

KENYA AND TANZANIA

Follow *the* Herds
on the Great Migration

AT A GLANCE

EAT

Book a bush breakfast (multiple courses served by waiters) out on the savannah.

DRINK

Down a cold Tusker (Kenya) or Serengeti (Tanzania) beer.

PRACTICALITIES

Research where to find the Migration throughout the year. *Book your safari months in advance throughsafaribookings.com*

IMAGINE YOURSELF ON THE savannah plains of Tanzania's Serengeti and Kenya's Masai Mara. Animals spread out in front of you to the horizon. Herds of nearly two million wildebeest and zebra seemingly moving as one. The earth itself appears to swarm. Sometimes there are so many zebras that everything blurs into a violent argument of stripes. When the herds cross rivers, hold your breath because crocodiles lie in wait. The Great Migration is one of nature's last, truly wild spectacles. Following instincts honed over millennia, the herds follow the rains and grasslands on their endless quest for survival, stalked all the while by predators. Following this quest and this contest is a journey into the storied nostalgia of the East African safari. Sleep under canvas and listen to lions roaring in the night. Sip G&Ts as elephant families move like cloud shadows across the landscape. Then watch in wonder as the sun sets in a great ball of fire behind a silhouetted acacia.

OMAN

Play Desert Explorer *in the* Empty Quarter

OMAN'S DESERT CAPTURES the essence of story-book Arabia better than anywhere else in the Gulf. Rippling dunes, camel trains and ingeniously built forts burn longer in the memory, and the ghosts of historical explorers Ibn Battuta, Bertram Thomas and Wilfred Thesiger haunt the horizon. The sand sea is a last frontier in another sense too: tourism is in its infancy here and, on a jeep safari into the Empty Quarter – or Rub' al Khali, as Omanis call it – you'll find yourself channeling the same energy as a true adventurer. Wahiba Sands, three hours south of capital Muscat, is a great introduction to desert life. With a maze of dunes to climb up and sand-board down, million-star skies to gawp at and only camels to share it with, this place immediately stirs the soul. Beyond, to the southwest, lies the mystical lost city of Ubar, the 'Atlantis of the Sands' which, still today, commands an oversized space in the imagination.

AT A GLANCE

EAT
Dine on gently-spiced goat meat and rice, known as *shuwa*.

DRINK
Welcome the sunrise with a dune-top mint tea or cardamom coffee.

PRACTICALITIES

The draining heat of June to August is best avoided; come from November to February for the coolest desert temperatures.

© PETER STUCKINGS / GETTY IMAGES

Asia

INDIA

Fall for Romantic Forts *and* Palaces

YOU HAVEN'T SEEN LUXURY until you've seen India's lavish forts and palaces. These are where the world's most pampered royals lived extraordinary lives defined by ambition and indulgence. The kingdoms of the North Indian plains were forged through conflict, but the monuments left behind tell a different tale of beauty, love and loss. To visit today is to leaf through a history book dripping with adoration and heartbreak.

The story begins the moment you enter Delhi's intoxicating sprawl. Amongst the honking traffic and frenetic bazaars selling everything from coloured *gulal* powder to steel tiffin boxes, you'll find fortresses, palaces and tombs left behind by eight great empires. It's easy to be overwhelmed, so focus on the big hitters – the Red Fort and Jama Masjid, the tomb of Mughal emperor Humayun, British-built New Delhi and the ruins at Qutb Minar. The Mughals' fiercest rivals and occasional allies, the Rajputs, controlled territory to the west, a patchwork of princely states stitched together to form modern-day

Opposite: the Peacock Gate of Jaipur's City Palace; *This page top:* Lake Palace hotel on Lake Pichola, Udaipur; *Bottom:* drinking chai in West Bengal; *Previous page:* a train crosses Sri Lanka's Nine Arches Bridge

AT A GLANCE

EAT
Dine on *dal bhati churma*, a nourishing Rajasthani staple of buttered, fire-cooked wheat-flour rolls, dunked into a richly spiced, lentil-based dipping sauce.

DRINK
Kulhad chai is sweet, milky tea infused with cardamom and ginger, served in an environmentally-friendly, unglazed earthenware cup that can be crushed back to dust after use.

STAY
Sleep in extravagant comfort in the former home of a maharaja. Palace hotels pop up everywhere in Rajasthan, from Jaipur's Rambagh and Jodhpur's swanky Umaid Bhawan Palace to Udaipur's floating Lake Palace.

EXPERIENCE
Book an overnight camel safari at Jaisalmer, the best way to avoid the crowds at Sam and Khuri and hit the open desert, eating and sleeping amongst the dunes beneath a light-pollution-free canopy of stars.

SHOP
Bargain for intricate miniature paintings of wildlife, deities and princely life; in Bundi, you can even have yourself painted into a royal scene.

A Traveller's Tale

Nowhere conjures up the magic of medieval India quite like Jaisalmer. On my first visit, I felt like I had been sucked into the scenery from Disney's *Aladdin*. Staggering bleary eyed from an overnight train, I wandered through a succession of elephant-sized gateways into a fortified city seemingly sculpted from the living golden stone of the desert. Combing the back lanes for a place to stay, every turn seemed to reveal another wonder. The intricate, filigree-carved frontage of a magnificent *haveli* home. A cobbled, butter-yellow courtyard, polished smooth by 800 years of footfalls. The astonishing, deity-bedecked tower of a jewel-box Jain temple. Everywhere, alleyways ended abruptly atop the city walls, gazing out towards the distant, dusty skyline. The intervening decades have changed the desert city, but watching sunrise from the top of the crenelated fortress walls with a cup of *masala chai* (spiced tea) remains one of northern India's great pleasures.

JOE BINDLOSS

"Palaces explode with gilded inlays and paintings of paradise, and courtyards present a riot of gardens and fountains"

Right: blue interior of Udaipur City Palace; *Opposite:* Hawa Mahal in Jaipur, constructed of red and pink sandstone

Rajasthan. These warrior clans were indefatigably proud, preferring death to dishonour; countless times, warriors rode out to certain death in battle while women and children immolated themselves inside the city walls. Exploring Rajasthan's royal capitals now is a powerfully emotional experience. Palaces explode with gilded inlays and paintings of paradise, and courtyards present a riot of gardens and fountains. But amongst all this opulence you'll see the tiny handprints of brides who died by ritual suicide on their husbands' funeral pyres.

The classic circuit begins in Jaipur, amidst a swagger of salmon-hued fortresses and follies erected by the rulers of the Kachhwaha clan. Head south and painted flowers, royal scenes and Hindu gods burst from every inch of wall and ceiling space in the royal palace of Bundi, while intricately carved victory towers rise like skyscrapers over 7th-century Chittorgarh, the

biggest fortress of them all. The romance ramps up to eleven once you roll into Udaipur, where ice-white palaces spill out onto the shimmering waters of Lake Pichola. White gives way to Brahmin blue in Jodhpur, where the fortified walls of the Mehrangarh form an evocative backdrop to candlelit dinners. Far out in the Thar Desert, the golden sandstone walls of Jaisalmer complete the colour quartet.

To close out India's Golden Triangle, loop back through Jaipur to Agra, perhaps with a stop at the tiger-stalked fortress in Ranthambhore National Park, and take an early morning tour around the Taj Mahal, built by the grieving emperor Shah Jahan for his lost bride. No other building captures so perfectly India's national tale of tragedy, beauty and wonder.

Opposite: ferrying a passenger past Delhi's Red Fort

Two Week Itinerary

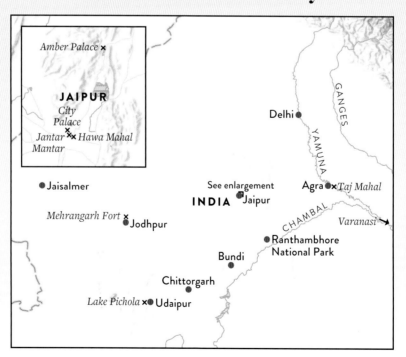

> Kick off with three atmospheric days wandering Delhi's tangled bazaars and Mughal forts, mosques and tombs. A five-hour train ride will deliver you to salmon-pink Jaipur – take two days absorbing the majesty of the City Palace, the Hawa Mahal, Amber Palace and Jai Singh II's extraordinary royal observatory.

>> Four hours south by bus, Bundi's painted palace and bottomless stepwells are worth a day of investigation, as are the victory towers of mighty Chittorgarh. It's two hours by train to Udaipur; allow two days to explore its many palaces and to enjoy dinners overlooking Lake Pichola.

>>> An overnight bus ride is an efficient way to reach Jodhpur, where you can get pleasurably lost in the maze-like, Brahmin-blue lanes surrounding Mehrangarh Fort.

>>>> For the full *Arabian Nights* experience, ride the rails to golden Jaisalmer (five to seven hours), adding on two more days for a camel safari into the dunes. It takes a day to reach tigerstalked Ranthambhore National Park by bus and train, and another six hours to reach Agra Fort train station and the wistful wonder that is the Taj Mahal.

MORE TIME? Extend the trip east from Agra to the sacred city of Varanasi to mingle with Hindu pilgrims by the sacred Ganges River.

PRACTICALITIES

GETTING THERE
AND AROUND
Delhi's Indira Gandhi International
Airport is the most convenient hub
for exploring the fortified cities
of North India. Hop from royal
capital to royal capital by train or
bus; book online using apps such
as Make My Trip, Yatra, Redbus and
12GoAsia for easy connections. For
speedier travel, Jaipur has regular
air connections to Delhi, Udaipur,
Jodhpur, Jaisalmer and Agra.

WHEN TO GO
North India is at its best from
October to March, avoiding the
soggy June-to-September monsoon
and the uncomfortably hot months
of April and May. Be ready for cool
nights and chilly morning starts
in the desert from December to
February. Book hotels and transport
well ahead over Christmas and
New Year.

THINGS TO NOTE
India can be a challenge for the
senses – and the immune system.
Carry earplugs, a facemask to
stop germs and air pollution, and
antibacterial soap or hand gel to
ward off infections. When dining
out, stick to busy places serving
food cooked fresh to order, and only
use purified water (including when
brushing your teeth).
For further information visit
incredibleindia.org

INDIA

Take it Slow
in Kerala

FROM SILENT BACKWATERS and jade-hued tea plantations to coconut-infused cuisine, Kerala is a feast for the senses. Here on southern India's palm-fringed west coast, life moves to a mellower beat, partly thanks to a unique geography of hundreds of inland waterways bordered by the biodiverse Western Ghats. Glorious beach activities await all along the 360-mile (580km) shoreline, from surfing in holy Varkala to escaping the world in the north, where undeveloped stretches of golden sand disappear into the distance and seaside towns like Kannur and Bekal host theatrical *theyyam* rituals. Cultural capital Kochi embodies everything that makes Kerala special, including traditional regional practices (such as colourful *kathakali* dance and holistic Ayurveda treatments) that rub shoulders with this ancient harbour city's booming contemporary creative scene. For a break from the coastal heat, there's no beating Kerala's cool, elevated Western Ghats – look for wild elephants in forested Wayanad, go overnight trekking in Periyar Tiger Reserve or dive into India's thriving tea industry in misty Munnar.

AT A GLANCE

EAT
Sadhya is a vegetarian feast and key part of the Onam harvest festival.

DRINK
Sip local *kaapi* (filter coffee), prepared differently across Kerala.

PRACTICALITIES

The best time to visit is October to March; December to February is peak season. If you're keen to travel by train, book ahead.

BHUTAN

Visit Blissful Mountains *and* Monasteries

AT A GLANCE

EAT

Ema datshi is chilli peppers stewed with yak cheese.

DRINK

Homemade grain alcohol *ara* helps you stay warm on mountain trails.

PRACTICALITIES

Contact a Bhutanese tour operator to arrange your visa, plan an itinerary and pay the daily tourist fee (currently US$100 per day).

FINDING SHANGRI-LA IS EASY. It's waiting for you in beautiful Bhutan, the last Buddhist kingdom of the high Himalaya. Though there's a wallet-crunching daily fee, Bhutan is a once-in-a-lifetime destination. To travel here is to step off the well-trodden map into pristine mountain valleys carved by glacial meltwater. It's a land of jangling temple bells and murmured mantras, defined by Gross National Happiness rather than Gross National Product. Days are spent on Himalayan trails in the pure mountain air and wandering the painted courtyards of centuries-old *dzongs* (fortress-monasteries). At night, you'll sleep in serene silence beneath star-filled skies; at mealtimes, you'll graze tantalisingly unfamiliar dishes of yak cheese and fiddlehead ferns. How you explore this paradise is up to you – climb to the precariously balanced chapels of Taktshang monastery, sip espresso with Buddhist monks in the cosmopolitan capital, cross cantilevered bridges to timeless Punakha Dzong. Even if you stop there, you'll have clocked up enough experiences to last a lifetime.

CHINA

Travel Through *the* Middle Kingdom's Golden Triangle

Opposite: dusk settles over Shanghai's Qibao Old Town; *This page:* traditional Chinese dancers at the Summer Palace in Běijīng

CHINA'S GOLDEN TRIANGLE of cities offers fascinating insights into the country. Five thousand years of history and the world wonder of the ancient Silk Road, a futuristic cityscape and bullet trains are all on the itinerary. Starting in Běijīng is crucial to understanding the country's long past, size and imperial grandeur. You'll feel like an ant standing in vast Tian'anmen Sq and wandering the courts and imposing halls of the Forbidden City, where the emperor once resided. The capital's sprawling grid can be overwhelming until you get into the maze of *hutong* courtyards, once home to imperial workers, now converted into cafes, breweries and boutiques. There are lingering hints of the city's old-world charm here – bicycles resting in stone doorway arches, laundry hanging from open windows.

To the south, Xī'ān is a city that has played an important part in China's story. The first emperor, Qin Shi Huang, had thousands of life-sized soldiers, horses and chariots built to see him into the afterlife, and today visitors can marvel at the unique expressions on each face of the Terracotta Army's soldiers in an aeroplane-hangar-sized warehouse outside the city. Xī'ān itself was built in the 500s CE as Chang'an, and was the largest

A Traveller's Tale

One January, I was working in Běijīng at the same time a friend from England was passing through. She asked if we could visit the Great Wall, so we booked a day trip with a private driver to the Mutianyu section of the ancient structure. It was a frosty morning, the temperature well below zero, when we set off in the dark to avoid the morning traffic. The deep winter had set in at that time of year, and when we reached the entrance to Mutianyu we found the mountains and wall dusted in snow. Given how freezing it was, few others had made the trek to visit that day and we virtually had the place to ourselves. We carefully made our way to the top, sidestepping patches of ice on the ramparts and snapping surreal selfies of the empty wall, which almost seemed made of gingerbread and icing.

MEGAN EAVES

AT A GLANCE

EAT
In Běijīng, sample crispy Peking duck; in Xī'ān, try *biangbiang mian* – spicy, hand-torn noodles; in Shanghai, slurp up some famous *xiaolongbao* soup dumplings.

DRINK
Spend the afternoon in a traditional teahouse, where endless hot water is brought to refresh the pot of your choice, accompanied by plates of different snacks.

STAY
Sleep in a converted *hutong* house in Běijīng, and in Shanghai opt for an opulent stay at a historic hotel along the Bund, such as the Fairmont Peace Hotel, a city landmark since 1929.

EXPERIENCE
Walk the shaded pavilions of the Summer Palace in Běijīng, where the emperor and court would retire to cool down in the hottest months.

SHOP
Wander the mazelike lanes of Xī'ān's Muslim Quarter in search of souvenirs, snacks and spices. In Shanghai, head to the French Concession to see the latest Chinese fashion trends in local boutiques.

"Běijīng's sprawling grid
can be overwhelming
until you get into
the maze of 'hutong'
courtyards, now
converted into
cafes, breweries
and boutiques"

Left: the Nanluoguxiang shopping
street in central Běijīng

city in the world. By the 700s, it was a world power and the eastern end of the Great Silk Road – a meeting point of cultures still present today in Xi'an's Muslim Quarter alleyways, in hand-pulled noodle shops and in ancient mosques containing both Chinese and Islamic architectural styles. Xī'ān was so important that, when the 50th emperor of neighbouring Japan ascended to the throne, he based the map for his new capital at Heian-kyō (now Kyōto) on Chang'an. In the 1300s, the city was surrounded by a huge wall with 18 gates, which still stands today – one of the country's most well-preserved. The best way to explore it is to cycle or walk the entire 8.5 miles (14km).

By contrast, Shanghai is where a hypermodern present is juxtaposed with a nostalgic past. The flashing lights and retro-futuristic architecture of Pudong's skyscrapers are a stark counterpoint to the British-built edifices of the Bund across the river. Contemporary art fills the likes of the Long and Rockbund Museums, themselves architectural marvels, but slip into the small streets surrounding Yu Gardens – part of Shanghai's disappearing Old Town – and you'll feel transported to a bygone century. And, of course, a shiny new bullet train will zip you on day trips to neighbouring Hángzhōu and Sūzhōu, where classical gardens and lakeside pavilions recall an era when scholars penned poetry in the shade of a draping willow tree.

Opposite: Shanghai's waterfront and spectacular skyline

Two Week Itinerary

>
Spends two days in Běijīng visiting Tian'anmen Sq, the Forbidden City and the Temple of Heaven. Get lost in the vibrant *hutongs* and enjoy a food tour.

>>
Day-trip to part of the Great Wall, such as Mutianyu. Head to Xī'ān on a high-speed train (four to five hours) and enjoy the sights, starting with the astonishing Army of Terracotta Warriors. Walk or cycle Xī'ān's ancient city walls, visit the Wild Goose Pagoda and shop and snack through the Muslim Quarter. Save one day for a trip to Hua Shan, one of China's most sacred mountains. On your final afternoon, board a sleeper train to Shanghai (14 hours).

>>>
Check out the Old Town, go shopping in Yu Garden and head up the country's tallest building, Shanghai Tower. In the evening, stroll the Bund taking in views of Pudong's skyscrapers.

>>>>
Use the next two days to discover the French Concession and the art scene, before spending your final two days in nearby Hángzhōu and Sūzhōu, both quick trips by high-speed rail. In Sūzhōu, visit the classical Chinese gardens, and in Hángzhōu, meander around West Lake to see why Marco Polo called it 'heaven on Earth'.

MORE TIME?

Take the train or fly to Hong Kong and Macau.

PRACTICALITIES

GETTING THERE AND AROUND

International flights get you to many of China's major cities – Běijīng is the best starting point for this trip. Travelling around by high-speed and sleeper trains offers the best value and atmosphere, but frequent domestic flights are also an option.

WHEN TO GO

Spring and autumn are the best times to visit China to avoid the sweltering summer heat and frigid winters. Avoid visiting during national holiday weeks, such as Spring Festival, 1 October and 1 May, when the crowds can be unmanageable.

THINGS TO NOTE

Be sure to buy your train tickets in advance (possible to do online). Pack face masks as they are still expected in many public places. If you wish to access international websites like Google and most social media platforms, you'll need to download a virtual private network (VPN) before you depart. Carry your passport with you during the day – you may be asked to show it for entry to attractions and museums. *Further information is available at china.org.cn*

JAPAN

Enjoy Temples *and* Cherry Blossoms *in* Kansai

IT'S SPRING IN THE KANSAI region of Japan, and the cherry blossoms are in bloom. Blanketing hills, parks and temple grounds in pale pink froth, this is one of the most classic and beloved of Japanese sights, depicted in art and music since antiquity. Today, visitors still flock to Kansai for *hanami* – flowering viewing parties. People spread blankets beneath the trees and spend hours eating, drinking sake and simply inhaling the delicate floral scent while feeling the spring sun on their faces.

Kyōto, the country's best-preserved ancient city, is central to these spring festivities. It's a place of temples and rock gardens and mossy Shinto shrines, of teahouses hidden behind sliding panels and candy shops with handmade sweets as intricate as flowers, of apprentice geishas padding softly through winding alleys (though far outnumbered by tourists dressed in geisha costumes). The attractions here are gentle and subtle: strolling the cherry tree-lined canal on the Philosopher's Path, bathing in steamy *sento* (public baths), admiring gardens, taking cooking classes.

A Traveller's Tale

I held a deer cookie in one hand, my four-month-old son in the other. It was his first trip abroad and we were in Nara, where deer are considered sacred and allowed to roam at will. The deer considered the cookie, but ultimately decided to nibble (ever so gently) on my son's sock. I laughed, the baby giggled and my husband snapped a picture. A charming memory and a legendary photograph.

EMILY MATCHAR

AT A GLANCE

EAT
A traditional, multi-course *kaiseki* meal, where each course is presented like a work of art.

DRINK
Visit one of Kyōto's numerous family-run sake breweries and sample the wares.

STAY
Sleep in a *ryokan*, a Japanese-style inn, with bedrolls on *tatami*-mat floors and communal baths.

EXPERIENCE
Participate in a tea ceremony, a ritualised affair combining food, art and spirituality.

Opposite: vendors at Nishiki Market in Kyoto; *This page:* walking among giants at Saganon bamboo forest in Arashiyama

In cherry blossom season, visitors head to busy Nishiki Market to gather picnics of seaweed salad, *onigiri* (rice balls with fillings), dried fish and more, then take their goodies to Maruyama-kōen. When darkness falls, the park's legendary weeping cherry tree is illuminated until midnight.

Just outside the city, Arashiyama is home to temples, shrines and an iconic bamboo grove that makes whistling sounds when the wind blows. Further afield, Nara was the capital of Japan in the 8th century and people come to see its historic temples, but the most-photographed things here are the fearless deer that wander freely throughout the city. Vendors sell special 'deer cookies' for visitors to feed them (they're known to gnaw shirtsleeves as well).

Less than an hour away by train, Osaka zooms you into the 21st century with bright lights, 24-hour karaoke bars, every kind of shopping imaginable and thousands of street vendors hawking fried skewers and octopus balls. There are plenty of higher-octane activities here too, from amusement parks to aquariums to *pachinko* (arcade game) parlours. A day in Osaka can balance out the tranquillity of Kyōto and its surrounds.

This page: punting down the river to Himeji Castle in cherry blossom season

PRACTICALITIES

GETTING THERE AND AROUND

From Tokyo, you can take the Shinkansen (bullet train) to Kyōto in about 2½ hours. From Osaka, the nearest major international airport, it's just 15 minutes by Shinkansen. Kyōto and Osaka are both well-supplied with local trains, buses and trams.

WHEN TO GO

Cherry-blossom season is generally from the last week of March into the first two weeks of April, though every year varies somewhat. Try to visit close to the start in case bad weather spoils the blooms earlier than normal.

THINGS TO NOTE

This is a hugely busy travel time in Japan, so accommodation books up quickly. The most popular *hanami* areas can be full of tour groups; get there early.
Further info at kyoto.travel/en

Five Day Itinerary

>

It's easy filling five days in Kyōto. Spend the first exploring the historic Higashiyama and Gion districts, visiting traditional shophouses and the Kiyomizu-dera, Kōdai-ji and Kennin-ji temples. Have a *kaiseki* dinner at famed Kikunoi restaurant.

>>

Next morning, take the train to Arashiyama to visit its famous bamboo grove early, then walk to the Tenryū-ji temple, founded in 1339. Have a Kyōto-style tempura lunch at century-old Tempura Endo Yasaka.

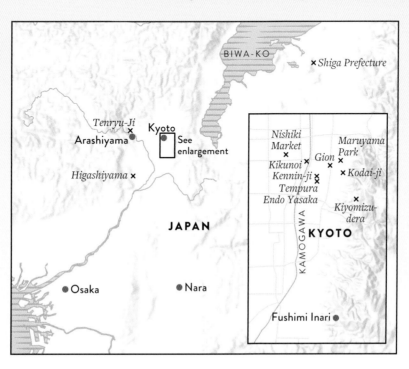

>>>

Begin your third day climbing through the brilliant orange *tori* (gates) of the Fushimi Inari shrine, before taking the train 30 minutes south to Nara for more temple-viewing and deer-feeding.

>>>>

Day four and it's all aboard again for the 45-minute journey to Osaka for street food, shopping, *pachinko*, bar-hopping and other fun. On your final day, grab a picnic at Nishiki Market then walk 15 minutes east for a day of *hanami* (blossom viewing) at Maruyama-kōen Park. Cap the trip with a soak at the local *sento* baths.

MORE TIME? Hike or cycle in bucolic Shiga Prefecture, just north of Kyōto.

JAPAN

Ski Hokkaidō's Legendary Powder

THIS IS NOT ORDINARY SNOW. This is 'Japow' – Japanese powder – considered by pro skiers and snowboarders to be the finest in the world. Here in Japan's northernmost island of Hokkaidō, steam rises from the sea to meet Siberian air currents, creating clouds that blanket the volcanic mountains in some 20ft (6m) of soft, dry snow a year. In Niseko, the heart of Japan's winter sports industry, snowboarders fly down the side of Mt Annupuri, ski the volcanic backcountry and snowshoe through silent pine forests. Afterwards, there's some of the best après-ski in the world: bubbling bowls of ramen or smoky *yakitori* followed by long soaks in the area's famed *onsen*. These geothermal hot springs steam in the frigid air, snowflakes melting on the water's surface. February brings the Sapporo Snow Festival, where hundreds of snow and ice sculptures gleam in the city lights, best enjoyed while savouring some traditional roasted sweet potatoes. Another perfect snow day in Hokkaidō.

AT A GLANCE

EAT

Miso ramen are thick noodles in a salty broth.

DRINK

Taste peaty local whiskies on a distillery tour.

PRACTICALITIES

Mid-December through March is the best snow season in Niseko; Chinese New Year brings bigger crowds and spiking prices.

SINGAPORE AND MALAYSIA

Follow a Southeast Asian Food Trail

AT A GLANCE

EAT

Mamak hawker stall cuisine fuses flavours from India, China and the Malay Peninsula.

DRINK

Teh tarik is 'pulled' tea sweetened with condensed milk.

PRACTICALITIES

Explore the peninsula by train – services run by Keretapi Tanah Melayu Berhad (KTMB) run from Singapore all the way to the Thai border.

THE BEST TRIPS ARE LED by the taste buds. And in Singapore and Malaysia, every snack-stop is a feast and every street corner is a banquet. Overlanding along the Malay Peninsula is one of Asia's greatest gastronomic journeys, taking in the culinary know-how of three great cooking cultures. Picking up your chopsticks in Singapore, you'll graze hawker courts crammed with Malay soups and stir fries, Chinese banquet halls piled with dim sum and Indian canteens perfumed by cardamom, cumin and coriander. Take a bus or train to reach Malaysia's culinary triumvirate – Kuala Lumpur, Melaka and Penang – and celebrate the nation's gourmet heritage with a carnival of open-air eating. Set your alarm clock early. You'll need every waking minute to fit in all the grilled seafood, *char kway teow* noodles and *roti canai* (Indian-style flatbread with curry sauce). And don't overlook Malaysia's food detours – Klang's *kopitiam* (coffeeshop) breakfasts, Kemaman's banana-leafed-steamed seafood, Selangor's family-run *warong* cafes and Ipoh's famed chicken-beansprout noodles.

Dive *to* Wrecks, Sharks *and* Rainbow Reefs

Opposite: Busuanga Island in the Philippines' Palawan province; *This page:* scuba diving among kaleidoscopic marine life

YOU'RE DEFINITELY GOING TO get wet. But in the Philippines, a monsoon archipelago of 7641 islands, that's rather the point because below the waves, a watery wonderland of wrecks and rainbow reefs awaits.

Arriving in the traffic-choked streets of capital Manila, first impressions of the Philippines are not always favourable, but the energy of the country will soon cast its spell. Head to calm, quiet islands nearby and you'll find sand so fine it sings, bacchanalian festivals spilling through the streets of Spanish-flavoured townships and shimmying curtains of fish, painting the deep, blue sea in a kaleidoscope of colours. Oh, and palm trees – lots of palm trees.

For a first bite of paradise, take the bus to Batangas and zip by pumpboat to Puerto Galera, the closest diving option from Manila. On land, waterfalls drop dramatically into rainforest glades; underwater, tuna, jacks, sweetlips and pelagic predators cruise confidently through submerged canyons. Having reached Mindoro Island, it would be remiss not to dive at Apo Reef for gasp-inducing encounters with everything from skittish

whitetip and blacktip sharks to mighty mantas, whale sharks and hammerheads.

From the southern tip of Mindoro, ferries chug to Caticlan, leaping-off point for the idyllic spray of sand known as Boracay – expect soul-recharging days basking on blinding white beaches and drift dives with big wrasse and rare mola. A few islands southeast, Cebu is legendary for glimmering shoals of sardines around Moalboal and close-enough-to-touch encounters with inquisitive thresher sharks off sand-sprinkled Malapascua

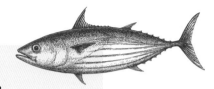

A Traveller's Tale

Diving at Coron was like nothing else I'd ever done. Dropping off the side of an outrigger pumpboat, I descended into the darkening blue, to be met by the masts of mighty warships and looming, coral-encrusted anti-aircraft guns. Deep in the gloom, I spotted silvery shoals of jacks darting through the holds of wartime supply ships, and menacing scorpion fish standing sentry on the prows of gunboats – a haunting and magical experience.

JOE BINDLOSS

This page: the paradisal Malcapuya beach in Palawan

Island. But it's not all reefs, reefs, reefs – surreal landscapes and pocket-sized primates await in the steamy forests and chocolate-drop hills of neighbouring Bohol.

From Cebu City, flights buzz northwest to wonderfully wild Palawan, where El Nido dishes out a convincing re-creation of heaven on Earth, with sparkling sands, coral lagoons framed by saw-tooth karst outcrops and dive sites frequented by turtles, barracuda and stingrays. We've saved the best till last. Ferries connect El Nido to the Calamian Archipelago, where more than a dozen Japanese warships from WWII lie wrecked in the dark, deep waters of Coron Bay.

PRACTICALITIES

GETTING THERE
AND AROUND

Flights, car ferries and outrigger boats link every corner of the Philippines, but be ready for disruption during the typhoon-prone rainy season from June to September. Travel across islands using buses or colourful *jeepneys* – stretched jeeps with bench seats and a riot of superfluous lights, horns and hood ornaments.

WHEN TO GO

November to June is the migration season for whale sharks, coinciding with peak visibility underwater and the driest weather on land. However, it pays to keep an umbrella handy year-round.

THINGS TO NOTE

With its karaoke bars, cacophonous boat engines and buses with overpowered sound systems, the Philippines is noisy: pack ear plugs. *For further information visit philippines.travel*

Two Week Itinerary

>

Manila is packed with bars, restaurants and museums, but you'll soon want to get into those cerulean waters. Take the bus and boat to Puerto Galera (three hours) to dive with rainbow shoals, then take another boat to Sablayan (1½ hours) to mingle with the big fish at Apo Reef.

>>

It's three hours from Roxas to Caticlan, a 15-minute boat ride from the blissful sands of Boracay. After a couple of days crossing Panay and Negros to Cebu by bus and boat, head north to Malapascua Island and its friendly sharks, then south to dive the teeming channels off Moalboal.

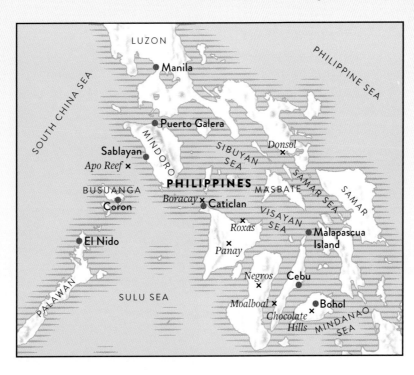

>>

Ferries connect Cebu City to nature-blessed Bohol and its Chocolate Hills. Fly on from Cebu City to El Nido (two hours) for spectacular beaches, diving and kayaking through the karst outcrops. It's another five hours by boat to Coron and some of Asia's most atmospheric wrecks, before flying back to Manila (1½ hours).

MORE TIME?

Head south from Manila to sleepy Donsol, which comes alive with migrating *butanding* (whale sharks) from November to June.

BORNEO

Admire a Rainbow *of* Wildlife

BORNEO IS THE STUFF of wildlife dreams: a rain-soaked haven for jungle-dwellers big and small, from elephants and rhinos to enigmatic orangutans. The easiest point of entry into this lost world of emerald-green foliage and cocoa-brown rivers is Malaysian Sarawak. Around multicultural Kuching, seven rainforest reserves offer a bumper serving of wildlife and wilderness, including almost guaranteed encounters with proboscis monkeys in Bako National Park. Ready for more? Bedding down in national park lodges, campgrounds and tribal longhouses, you can hike into the hot and humid rainforest in search of rhinoceros hornbills, clouded leopards and tiny tarsiers, or just settle in at the Semenggoh orangutan sanctuary near Kuching and let the 'old man of the forest' come to you. Sleeping out in the forest is an experience all by itself – a cacophonic chorus of unidentified whistles, shrieks and rattles will fill the air, while supersized bugs clamber across your mosquito net. Always tip out your boots before putting them on in the morning!

AT A GLANCE

EAT
Try *linut*, gloopy sago starch, dipped into *sambal belacan* chilli paste.

DRINK
Tuak is a traditional rice wine, served at homestays.

PRACTICALITIES

You're going to get wet in Borneo – April to September is the driest season, but keep an umbrella or raincoat handy any time.

INDONESIA

Visit Bali *with a* Gentle Footprint

AT A GLANCE

EAT

Taste Bali on a plate with *nasi campur*, rice with meat or veg side dishes.

DRINK

An ancient turmeric-and-ginger-based elixir, *jamu* is a vitality boost in a glass.

PRACTICALITIES

Avoid spending precious vacation time in Bali's notorious traffic jams and choose fewer destinations to explore at a more relaxed pace.

COCONUT PALMS BEND over golden beaches, conical-hatted farmers tend to rice terraces and the aroma of incense fills the air. This is the image of Bali that draws millions of visitors each year, and travellers can help to preserve the island's unique charms by exploring it in ways that enrich a stay without harming its lush setting or the locals who call it home. Connect with nature and off-the-beaten-track Balinese communities on the Astungkara Way, a mindful hiking experience linking the north and south coasts. Immerse yourself in Balinese village life responsibly on an excursion operated by Jaringan Ekowisata Desa, an eco-tourism network designed and owned by the people of four villages. Or go diving with a member of Green Fins, a joint initiative by the Reef-World Foundation and the United Nations Environment Programme that recognises dive and snorkelling centres (and live-aboards) committed to protecting and preserving coral reefs. That way you can leave Bali just as beautiful as you found it.

VIETNAM

Tour Hanoi *and* its Hinterland

HANOI IS A CITY THAT refuses to grow old gracefully. This millennium-old capital of ancient pagodas and labyrinthine streets is partway through a transformation into a 21st-century Asian metropolis. It also serves as a gateway to northern Vietnam – take a bus or train away from the urban clamour, and within a few hours you might be on boat gliding amongst the limestone monoliths of Halong Bay, or climbing a stairway of emerald rice paddies around Sapa. A journey from the capital to the hinterland is to see this country in all its contradictory glory: both raucous and rustic, exhilarating and eternal.

Begin your exploration in Hanoi's old quarter, where temples neighbour karaoke joints, and dynasties of artisans ply their trade next to shops selling cuddly toys the size of grizzly bears. Its streets throng and thrum with life – this is a place that is forever on the move. Witness its famous rush-hour traffic, when a tidal wave of scooters floods the grid of avenues; pedestrian crossings exist more as a personal challenge than a guarantee of safe passage. These are streets where Evel Knievel might have written the highway code, but amongst them are pockets of tranquillity; backstreets where caged birds sing and the aromas

Opposite: rickshaws and frtuit vendors in Hanoi; *This page top:* lunch in Lao Cai province; *Bottom:* there are thousands of islets in Halong Bay

AT A GLANCE

EAT

Hanoi gave Vietnam its national dish of *pho*, a steaming hot noodle soup, often made with beef. Its name is thought to derive from the French *pot au feu*.

DRINK

Bia hoi is a popular drink in northern Vietnam, a refreshing light beer suited to the climate, served on street corners at low prices.

STAY

Hanoi's Metropole dates to the French colonial era, with interiors featuring wooden floors and whirring ceiling fans. Guests can also visit a rediscovered bunker, where staff and residents sheltered during the bombing of Hanoi in 1972.

EXPERIENCE

Be sure to make a crossing of Long Biên Bridge – blown to pieces by American bombs fifty years ago, the structure has long since been repaired and is a symbol of defiance and pride.

SHOP

Vietnam is renowned for its silk products and just south of the capital you'll find the weaving village of Vạn Phúc Phúc, where stalls are resplendent with colourful scarves and gowns.

A Traveller's Tale

On my visit to Vietnam, I met the artist Do Hien, a man who has spent much of his life painting Hanoi's streets. He welcomed me into his studio to show me sketches of modern city life, including couples waltzing by Hoan Kiem Lake.

'Hanoi is a place that runs in your blood', he said. 'Had I not lived in this city I might not be able to paint like I do.'

There were darker chapters in Hien's collection too. He began his career as a Viet Cong propaganda artist with prints of anti-aircraft guns firing into the skies, but today, he can't paint with the ferocity of his youth.

'I try to remember what I was feeling, but I don't have the anger any more.'

I purchased two of his prints to take home. Whenever I look at them, I think of Hanoi, the lake – and that peaceful day in the studio.

OLIVER SMITH

"A journey from Hanoi to the hinterland is to see Vietnam in all its contradictory glory: both raucous and rustic, exhilarating and eternal"

Right: rice terraces beneath the mountains of Lao Cai; *Opposite:* Turtle Tower on Hoan Kiem Lake in Hanoi

of spices drift in the air. Also among these oases of calm is Hoan Kiem Lake, on which you'll find a little island with a 19th-century temple, enshrined by the surrounding water.

A deeper peace can be found in the mountains to the north-west of Hanoi. A sleeper train from the capital stops short of the Chinese border, where winding roads lead skywards to Sapa. A hill station settled by Vietnam's French colonists, Sapa stands in a spectacular Alpine landscape – the cloud-cloaked summits of the Hoang Lien Son mountain range brooding above, and rice terraces extending below – arranged as neatly as the folds in origami paper. Here and there, water buffalo stumble about rice paddies. Walkers too strike out on the trails, passing bucolic highland villages that Vietnam's minority hill tribes call home.

For many, the defining vision of northern Vietnam lies on the other side of Hanoi. Halong Bay contains thousands of islets rising sheer from the shallows of the Gulf of Tonkin, its geography formed – so legend tells – when a dragon crash-landed here to form a barrier that might protect the Vietnamese homeland. Today, thousands come on charter sailings to nose about the narrow straits and hidden bays. It remains a place seared into national myth; still a gateway guarding the seascapes, summits and cities beyond.

Opposite: a village in the foothills of the Hoang Lien Son mountains

10 Day Itinerary

>

Start your adventure in Hanoi. The capital deserves at least two days for wandering around its temples and museums, and stopping by Ho Chi Minh's mausoleum, where you can see the father of the modern nation in repose.

>>

Early on day three, take a three-hour bus ride east to Bai Chay, the harbour from which most boats depart for Halong Bay. Sailings vary in duration and luxury, but two days is plenty, giving you a chance to moor at Titop Island, and climb the stone steps for a view over the archipelago.

>>>

Halong voyage completed, head back to Hanoi and catch the night train to Lao Cai. Relax in the cool air of Sapa for two days – or work up a sweat ascending misty Fansipan, the 10,312ft (3143m) peak once known as the 'Roof of Indochina'.

>>>>

With your final three days, you might choose to explore more remote parts of these mountains around Ha Giang or ride the legendary Reunification Express to central Vietnam. Here you can stride through the Imperial City of Hue and the colourful merchant's warehouses of Hoi An.

MORE TIME?

Continue south to Hanoi's spirited southern rival, Ho Chi Minh City, aka Saigon.

PRACTICALITIES

GETTING THERE AND AROUND

Though Ho Chi Minh (Saigon) is the nation's main entry point, Hanoi International is served by an ever-broadening range of international flights. The country's reliable railway network runs not just to Sapa, but also to Hue, Danang, Nha Trang and Ho Chi Minh City – there's plenty of sleeper options on board. To get to Halong Bay ports you'll need to take a bus.

WHEN TO GO

October to March is the best time to go to northern Vietnam, when cooler, less humid air makes pacing the streets of Hanoi and trekking around Sapa more pleasant (though don't be surprised by the odd flurry of winter snow). Look out for Tet – the Lunar New Year around January and February sees the whole country on the move, and train and bus tickets can sell out.

THINGS TO NOTE

Wildly divergent climates in northern Vietnam will mean you need to pack for all eventualities – take a waterproof, warm layers and hiking boots for the trails around Sapa, as well as sunglasses, suntan lotion and swimwear for the hot and often humid coastline. *Further information is available at vietnam.travel*

CAMBODIA

Discover Lost Cities

FEW 'LOST CITIES' COME CLOSE to the grandeur of Angkor. While many such places emerge from undergrowth all over the planet, this vision of heaven on Earth, executed in finely chiselled stone, is exceptional. Ease yourself in by watching dawn creep over the Bayon temple, fruit bats swooping past monumental faces of the Buddhist deity of compassion. Spend the day wandering the many other ruins, then catch sunset over the *prangs* (spires) of Angkor Wat, the grandest temple of them all. Southeast Asia's most famous site is just the grand front door, however, to a profusion of ruined cities, scattered across the jungles of northern Cambodia. Calmer insights into the country's past await in the peaceful ruins of Banteay Srei and Beng Mealea, enveloped by jungle north of Siem Reap, and amongst the silent stones of Koh Ker and Prasat Preah Vihear to the northeast. Spend the night here in a simple homestay for a deep immersion into Cambodian village life.

AT A GLANCE

EAT
Amok trey, Cambodian fish curry, is infused with coconut and turmeric.

DRINK
Angkor Beer, with Angkor Wat on the label, is the nation's favourite.

PRACTICALITIES

Rather than flying from Phnom Penh to Angkor, take the scenic route by boat or bus for a window onto rural life in Cambodia.

INDONESIA

Delve Into the Heart
of the Coral Triangle

AT A GLANCE

EAT

Enjoy fresh-caught barbecued fish with spicy *sambal* chilli paste.

DRINK

Nothing quenches a post-dive thirst like a fresh local coconut water.

PRACTICALITIES

Visit between October and April for calm waters, mostly clear skies and the best visibility for underwater exploration.

'**THE SEA, ONCE IT CASTS ITS SPELL**, holds one in its net of wonder forever', Jacques Cousteau once mused. It's anyone guess whether Raja Ampat was front-of-mind when the legendary scuba diver shared this famous quote. But the sentiment is certainly true of the now-rare marine ecosystem found in West Papua's Raja Ampat archipelago, where nutrient-rich waters and fast-moving currents create an ideal environment for a staggering diversity of marine life, including nearly 600 species of reef-building corals. Naturally resilient to coral bleaching and largely spared from destructive fishing practices, the region's tropical waters are a scuba diver's holy grail – whether you're into tiny, technicolour nudibranchs or enormous manta rays and whale sharks, they're all here. Commonly visited on a live-aboard cruise (with options for snorkellers), the jungle-covered islands of Raja Ampat also house a handful of dive resorts that are perfect for visitors who prefer a dry-land base with coral reefs just steps from their bungalow door.

THAILAND

Travel Back *in* Time

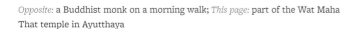
Opposite: a Buddhist monk on a morning walk; *This page:* part of the Wat Maha That temple in Ayutthaya

SOME TRAVELLERS TO THAILAND set their sights on the beaches and islands. For others, it's all about the food and national parks. But history buffs plan trips around the meandering railway line linking Bangkok to Chiang Mai, which whisks sightseers from ancient capital to ancient capital in air-conditioned comfort.

Bangkok is where the royal story unfolds most vividly. It's a newcomer as the capital of Thailand – the time-scarred ruins of previous capitals lie scattered around the countryside, recalling centuries of dynastic history in the one nation in Southeast Asia never colonised by European powers. In the streets of Krung Thep Maha Nakhon (Great City of Angels), to use Bangkok's official title, the air is perfumed by durians, jasmine and spices, and food carts and fruit markets jostle for space with backpacker bars and sacred shrines constructed during the golden age of Rattanakosin, the island capital of King Rama I (r 1782–1809).

When people talk about the 'golden East', this is what they mean. Everywhere, magnificent *wat* (Buddhist monasteries) spill out of gilded courtyards, and royal palaces shimmer with mirrored mosaics and gleaming gold leaf. It's a richness of decoration that intoxicates the senses – indeed, Thailand burns through tonnes of gold leaf every year, applying it in lavish layers to stupas, statues and temple spires.

A Traveller's Tale

You never forget your first bite of Bangkok. It's a city that grabs visitors by both ears and beats them into submission, but also a place of remarkable serenity. Arriving for the first time in the 1990s, I spent blissful days rising before dawn to catch the sunrise with novice monks in the prayer halls of ancient Buddhist monasteries. Few cities anywhere feel quite so alive with energy and belief.

JOE BINDLOSS

AT A GLANCE

EAT
Thailand's spectacular street food is best experienced in the busy night markets fringing Chiang Mai's medieval walls.

DRINK
Quench your thirst with fruit smoothies, prepared using an astounding array of tropical fruits.

STAY
Staying in old-fashioned guesthouses in traditional wooden homes offers the chance to sample delicious Thai home-cooking.

EXPERIENCE
Explore monasteries, markets and palaces using Bangkok's atmospheric Chao Phraya Express river ferry.

The backstory of the Thai monarchy unfolds to the north of Bangkok. In 14th-century Ayutthaya, the remains of monasteries, monumental Buddhas and soaring *prangs* (reliquary towers) from Thailand's second capital lie in a curve of the Chao Phraya River, stripped of gold and stucco and partly reclaimed by greenery. Further north in Sukhothai, Thailand's first capital, peaceful parklands are punctuated by more ruined temples, huge Buddhas and lotus-bud *chedis* (stupas) – a perfect antidote to the urban crush of Bangkok. A different royal tale unfolds in Chiang Mai, once a proudly independent kingdom, with its own ruined capital on the city fringes at Wiang Kum Kam. In between learning to make green curry and pad thai in the city's famed cooking schools, you can wander back-lanes dotted with the remains of stupas, soaking up seven humbling centuries of history.

Opposite: open for business at Bangkok's Amphawa floating market

Eight Day Itinerary

>

Begin the journey back to imperial Siam in Bangkok, with three days of temple hopping, palace touring and riverboating around historic Rattanakosin Island. Block out one afternoon for a trip to Chatuchak, Thailand's most mesmerising weekend market.

>>

A 1½-hour train ride gets you to the plain of ruined temples in atmospheric Ayutthaya, serving up a rewarding experience of small-town life. Take a turn around Ayutthaya's museums, from the gold-filled Chao Sam Phraya National Museum to the quirky Million Toy Museum.

>>>

Continue by train to Phitsanulok (3½ hours) and take a one-hour bus ride to Sukhothai, where you'll easily fill two history packed days visiting temples by bicycle and staring in awe at house-size Buddha statues.

>>>>

Returning to Phitsanulok, take the train to Chiang Mai (seven hours) and settle in for cooking courses, full-flavoured night markets, rainbow-coloured prayer halls and strolls around the sleepy ruins of Wiang Kum Kam.

MORE TIME?

Head southwest from Bangkok to historic Phetchaburi, used as a summertime escape by King Rama IV and crammed with palaces and gilded *wat*.

PRACTICALITIES

GETTING THERE AND AROUND
Bangkok's Suvarnabhumi Airport has connections worldwide. Explore the capital by taxi, BTS and MRT trains, or the ferries of the Chao Phraya Express. For travel to Ayutthaya, Sukhothai and Chiang Mai, book train travel ahead at stations (or via 12go.asia).

WHEN TO GO
Northern Thailand sees blue skies from November to April, but it's hot and humid year-round, so pack accordingly (a sun hat and battery-powered hand fan will come in useful).

THINGS TO NOTE
Not all Thai dishes are spicy, but those that are can be incendiary – don't be afraid to step outside your comfort zone, but order a sweet fruit juice on the side to dampen the chilli heat.

Further information is available at tourismthailand.org

SRI LANKA

Seek Out Ancient Cities *by* Road *and* Rail

SRI LANKA PACKS INFINITE WONDER into one small space. Golden beaches, pounding surf, wildlife-filled national parks, emerald tea plantations and the toppled ruins of ancient cities tumbling from the jungle. The island formerly known as Ceylon measures just 435km by 240km (270 miles by 150 miles), so nothing is too far from those jewel-bright beaches. Indeed, you may be tempted to spend your whole trip soaking in the bathtub-warm Indian Ocean. But be brave and pack away the beach towel – inland from the sand lie the intricately carved ruins of a succession of ancient cities, abandoned to the forest before the first Europeans set eyes on the cinnamon isle.

The adventure begins on the atmospheric hill railway from Colombo, which climbs through lush vegetation to Kandy, where Sri Lanka's most sacred shrine holds what may well be a genuine tooth of the Buddha. Step even further back in time at Dambulla, where cave temples that have been used by pilgrims since the 1st century BCE explode in a riot of primary colours.

A Traveller's Tale

Walking onto the plain of stupas at Anuradhapura was like stepping into a story book. In my case, I had the actual book, a pamphlet of Sri Lankan legends my grandfather purchased in the 1920s while visiting as a merchant sailor. The sense of connection to the past was tangible – pilgrims still adorn the *dagobas* with bolts of cloth, as they did 2000 years ago when these stupas were new and stucco-covered.

JOE BINDLOSS

AT A GLANCE

EAT
Curry and rice is Sri Lanka's national dish, so expect a wonderful spread of whatever the cook has available.

DRINK
Tasty *toddy* is prepared from fermented palm flowers and served fresh or distilled into potent *arrack*.

STAY
Bed down in a family-run guesthouse, enjoying fiery home-cooked flavours from the kitchen.

EXPERIENCE
Spot elephants, crocodiles and tropical birds at Minneriya National Park, an hour from Sigiriya.

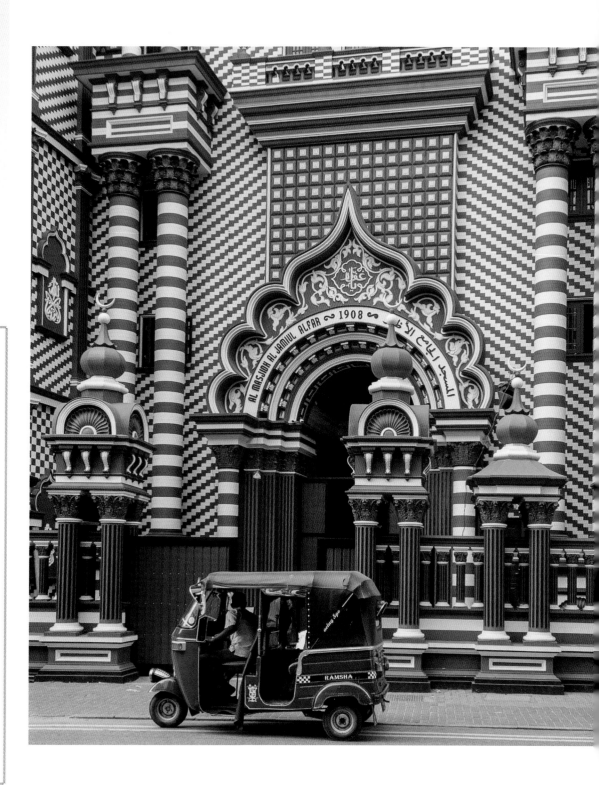

Opposite: a steaming pot of Jaffna crab curry; *This page:* the decorative exterior of Jami Ul-Alfar mosque in Colombo

King Valagamba took refuge in these caves after being driven from his capital by a jealous rival, and he set his artisans to work creating some of Sri Lanka's most remarkable carvings and murals in thanks for his salvation.

Just north lies one of the most spectacular sights of them all – lofty Sigiriya, where a breathless climb up a sheer-faced outcrop reveals the remains of the ancient royal seat of King Kashyapa I. Take in the views, then continue northeast to Polonnaruwa, capital of Sri Lanka for three centuries from 1070 CE. This is ancient architecture with atmosphere – on all sides, chiselled masonry bursts from the undergrowth and monumental Buddhas gaze out serenely from centuries-old brick stupas. Polonnaruwa was preceded by the country's first capital, fabulous Anuradhapura, whose 2000-year-old stupas are still vital, vibrant places of worship. To visit on a full moon *poya* day – watching white-clad pilgrims pay their respects at the Bodhi tree grown from a cutting from the original tree under which Buddha attained enlightenment – is to plug into the very soul of Sri Lanka.

This page top: the Sigiriya Lion Rock fortress soars dramatically over the landscape

PRACTICALITIES

GETTING THERE AND AROUND

Bandaranaike International Airport is closer to Negombo than Colombo, so it's easy to head straight to the sand. To reach the ancient cities, book ahead for the train ride from Colombo to Kandy, then zip around by local bus. Alternatively, hire a car and driver and be chauffeured all the way.

WHEN TO GO

The ancient cities are mostly dry from January to March and May to September, outside the country's twin monsoons. At any time of year, expect warm temperatures and high humidity.

THINGS TO NOTE

A pair of binoculars is a worthy addition to your packing list – rainbow-coloured tropical birds frequent the forests around the ancient cities, from pied hornbills and vivid Sri Lanka blue magpies to jewel-like kingfishers. *Further information is available at srilanka.travel*

10 Day Itinerary

>

Arriving at Bandaranaike International Airport, start the trip with a day on the sand at Negombo, then head into Colombo for fine dining, colonial-era history and the delights of the National Museum. Trundle up to Kandy on the hill railway and pay your respects at the Temple of the Sacred Tooth Relic.

>>

Delve into the local food and culture for a day or two – perhaps taking in a show of traditional Sri Lankan dance – before taking a two-hour bus ride to Dambulla. Gasp at the vividly colourful carvings inside the cave temples, then take the bus on to Sigiriya (45 minutes), ready for a first-light visit to the ruins on the rock.

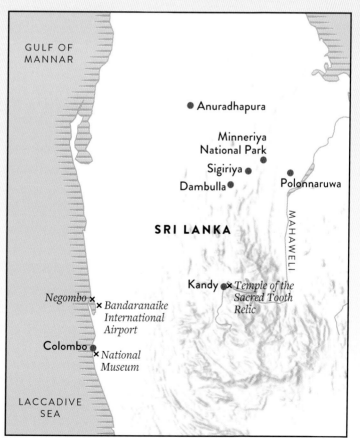

>>>

Another two-hour bus ride brings spectacular Polonnaruwa into view; devote two days to exploring supersized Buddhas and toppled temples, and consider an elephant-spotting day trip to nearby Minneriya National Park.

>>>>

End with a three-hour ride to the most stunning ancient city of all – two days is the minimum to get the best from Anuradhapura's towering *dagobas* (stupas) and tumbledown temples.

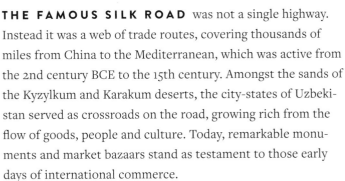

UZBEKISTAN

Travel *the* Silk Road

Opposite: a traditional teahouse in the Uzbek city of Kokand; *This page:* plenty to browse in a local bazaar

THE FAMOUS SILK ROAD was not a single highway. Instead it was a web of trade routes, covering thousands of miles from China to the Mediterranean, which was active from the 2nd century BCE to the 15th century. Amongst the sands of the Kyzylkum and Karakum deserts, the city-states of Uzbekistan served as crossroads on the road, growing rich from the flow of goods, people and culture. Today, remarkable monuments and market bazaars stand as testament to those early days of international commerce.

As the evening breeze carries the call to prayer, fading sunlight sparkles on the blue majolica tiles of Shah-i-Zinda's mausoleums. But even this Samarkand marvel is overshadowed by the monumental *medressahs* (Islamic schools) of the nearby Registan – where students once hurried to class, artisans now produce miniature paintings, earthenware and carpets.

While Samarkand's monuments are found within a modern city, many find Bukhara more charming thanks to its sense of

completeness – in the quiet hours, it almost feels as if a ghost of the Silk Road is just out of focus or right around the next curving alley. In legendary domed bazaars here, bartering for goods carries on into the modern era, as does the seemingly endless stretch of ceramic-dish vendors beneath the fortress walls in the shadow of the Kalon Minaret. But in the *chaikanaas* (teahouses), where relationships are built on squat wooden platforms over endless pots of tea or a shared platter of steaming *plov* (rice and meat), the passage of time seems to disappear a little further with every sip.

A Traveller's Tale

I didn't imagine a chance Bukhara teahouse interaction would lead to a week of dancing, singing and untranslated congratulatory speeches. Uzbekistan is a hospitable place, but Sadriddin's invitation to join him at a wedding the next day was something else – as were three more such invitations later that week, where he sang and played the tambur. And me? Well, I was just with the band.

STEPHEN LIOY

AT A GLANCE

EAT

Plov is the must-try dish, a bubbling cauldron of rice simmering with rich meat and spices.

DRINK

Green tea, Uzbekistan's favourite drink, is found everywhere, all the time.

STAY

Bukhara's boutique hotels, converted from restored *medressahs*, are among the most memorable in Central Asia.

EXPERIENCE

The crumbling desert fortresses of the Elliq Qala, beyond Khiva, impress with faded grandeur.

This page: the UNESCO-listed Ichon Qala, the old walled town of Khiva

On the edge of the Kyzylkum, Khiva's location made it a trading hub for one thing above all – enslaved people captured in raids on the very Silk Road caravans that made the region rich. The last of the three great cities to be folded into the Russian Empire, in large part due to this dangerous location, the walled inner section is preserved to a remarkable degree. Stretching out from the end of the long circular staircase that leads to the top of the Islom Hoja Minaret, the Old Town disappears like a mirage into the sands beyond.

PRACTICALITIES

GETTING THERE
AND AROUND

Tashkent airport is the country's international hub, and the city is well connected by fast trains to the major Silk Road destinations. Try to book at least a week in advance, but if trains are sold out there are also domestic flights and inter-city shared taxis to fall back on.

WHEN TO GO

September to November is the ideal time to travel to Uzbekistan's Silk Road cities - the scorching high temperatures of summer are gone but the cold hasn't yet set in, and the bounty of fruit harvest around this time mean there's always something fresh and sweet in the bazaars.

THINGS TO NOTE

Citizens of 90 countries can enter Uzbekistan for 30 days, though notably the United States is not on this list.
For further information visit uzbekistan.travel

One Week Itinerary

>

Spend a day upon arrival in Tashkent to visit Chorsu Bazaar and the Khast Imom religious complex, then hop on a train for the renowned Silk Road cities.

>>

Samarkand is two to three hours and Bukhara four to six from Tashkent, both warranting two-to three-day stops. The former's Registan Square is the Silk Road postcard of the country (though the Shah-i-Zinda mausoleums beat it for pure mosaicked beauty), while Bukhara's quiet Old Town streets are as much a draw as any single sight.

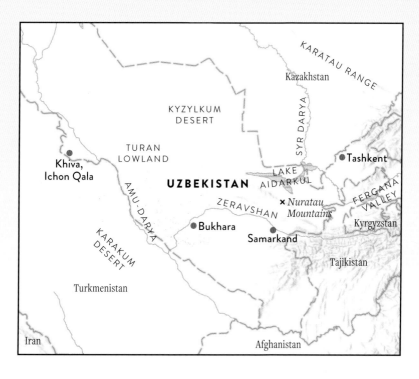

>>>

Spare a couple more days for Khiva – six hours by train from Samarkand, though 2024 saw a new high-speed line drop that to two. The Ichon Qala walled city is the best-preserved medieval town in the country – most beautiful as the fading sun lights the tiled minarets.

MORE TIME?

Travel between Samarkand and Bukhara via the Nuratau Mountains, where community based tourism initiatives welcome travellers into local homes for guided hikes on easy shepherds' paths to abandoned villages and high pastures studded with lakes.

Enjoy Paradise *in the* Andaman Islands

IF PARADISE WAS A BEACH, it'd likely be found in the islands of Thailand's Andaman Sea. Here, jungle-draped limestone pinnacles shoot out of sparkling cyan waters, protecting hidden bays fringed by golden beaches. This is the Thailand made famous by *The Beach* – its Maya Bay setting is now open to visitors again following a years-long restoration project designed to protect its natural beauty into the future. But the Phi Phi Islands aren't the only place to revel in this surreal seascape. Within easy reach of Phuket and Krabi, the larger islands of Phang Nga Bay offer sojourns at luxury resorts and traditional village homestays, feasting on the seafood bounty hauled in by local fishers. Further south, Ko Lanta pairs superb beaches with one of the nation's most responsible elephant experiences, while the more remote Trang Islands transport visitors back to the Thailand of yesteryear, where enjoying a jungle-backed beach all to yourself is still well within the realm of possibility.

AT A GLANCE

EAT
Yellow-crab curry is a quintessential regional dish worth sampling.

DRINK
Wash down a spicy meal with a fresh mango smoothie.

PRACTICALITIES

The November to April dry season is the best time to visit the Andaman Islands. *For more information, visit tourismthailand.org*

NEPAL

Trek *the* Serene Langtang Valley

AT A GLANCE

EAT
Simple, nourishing *dal bhaat* (rice and lentils) is the fuel of the Himalaya hiker.

DRINK
Chhaang is Nepal's traditional grain-based wine.

PRACTICALITIES
To trek Langtang, you'll need a local guide, a Trekkers Information Management System card, and a permit for Langtang National Park.

NOWHERE HAS TREKKING quite like Nepal. Breathless trails strain over the highest mountains on Earth, and the reward for a hard day's hiking is a slice of apple pie and a cold beer by a yak-dung fire. You'll need a permit to take on the most popular trails, but beyond that, the sky is literally the limit. Everest (Sagarmatha) and the Annapurna massif offer weeks of rugged hiking on the shoulders of giants, but for a compact taste of Nepal's mountain magic, head for the scenic Langtang Valley. Starting by bus from Kathmandu, this seven-day loop will marinade you in the majesty of the mountains, linking dizzying high passes, ancient Buddhist monasteries and yak pastures guarded by a curtain wall of snow peaks. Best of all, you'll immerse yourself in the culture of the Himalaya, staying in rustic village teahouses and carb-cramming for the trails with hearty, healthy meals. Bring extra camera cards – you'll need them.

Oceania

AUSTRALIA

Embark *on a* Classic East Coast Road Trip

Opposite: coastal scenes around Newcastle, New South Wales; *This page:* a classic Aussie pie, baked in Surry Hills; *Previous page:* Sydney Harbour and Opera House

THE SWEEP OF COASTLINE from Sydney north to Byron Bay is sublime. Few sections of Australia's seaboard have had a more defining impact on the nation's road-trip culture than this stretch of the country's east coast. When American filmmaker Bruce Brown (of *Endless Summer* fame) brought Byron's now-iconic surf breaks to the silver screen in the 1961 film *Surfing Hollow Days*, car engines rumbled to life across Sydney. With surfboards strapped to roofs and sleeping bags stuffed into backpacks, the east coast surf trip was born. Today, a 472-mile (760km) motorway bypasses nearly every town between the two urban hubs, yet travellers continue to trace the original, winding route taken by the wave-chasers who put this classic journey on the map.

Directly north of Sydney, golden sandstone cliffs frame the sapphire beaches and seaside national parks of the Central Coast region. The road here quickly flattens out, travelling by scenic inlets and past sparkling lakes up into the heart of Newcastle, a seaside city reborn, while the cellar doors of Australia's oldest wine region, the Hunter Valley, beckon just a short drive inland. The immense bay at the mouth of the Karuah River sets the

A Traveller's Tale

It was still dark when my alarm went off, and I was tempted to stay in bed. But I'd never hiked to the summit of Tomaree Head in Port Stephens before, and I figured sunrise was the time to do it. Within 15 minutes I was striding up the steepest trail in Tomaree National Park, which ribbons along the coast towards the southern hemisphere's largest shifting sand dunes in the Worimi Conservation Lands, north of Newcastle. The calming scent of the Australian bush filled my nose as I followed the trail up past granite boulders and angophora forest, sweat beading on my forehead as I raced against the sun. It beat me by a whisker in the end, but I wasn't bothered, having reached the top just in time to see the first rays of light illuminate the almighty splash of a breaching whale in a halo of silver.

SARAH REID

AT A GLANCE

EAT
Stopping into a small-town bakery for a pie or sausage roll is a rite of passage on this road trip. Tucking into takeaway fish and chips by the seafront is another favourite pastime.

DRINK
Stock up on Hunter Valley wines from the region's vineyards to enjoy during journey overnights, and seek out independent coffee shops in coastal towns for the best brews.

STAY
There's excellent camping in coastal national parks in the region. A growing number of retro-inspired boutique hotels, meanwhile, are loaded with beach-holiday nostalgia.

EXPERIENCE
Make a pit stop in Coffs Harbour to snap an obligatory selfie in front of the Big Banana, the most famous of Australia's Big Things.

SHOP
Held weekly in most large coastal towns, farmers markets offer an atmospheric opportunity to sample locally grown and harvested produce, and immerse in the local community.

"Sydney feels very far away as backroads weave through flooded gum forests, skirt a string of lakes and follow the contours of an ancient landscape"

Left: kangaroos bound across Hunter Valley, Australia's oldest wine region

scene for a picturesque sojourn in Port Stephens, with walking trails, gorgeous beaches, koalas and history to uncover in its headland national park.

Sydney begins to feel very far away as backroads weave through flooded gum forests, skirt a string of lakes and follow the contours of an ancient landscape, shaped by long-dormant volcanoes and a 300-million-year-old continental collision that formed the Great Dividing Range rising up to the west. To the east, the sight of humpback and southern right whales is common between May and November as these gentle giants frolic in the ocean on their annual migration. Kangaroos and wallabies graze contentedly in coastal parks as white-bellied sea eagles ride the currents above, and brush-turkeys scratch along

the rainforest floor. Echoes of penal settlements, WWII history and abandoned industries linger in shore-hugging cities and towns, while Aboriginal cultures continue to pulse through the land. Interpretive signage offers some insights, but the stories of this landscape are best shared by its Traditional Custodians, who lead an array of tours along the coast.

Continuing north, a seemingly endless series of side roads invite travellers to uncover epic surf spots, wilderness trails and charming hinterland towns including boho Bellingen and pretty Bangalow. And then you reach your destination, Byron Bay, the genetically blessed beach town that now offers a delicious food scene and much more, alongside the great waves that made it famous.

Opposite: paddleboarding the clear waters near the town of Byron Bay

10 Day Itinerary

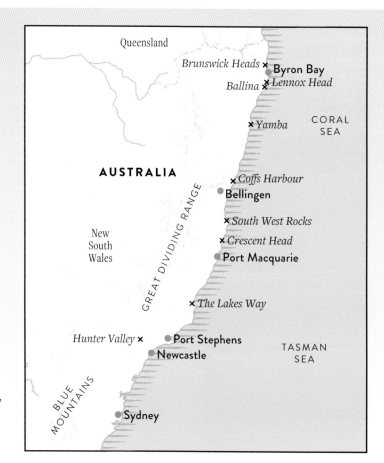

>

Kick-start your road trip in the New South Wales capital, checking out Sydney's big-ticket sights, seeing and being seen on its beaches, bar-hopping, shopping and dining out to your heart's content.

>>

Two hours to the north of Sydney is the historic steel city of Newcastle, now home to a blossoming culinary scene of its own. Detour inland to the verdant vineyards of the Hunter Valley for tastings and top meals before making an easy trip back to the coast to explore Port Stephens. Then follow the scenic Lakes Way along the coast before rejoining the Pacific Motorway en route to Port Macquarie, to visit a koala hospital and enjoy oceanside walks.

>>>

Consider side trips to the surf town of Crescent Head and to South West Rocks to see its colonial jail (or go diving) before heading a short way inland to the historic hinterland town of Bellingen.

>>>>

Round off the route by cruising through Coffs Harbour, Yamba, Ballina and Lennox Head on your way to Byron Bay, where more sun, surf, walks and some of regional Australia's hottest restaurants await.

MORE TIME?

From Byron Bay, travel 20 minutes up the motorway to riverside Brunswick Heads for a more bucolic beach-town vibe.

PRACTICALITIES

GETTING THERE AND AROUND

Most travellers will arrive into Sydney airport, from where trains run frequently to the city centre (13 minutes). Or rent a car at the airport and begin your journey straight from there (ensure parking is available at your first night's accommodation) – one-way car hire is available with drop-off at Gold Coast Airport, a 45-minute drive north of Byron.

WHEN TO GO

New South Wales' North Coast is a year-round destination, though the spring and autumn months (March to May and September to November) offer some of the best beach weather, and fewer crowds outside of Easter and the late September/October school holidays. Winter swells typically generate bigger surf, while onshore winds are more common during summer.

THINGS TO NOTE

Comfortable walking shoes and a jacket to protect from rain and wind are essentials on this road trip. While the winter months are typically drier, the weather can change at any time and evenings can be cool, even in summer. A picnic set also comes in handy – most coastal parks have free barbecues.
For more information see visitnsw.com

AUSTRALIA

Embrace *the* Spirituality *of* Uluṟu

THERE'S NOWHERE ELSE ON EARTH quite like
Uluṟu. It's almost impossible to look away from the vast,
sandstone monolith, rising as it does from the red sands of the
desert like an apparition, riven with crevices and animated by
ancient stories from its Traditional Owners, the Anangu. At
sunrise and sunset Uluṟu appears almost luminous. After a rare
desert rainstorm, rivulets seemingly of molten silver stream
down its many faces. And in the long daylight hours, it glowers out across the desert over which it presides, moody and
magnificent. Uluṟu is part of a national park, which it shares
with Kata Tjuṯa, a series of nearly 40 granite domes in weirdly
wonderful forms that dominate the horizon for miles in every
direction. Together, Uluṟu and Kata Tjuṯa carry deep spiritual
significance; learn more on walks led by Anangu guides or
at the Uluṟu-Kata Tjuṯa Cultural Centre. And together these
two geological marvels form the compelling centrepiece of
Australia's storied Red Centre.

AT A GLANCE

EAT
Fine-dine under the stars at Sounds
of Silence.

DRINK
Enjoy a glass of Australian
Chardonnay or Cabernet Sauvignon
at the Uluṟu sunset site.

PRACTICALITIES

Most walks close by 11am if the
forecast temperature passes 36°C
(97°F) so, if you can, visit May-
September when such highs are
unlikely.

AUSTRALIA

Walk *in the* Footsteps *of* Lutruwita's (Tasmania's) Traditional Custodians

AT A GLANCE

EAT
Get a taste for muttonbird, a traditional Palawa protein.

DRINK
Match refined bush tucker with fine Tasmanian wine.

PRACTICALITIES

Wukalina Walk (wukalinawalk.com.au) departs Launceston up to five times monthly from September to April or May.

AUSTRALIA'S WILD AND RUGGED landscapes aren't only layered with natural beauty, but also threaded with ancestral stories. Storytelling is at the heart of wukalina Walk, a four-day, three-night Palawa (Aboriginal person) guided hike that immerses guests in the soul-stirring scenery of Wukalina (Mt William National Park) in the Larapuna (Bay of Fires) region of northeastern Lutruwita (Tasmania). Along the way, guests sleep in architect-designed domed huts modelled on a traditional standing camp surrounded by coastal heathland, sample bush tucker that has sustained local people for millennia, learn about ancestral connections to the land and sea, and enjoy bush yarns by the light of a flickering fire – with just two main days of hiking, there's plenty of time to chat. Small group sizes of up to 10 add an intimacy to the experience, which for many is transformative. And not only for visitors. The hike also provides meaningful opportunities for a new generation of Palawa to share culture on Country (traditional lands).

AUSTRALIA

Spot Rare Animals *on* Kangaroo Island

WILDLIFE SIGHTINGS IN AUSTRALIA don't come better than spotting a koala. On Kangaroo Island (KI), it's not uncommon to see half a dozen curled up in one tree. Just a short ferry ride (or flight) from the South Australian mainland, KI is a magnet for wildlife watchers. Many come to see its robust koala population, others its eponymous kangaroos. Like much of the wildlife on the island – which is also a stronghold for the beautifully patterned Rosenberg's goanna – these species have evolved in isolation to become a subspecies of their mainland relatives. But these critters aren't the only highlight. National parks cover more than 40% of the 1700 sq mile (4405 sq km) island, now recovering well following devastating 2019–20 bushfires. KI is also well known for its gourmet produce, from Bordeaux-style wine blends to native honey. And there are walking trails to explore and sea-lion-studded beaches to soak up, lapped by the dreamy blues of the Southern Ocean.

AT A GLANCE

EAT
The island's seafood bounty includes fresh oysters and melt-in-your-mouth kingfish.

DRINK
Sip award-winning craft gin and excellent local wine at cellar doors.

PRACTICALITIES

The best way to see Kangaroo Island is on a self-drive adventure or an organised tour.
For more information, visit tourkangarooisland.com.au

AUSTRALIA

Sip Victoria's King Valley

AT A GLANCE

EAT
The restaurant at Chrismont has arguably the best views of the valley.

DRINK
King River Brewing serves hoppy alternatives to the grape.

PRACTICALITIES

Private tours from Whitfield cover King Valley but your own transport offers more options. Direct trains from Melbourne to Wangaratta take two hours.

WHEN ITALIAN IMMIGRANTS FIRST arrived in Australia, many made their way north of Melbourne to an area known as King Valley in Victoria's High Country. Here, families introduced many of their cherished traditions from home. They created vineyards of traditional Italian grape varieties, including Sangiovese, Nebbiolo and Glera, which is used to make prosecco. Walnut trees were planted and Italian sausages and cheeses produced. Today, the King Valley is a superb setting for a wine-tasting weekend at cellar doors still owned by some of those Italian families such as Pizzini and Corsini (owners of La Cantina). More recent openings include the Star family's welcoming Red Feet Wines. At the north end of the Prosecco Road, drop in on some of the region's world-class producers or sample a tasting menu at the Brown Brothers restaurant. You're also on the doorstep of Beechworth, which has more great restaurants, wineries and pubs. Burn off calories on the alpine region's hiking and biking trails. Book ahead for accommodation in November during La Dolce Vita, King Valley's annual festival of food and wine.

Dive *into the* Southern Great Barrier Reef

THE SIGHT OF THE Great Barrier Reef is a salve for the soul. And that's before you've been dazzled by the spectacle of colour, texture and activity below the surface. Most visitors to the reef stick to the northern hubs of Cairns and the Whitsunday Islands, but some of the most rewarding and low-impact opportunities to experience this World Heritage wonder occur in the Southern Great Barrier Reef. Rehabilitated from a barren coral cay left to feral goats, Lady Elliot Island is now one of Australia's foremost eco-resorts. A short hop to the north, uninhabited Lady Musgrave Island provides a wild backdrop for camping and day trips to its idyllic coral lagoon; you can even upgrade to an eco-certified glamping experience on a floating pontoon. Most tours operate from the mainland hub of Bundaberg in a relaxed agricultural region that is also home to the state-of-the-art Mon Repos turtle education centre, which runs turtle viewing tours during the nesting season (November to March).

AT A GLANCE

EAT
Slurp homemade ice-cream and other local produce at Bundaberg farm gates.

DRINK
A trip to Bundaberg isn't complete without some of its eponymous rum.

PRACTICALITIES

Bundaberg is a 4½-hr drive north from Brisbane, or a one-hour flight. Aim to stay in the seaside suburb of Bargara.

AUSTRALIA

Swim *with* Whale Sharks *at* Ningaloo

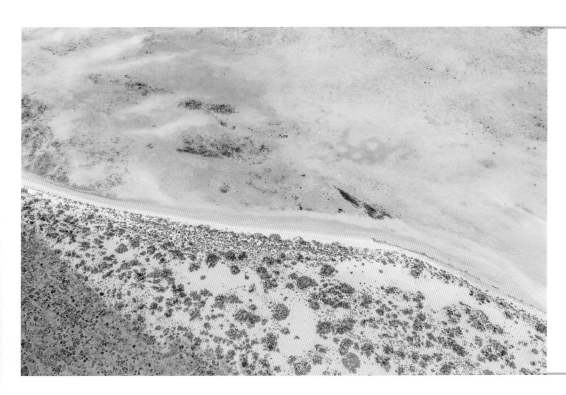

AT A GLANCE

EAT
Dig into Exmouth-caught tiger prawns and snapper.

EXPERIENCE
Join conservation-focused whale shark swims from Exmouth or Coral Bay.

PRACTICALITIES

Stay in Coral Bay, Exmouth or Cape Range National Park. Qantas connects Perth and Learmonth, the closest airport to the reef. Further information at *westernaustralia.com*

WHOA, THAT'S ONE BIG FISH. There's no place on Earth like the Ningaloo Reef for popping on snorkel and flippers to frantically swim alongside a whale shark – close enough to glimpse its distinctive patterning, mesh-fine gills and gaping mouth hoovering up plankton and krill. Swimming with a gentle giant as big as a minibus and weighing up to 20 tonnes is an experience you'll be talking about forever. Spreading across some 2300 sq miles (6000 sq km), the remote Ningaloo Reef in Western Australia is one of the largest near-shore coral reefs on the planet. Though every bit as beautiful as the Great Barrier Reef, it receives just a trickle of the visitors. By day, it's just you and the deep blue, as you glide above the corals aboard a catamaran and slip into glassy turquoise water to swim with dancing manta rays, chilled-out turtles, dugongs, sharks, whales and shoals of tropical fish straight out of *Finding Nemo*. By night, a galaxy of stars twinkles overhead.

NEW ZEALAND/AOTEAROA

Experience Māori Culture *in* Northland

Opposite: Māori meeting house at Waitangi Treaty Grounds; *This page:* the lighthouse at Cape Reinga, New Zealand's northern tip

WELCOME TO THE BIRTHPLACE of modern New Zealand and to an essential Kiwi road trip. Begin at the Waitangi Treaty Grounds, where in 1840 chiefs representing New Zealand's Māori tribes signed a covenant with the British Crown, laying the foundations for the country also known as Aotearoa. Guided tours, infused with *tikanga* (Māori customary practices), explore the site's intricate wooden carvings and *tukutuku* (woven panels) amid the spiritual half-light of Te Whare Rūnanga, a traditional meeting house erected for the treaty's centenary in 1940. Cultural performances, infused with energy, humour and heavenly harmonies, begin with a traditional *powhiri* (Māori welcome) and include the *haka*, the stirring challenge performed by the All Blacks rugby team.

On New Zealand's northern tip, Cape Reinga/Te Rerenga Wairua is regarded by Māori as the traditional departure point for the souls of the dead when they embark on a final journey back to Hawaiki, the legendary Polynesian homeland. Follow the 0.6 mile (1km) trail from the car park to the cape's lighthouse,

an often windy walk thanks to competing breezes gusting in from both the Tasman Sea and the Pacific Ocean. Where the two meet, off the sandy arc of Spirits Bay/Piwhane, swells surge from the west and the east to produce crashing waves up to 32ft (10m) high.

A Traveller's Tale

Four decades after visiting Waipoua Forest with my parents, I'm now the one steering carefully around bush-shaded serpentine curves. My dad and I stroll on a verdant boardwalk to Tāne Mahuta (Lord of the Forest), the biggest tree amongst many. Effortlessly confirming its longevity, it soars to 60ft (18m) and has a girth of 52ft (16m). It's now also a poignant memory of a final, special road trip with my parents.

BRETT ATKINSON

AT A GLANCE

EAT
Enjoy local Orongo Bay oysters on the waterfront verandah at Russell's historic Duke of Marlborough Hotel.

DRINK
Try Northland-brewed craft beers from Waipū-based McLeods Brewery at Hone's Garden in Russell.

STAY
Relax in a self-contained apartment at GEMS Seaside Lodge near the surf in sleepy Ahipara.

EXPERIENCE
Bounce around Waitangi Mountain Bike Park on forested trails named after Waitangi's Māori heritage.

A sheltered anchorage away from the roiling surf of the west coast, Hokianga Harbour is reputedly where legendary Polynesian navigator Kupe first made landfall in Aotearoa over a thousand years ago. Towering sand dunes frame the harbour's narrow entrance, and the arrival and subsequent return of Kupe across the South Pacific back to Polynesia is recounted at Opononi's Manea Footprints of Kupe Experience. The multimedia and multisensory experience incorporates another spirited performance and more stellar harmonies from descendants of the ocean-crossing explorer. South in the Waipoua Forest, the local Te Roroa *iwi* (tribe) conduct intimate and spiritual after-dark experiences amid the imposing kauri trees of Northland's largest stand of native bush. Māori legends and *mātauranga* (traditional Māori knowledge) combine with a visit to Te Matua Ngahere, (Father of the Forest), a massive kauri tree that's up to 3000 years old.

Opposite: Tāne Mahuta, a giant kauri tree in the Waipoua Forest

One Week Itinerary

>

Head north from Auckland, stopping at Whangārei to visit the Wairau Māori Art Gallery at the Hundertwasser Art Centre. It's then another hour to Paihia in the Bay of Islands, a total drive of around three hours. Stay in Paihia for three nights, a good base for exploring Waitangi. Cross by ferry to sleepy Russell/Kororāreka. This was New Zealand's first capital from 1840 to 1841.

>>

From the Bay of Islands, travel three hours north to Cape Reinga/Te Rerenga, New Zealand's northernmost point, before continuing 90 minutes back south to overnight in the surf settlement of Ahipara.

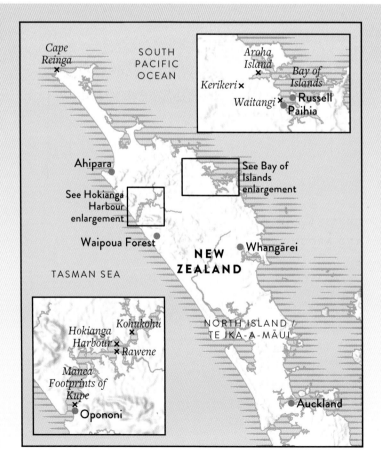

>>>

Negotiating the vehicle ferry across the Hokianga Harbour from Kohukohu to Rawene, it's a two-hour drive from Ahipara to Opononi. Spend two nights visiting Manea Footprints of Kupe, and experiencing the Waipoua Forest with Footprints Waipoua. From Opononi, it's around four hours back to Auckland.

MORE TIME?

Spend a night at Aroha Island near Kerikeri, embarking on an after-dark forest walk to hear, and maybe see, kiwi, New Zealand's national bird.

PRACTICALITIES

GETTING THERE AND AROUND

Around three hours south of Waitangi and the Bay of Islands, Auckland is New Zealand's main international transport hub with regular flights from Australia, North America and Asia. InterCity buses link Auckland to Paihia, but a rental car is needed to travel further. Cars are more easily rented in Auckland.

WHEN TO GO

December to April is best for warm and settled weather. Avoid Christmas/New Year and Easter as the Bay of Islands is a popular family holiday destination. Waitangi is crowded on 6 February for Waitangi Day celebrations commemorating the treaty's signing.

THINGS TO NOTE

Dining options are limited in Ahipara and Opononi. Stock up on groceries in Kaitaia and stay in accommodation with a kitchen. For more info see *northlandnz.com*

NEW ZEALAND/AOTEAROA

Discover *the* South Island's Legendary Landscapes

NEW ZEALAND'S WILDERNESS makes you feel lost in time. The forests, draped in moss and carpeted with ferns, blot out all sounds except birdsong. The fjords, where towering granite meets sapphire water, are utterly serene. Surrounded by natural beauty, it's easy to forget civilisation – especially on the sparsely populated South Island (Te Waipounamu).

The Southern Alps form a mountainous spine down the island. To the east are traveller hubs like Queenstown, and to the west is the remote West Coast – by touring both, you can experience all the variety of the Land of the Long White Cloud (Aotearoa).

Start in lively Queenstown, where adrenaline junkies indulge in mountain biking, skiing and bungee jumping. After this bracing start, Te Anau, to the southwest, feels comparatively placid. This lakeside town is the starting point for the 75 mile (120km) Milford Rd, a showcase of Fiordland's geological variety. The scenery is quite literally mind-boggling, tripping up your senses with its symmetry and scale. The Mirror Lakes give an eerily perfect reflection of the Earl Mountains, while the Homer Tunnel reveals the granite innards of the Darran Mountains.

Opposite: waterside on the Pororari River Track; *This page top:* Fox Glacier in the Southern Alps; *Bottom:* mountain biking near Queenstown

AT A GLANCE

EAT

A mania for whitebait (fish fry) grips the West Coast between September and October. Try these tiddlers fried, whipped into an egg patty, or even as a pizza topping.

DRINK

Sip wines from Otago, a cool-climate wine region known for smooth, fragrant Pinot Noirs. Sample them at vineyards along the Kawarau River near Queenstown, and tasting rooms by Lake Wānaka.

STAY

Overnight huts in national parks offer camaraderie with fellow trampers (hikers) and the chance to enjoy misty mornings in the middle of New Zealand's forests.

EXPERIENCE

Get high! The South Island's vertically oriented sights are even more spectacular from the air, whether you're bungee jumping in Queenstown or taking a helicopter ride above Fox Glacier.

SHOP

Pounamu (greenstone) is gathered from riverbeds all over the South Island and carved into jewellery and ornaments. Look out for fish-hook and fern designs, which represent safety and new beginnings.

A Traveller's Tale

It was the longest seven minutes of my life. Small aircraft send me into a cold sweat, and the helicopter ride to Fox Glacier was no exception. Fortunately, the roar of the rotor blades helps drown out my anxious thoughts. I look through the fishbowl windows and a carpet of meadows and trees unfurls beneath us, while the fang-like peaks of the Southern Alps are dead ahead.

When the helicopter corkscrews slowly down to land on the glacier, we're instantly in another realm. We step out onto a river of compacted snow sandwiched between two cliffs, which rise like dark grey curtains. The glacier's surface has the dimpled appearance of a honeycomb. There are cracks running across the ice, almost as though the glacier has veins extending from a deep blue heart. The frenetic seven-minute helicopter ride is soon forgotten. Here, time is measured in centuries of slow-moving ice.

ANITA ISALSKA

"The Fiordland scenery is mind-boggling, tripping up your senses with its symmetry and scale"

Left: the Darran Mountains above Lake Marian, Fiordland National Park

At road's end is one of New Zealand's most celebrated destinations, Milford Sound (Piopiotahi), where high cliffs and conical mountains frame a pristine fjord. On a boat cruise, you can spot feather-browed Fiordland penguins on the banks, and humpbacks and bottlenose dolphins somersaulting in the water. In this peaceful place, humanity feels like an imposition – as though you're sailing uninvited into Mother Nature's walled garden.

Civilisation feels even further away at Fox and Franz Josef Glaciers, though the impact of people quickly becomes clear. In Māori legend, these glaciers are the frozen tears of Hine Hukatere, whose lover was swept to his death in an avalanche. The mythical tears took thousands of years to form, but the real ice is drying up in the space of decades as human-created climate change sends the glaciers into retreat.

Continuing north, rejoin the windswept West Coast road to Punakaiki for another ancient phenomenon, the Pancake Rocks. These limestone stacks were formed over 30 million years ago from layers of dead marine organisms, and they've been gradually sculpted by lashing wind and waves.

You've saved full communion with nature until last. Park at Smoke-ho, near Blackball, and embark on one of New Zealand's Great Walks, the Paparoa Track. The trail carves through nīkau palms and fern-fringed rainforest up to a sheer gorge; stay overnight in Pororari Hut. Come morning, step outside to a chorus of bellbirds and wood pigeons before walking back with renewed appreciation for the South Island's vast and fragile beauty.

This page: Pancake Rocks at Punakaiki; preparing to embark on a scenic cruise around Milford Sound

PRACTICALITIES

GETTING THERE
AND AROUND

International flights serve Queenstown and Christchurch airports. If coming from the North Island, take a ferry from Wellington to Picton. Cars and campervans are convenient for roving around, especially along the West Coast, but InterCity buses travel between Queenstown and Te Anau; services to Franz Josef and Fox Glaciers and Punakaiki (for Paparoa National Park) are seasonal. Book shuttles from Greymouth or Punakaiki to reach the Paparoa Track's Blackball trailhead.

WHEN TO GO

Summer (December to February) is prime time for road trips and hikes. Book overnight accommodation well in advance, and expect crowded hiking huts and multitudes of visitors at Milford Sound. The shoulder seasons (October to November and March to April) have smaller crowds but less predictable weather.

THINGS TO NOTE

There's a reason New Zealand is so lush and green – expect downpours and bring layers, especially on overnight hikes. Another outdoor annoyance is the ravenous sandfly, which leaves very itchy bites. Bring repellent and cover up, especially in summer.

Further information is available at newzealand.com.

Eight Day Itinerary

>

Begin in Queenstown, a playground for hikers, bikers and skiers amid the Remarkables mountain range. On your second day, drive two hours to Te Anau, stopping at the Devil's Staircase for views of Lake Wakatipu and the mountain-backed town of Mossburn. When you arrive, stroll by the lake and take a boat ride to the glow-worm caves.

>>

Day three is for driving the serpentine Milford Rd (2½ hours) to reach Milford Sound for a scenic cruise. Back in Te Anau, set out on day four on the long, six-hour drive to Fox Glacier, breaking it up with lakeside coffee in Wānaka, and a bite and beach walk in remote Haast.

>>>

If weather allows, start day five with a helicopter ride to Fox Glacier, before spending the afternoon cycling. Next day, drive 30 minutes to Franz Josef – it's your second shot at a chopper ride above a glacier (the weather is fickle).

>>>>

Drive on to Paparoa National Park (2¾ hours) before nightfall, via Punakaiki's Pancake Rocks. Awake early on day seven to tackle a stretch of the Paparoa Track: hike to Pororari Hut and head back the following day (10 miles/16km each way).

MORE TIME?

Walk the full Paparoa Track over three days.

NEW ZEALAND/AOTEAROA

Make a Gourmet Escape *to* Waiheke Island

SLOW DOWN. YOU'RE HERE. Waiheke Island's most famous sign urges arrivals from downtown Auckland to quickly adapt to island time, New Zealand–style. Welcome to a self-proclaimed 'island of wine' – more than 20 vineyards take advantage of the balmy Mediterranean–style microclimate – but travelling wine buffs now share the place with fans of beer, whisky and good food. Food trucks span the globe from Sri Lanka and Mexico to France and Argentina, local oysters are served at relaxed bistros along the sandy bay of Onetangi Beach, and a leisurely lunch at The Heke could include shared plates of organic produce, island-crafted beer and award-winning whisky. Enjoy a lazy, Kiwi summer's day at Man O' War Vineyard, its remote location on Waiheke's isolated east coast reached by a winding, unsealed road with elevated views of Auckland's Hauraki Gulf on the way. Play cricket on the beach, jump off the wharf, or ride an e-bike through vineyard rows. Now you've really slowed down.

AT A GLANCE

EAT
Wood-fired pizza from Dragonfired's food truck on Little Oneroa Beach.

DRINK
Award-winning gin with island botanicals at Waiheke Distilling Co.

PRACTICALITIES

Stopping at vineyards and beaches, Fullers' Hop-On Hop-Off Explorer Bus is the most convenient way to get around Waiheke Island.

COOK ISLANDS

Drive Around Paradise

AT A GLANCE

EAT
Dig into *ika mata*, raw fish with lime and coconut sauce.

DRINK
Enjoy bush beer, made from oranges, sugar, malt and hops.

PRACTICALITIES

Hawaiian Airlines, Air New Zealand, Air Rarotonga and Jetstar Airways offer flights to the Cook Islands.

IMAGINE HAWAI'I 90 YEARS AGO – that's the Cook Islands now. Beaches are never crowded, traffic is nonexistent and there are no buildings taller than a coconut tree. The 20-mile (32km) road that goes around main island, Rarotonga, takes about 45 minutes to drive without stopping, passing orchards and goats wandering among banana trees, with lush jungle views as far as the eye can see. Salty air mixes with a cool breeze and the glorious scent of jasmine and gardenia. Black Rock, a worthy stop on the route, draws cliff jumpers and enthusiastic snorkellers. The dreamscape of turquoises and teals surrounding the islands is called Marae Moana, one the world's largest marine parks. This protected area is teeming with life, from Napoleon wrasse weighing up to 400lb (181kg) and humpbacks whales who gather here from July through October to pastel-purple coral gardens that could easily win the next Pantone Color of the Year award.

SAMOA, FIJI AND VANUATU

Find Adventure
and Culture *in the*
South Pacific

Opposite: To-Sua Ocean Trench in the Samoan rainforest; *This page*: ceremonial lighting of the beach torches at Nadi in Fiji

TIME SLOWS DOWN in the Pacific Islands. On a road trip around Samoa's main island, jungle-covered mountains rise up in the rear-view mirror and aquamarine waters lap at white-sand beaches fringing the coastal road. The maximum speed is 34mph (55kp/h), but most drivers go slower. Indeed why rush? Relish the opportunity to pause at thundering waterfalls and unique coastal swimming spots formed by ancient lava tubes before nodding off to the sounds of the ocean at night in a simple beach *fale* (hut).

It's relatively easy to fly between the larger Pacific Island nations, making a good case for a multi-country adventure. World-renowned for its hospitality, more developed Fiji lies in the heart of the region. Leave the resort tourists behind and embark on a hike linking remote villages in the lush mountains of Viti Levu, the main island. Marvel at the subterranean majesty of Somosomo Strait's blockbuster Great White Wall on a scuba diving live-aboard, or escape to an ecofriendly small-island resort far from the crowds to snorkel, dive or surf until the sun sets in a blaze of colour on the blue horizon. And you'll likely be welcomed with a friendly *bula* (welcome/hello) wherever you go.

The easy-going vibe continues in Vanuatu, ranked the world's second-happiest nation by the Happy Planet Index. Select from an appealing mix of island adventures – from scuba diving one of the world's most famous wrecks on Espiritu Santo to watching the famed 'land divers' of Pentecost Island in action. But nothing stirs the soul – or gets the adrenaline pumping – like a visit to Tanna Island. Here *kastom* tribes offer a taste of the traditional lifestyles they continue to maintain as the world changes around them, and the Mt Yasur volcano mesmerises with its near-constant lava show. It's not only one of

A Traveller's Tale

First there was a deep, almost guttural rumble. And then, boom! Before I even registered the sound – or raised my camera – a neon spray of lava spewed up into the sky, like an upside-down shower of molten tangerine rock. I'll be ready for the next one, I told myself, as I settled in on the rim of Tanna Island's Mt Yasur volcano for an electrifying afternoon of live entertainment.

SARAH REID

AT A GLANCE

EAT
You haven't been to Fiji if you haven't enjoyed a *lovo* (underground oven) feast.

DRINK
Visitors are often welcomed to the region with *kava*, a traditional drink with relaxing properties.

STAY
With epic dive sites on its doorstep, White Grass Ocean Resort is the pick of accommodation on Vanuatu's Tanna Island.

EXPERIENCE
Learn about the ancient custom of sand drawing at Vanuatu's National Museum in Efate.

Opposite: searching for treasures among sunken US military hardware at Million Dollar Point, Vanuatu

the world's most active volcanos, but also among the most accessible, with just a short climb to the rim following a bumpy 4WD journey across an otherworldly, ash-covered landscape. Feel humbled by the power of nature as lava spurts up into the air during the frequent eruptions. And thoroughly revitalised after your island-nation-hopping adventures.

PRACTICALITIES

GETTING THERE AND AROUND

Samoa receives flights from Australia, New Zealand, Fiji and Honolulu, while Vanuatu has flights to Australia, New Zealand, the Solomon Islands and New Caledonia. Fiji is easier to access, with the national carrier servicing more than 100 destinations. Taxis and shuttles greet planes in all destinations.

WHEN TO GO

The dry season from May through September is generally the best time to visit, with good visibility for diving and a low risk of crossing paths with a cyclone.

THINGS TO NOTE

It's a good idea to book hotels in advance in all destinations (as well as domestic flights in Fiji and Vanuatu), though it's usually easy to find a beach *fale* in Samoa for the night.

For further information see samoa.travel, fiji.travel and vanuatu.travel

Three Week Itinerary

>

Start in Samoa. Hire a car in capital Apia and spend a week circumnavigating the main island at a leisurely pace – aim to spend most of your time on the glorious south coast.

>>

Next, fly to Nadi in Fiji. Embark on a hiking adventure with Talanoa Treks, book a live-aboard diving adventure or take a short flight or ferry to an island resort for a week of surfing, diving or Fijian village life.

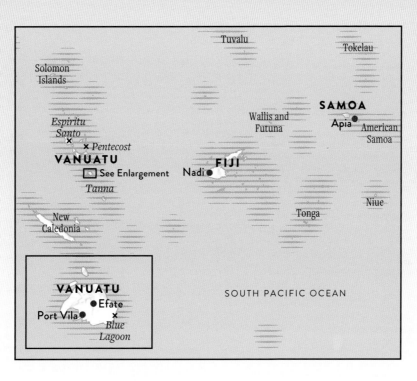

>>>

Finish your adventure in Vanuatu. Fly into the capital Port Vila and take a connecting flight to Espiritu Santo for diving, Pentecost for cultural immersion, or Tanna for more diving and culture, and a front-row seat to an erupting volcano. Save a day or two to explore the magical Blue Lagoon and gin-clear jungle cascades on the main island of Efate before your departure.

MORE TIME?

Choose another Fijian island to explore if you're transiting back through the country, or make the most of Vanuatu's connections to other Pacific Island destinations including the Solomon Islands and New Caledonia.

Index

Dream Trips of the World

October 2024

Published by Lonely Planet Global Limited

CRN 554153

www.lonelyplanet.com

10 9 8 7 6 5 4 3 2 1

Printed in Malaysia

ISBN 978 18375 8302 7

© Lonely Planet 2024

© photographers as indicated 2024

Publishing Director Piers Pickard

Gift & Illustrated Publisher Becca Hunt

Senior Editor Robin Barton

Designer Emily Dubin

Typesetter Howie Severson

Editors Dora Ball, Cliff Wilkinson, Polly Thomas, Nick Mee

Print Production Nigel Longuet

Lonely Planet Global Limited

Digital Depot, Roe Lane (off Thomas St), Digital Hub, Dublin 8, D08 TCV4 Ireland

STAY IN TOUCH lonelyplanet.com/contact

Writers: Amy Balfour, Anita Isalska, Anthony Ham, Brendan Sainsbury, Brett Atkinson, Emily Matchar, Isabella Noble, James Bainbridge, Jesse Scott, Joe Bindloss, Kerry Walker, Megan Eaves, Mike MacEacheran, Nicola Williams, Oliver Smith, Paul Bloomfield, Regis St Louis, Rudolf Abraham, Sarah Reid, Sarah Sekula, Stephen Lioy, Sue Watt

Cover image: Tiger's Nest monastery, Bhutan © cannaD750 / Shutterstock

Back cover images: © Eric Lafforgue, Pete Seaward, Justin Foulkes, Jonathan Gregson / Lonely Planet; Fabio Lamanna, Peter Zelei Images, Igor Tichonow/EyeEm / Getty Images; Nikada / iStock; Sean Pavone / Shutterstock